A series of diaries and letters, journals and memoirs

LORD HERVEY'S MEMOIRS

Lord Hervey was born in 1696, the second son of a wealthy Suffolk country gentleman, who was made a peer under Queen Anne and created Earl of Bristol on George I's accession. He was educated at Westminster School and Clare Hall, Cambridge. In 1716 he went on the Grand Tour and visited Hanover where he became a friend of Prince Frederick (Prince of Wales and later George II). He married Mary Lepell, a maid of honour to the Princess, in 1720. After the death of his elder brother, Lord Hervey was returned as Member of Parliament for the family seat of Bury St Edmunds in 1725. On joining the supporters of Walpole he became Vice-Chamberlain to the royal household and a Privy Councillor. As a favourite of Queen Caroline's he had considerable influence at court. He was raised to the Lords in 1733 and became Lord Privy Seal in 1740, but after Walpole's fall in 1742 he lost his place and went into opposition. Lord Hervey died on 8 August 1743. A clever and knowledgeable observer of the political scene, his memoirs have been ranked with those of Saint-Simon and they give a vivid, satirical picture of the power and personality struggles at court.

Richard Romney Sedgwick was born in 1894 and educated at Westminster School and Trinity College, Cambridge. From 1949 until his retirement in 1954 he was Assistant Under-Secretary of State, Commonwealth Relations Office. He became a Fellow of Trinity College in 1919 and was made a Companion of St Michael and St George in 1945. His other publications include *Letters from George III to Lord Bute* (1939) and he was editor of *History of Parliament, 1715–1754*. He died on 20 January 1972.

LORD HERVEY'S MEMOIRS

EDITED BY

ROMNEY SEDGWICK

PENGUIN BOOKS

Penguin Books Ltd, Harmondsworth, Middlesex, England
Penguin Books, 40 West 23rd Street, New York, New York 10010, U.S.A.
Penguin Books Australia Ltd, Ringwood, Victoria, Australia
Penguin Books Canada Ltd, 2801 John Street, Markham, Ontario, Canada L3R 1B4
Penguin Books (N.Z.) Ltd, 182–190 Wairau Road, Auckland 10, New Zealand

First published by B. T. Batsford Ltd 1963
Published in Penguin Books 1984

Copyright © the Estate of Romney Sedgwick, 1963
All rights reserved

Made and printed in Singapore by
Richard Clay (S.E. Asia) Pte Ltd

Contents

Introductory Note

LORD HERVEY, the author of these memoirs, was born in 1696, the second son of a wealthy Suffolk country gentleman, who was made a peer under Anne and created Earl of Bristol on George I's accession. After the death of his elder brother he was returned to Parliament in 1725 for the family seat at Bury St. Edmunds, attaching himself to Walpole, at the cost of a breach, ending in a duel, with his former friend, William Pulteney, the leader of the Whig opposition. Appointed Vice-Chamberlain to the royal household in 1730, he became a great favourite with Queen Caroline and, for a time, with her son, Frederick, Prince of Wales, with whom, however, he quarrelled fiercely in 1732. Raised to the Lords in 1733 to strengthen ministerial debating power there, he was brought into the Cabinet as Lord Privy Seal in 1740, lost his place on Walpole's fall in 1742, went into opposition, and died on 8th August, 1743, aged forty-six.

For over a century Hervey was remembered merely as a minor politician, whose effeminate good looks had given rise to the saying that there were three sexes, men, women, and Herveys, and who had been scarified by Pope in the famous lines on Sporus. It was not till 1848 that his descendants released his memoirs of the first ten years of the reign of George I, based on his experiences at the Court, put down while they were fresh in his memory. The work is a historical masterpiece, ranking Hervey with St. Simon among the great memoir writers whom Macaulay considered to be the only modern historians comparable to Herodotus, Thucydides, and Tacitus, 'the ancient masters of history.'

The 1848 edition of the memoirs was based on a censored manuscript, from which Hervey's descendants had removed a number of passages, mostly relating to the royal family. In 1931 a new edition was published from a more complete manuscript in the Windsor archives, containing most of the missing passages, but not those covering the period May 1730 – November 1732, which must have contained the story of Hervey's relations with the Prince of Wales. An abbreviation of the 1931 edition was published in 1952. The present volume reproduces the text of the 1952 edition, which is now out of print.   R. S.

chapter one

The New Reign

1727

THE LATE KING died on the road to Hanover, on the 11th of June, 1727, at Osnaburg, in the very same room where he was born. On Wednesday, June 14th, news was brought by an express to Sir Robert Walpole, who was at dinner at Chelsea[1] when it arrived. He went immediately to Richmond (where the Prince of Wales then was) to acquaint him with what had happened and receive his orders. The Prince was laid to sleep (as his custom had been for many years after dinner), and the Princess was in the bedchamber with him, when the Duchess of Dorset, the lady-in-waiting, went in to let them know Sir Robert Walpole was there, who was immediately brought in. All he said was, 'I am come to acquaint Your Majesty with the death of your father.' The King seemed extremely surprised, but not enough to forget his resentment to Sir Robert one moment; neither his confusion, nor his joy at this great change, nor the benevolence so naturally felt by almost everybody towards the messenger of such good news, softened his voice or his countenance in one word or look. Whatever questions Sir Robert asked him with regard to the council being summoned, his being proclaimed, or other things necessary immediately to be provided, the King gave him no other answer than 'Go to Chiswick, and take your directions from Sir Spencer Compton.'

This interview therefore was very short. Sir Robert went as commanded to Chiswick, and the King and Queen immediately went to London.

As Sir Robert Walpole had not the least hope of making his peace so far as to be employed in the new reign, he did not endeavour

[1] Orford House, Walpole's chief London residence.

I

to disguise to Sir Spencer Compton any one circumstance that had passed at Richmond, but naturally and openly told him:

'The King, Sir, has sent me to you in such a manner as declares he intends you for his minister, and has commanded me to receive all my instructions from your mouth. It is what I as well as the rest of the world expected would be whenever this accident happened. You have been the Prince's Treasurer ever since he came to England; it is a natural promotion to continue you upon his being King; your services entitle you to that mark of his favour, and your abilities and experience in business will both enable you to support the employment and justify him in bestowing it. Everything is in your hands; I neither could shake your power if I would, nor would I if I could. My time has been, yours is beginning; but as we all must depend in some degree upon our successors, and that it is always prudent for these successors by way of example to have some regard for their predecessors, that with the measure they mete it may be measured to them again, for this reason I put myself under your protection, and for this reason I expect you will give it. I desire no share of power or business; one of your white sticks, or any employment of that sort, is all I ask as a mark from the Crown that I am not abandoned to the enmity of those whose envy is the only source of their hate, and who consequently will wish you no better than they have done me the moment you are vested with those honours and that authority, the possession of which they will always covet, and the possessor of which, of course, they will always hate.'

Sir Spencer Compton was at this time Speaker of the House of Commons, Treasurer to the Prince, and Paymaster to the Army. He was a plodding, heavy fellow, with great application, but no talents, and vast complaisance for a Court without any address. He was always more concerned for the manner and form in which a thing was to be done than about the propriety or expediency of the thing itself; and as he was calculated to execute rather than to project, for a subaltern rather than a commander, so he was much fitter for a clerk to a minister than for a minister to a Prince. Whatever was resolved upon he would often know how properly to perform, but seldom how to advise what was proper to be resolved upon.

His only pleasures were money and eating; his only knowledge forms and precedents; and his only insinuation bows and smiles.

But as he did not want pride or ambition, though he wanted parts to feed them, he was extremely pleased with this speech of Sir Robert Walpole's, and looking upon himself, dazzled with the lustre of so bright a prospect, as possessed already of all the favour and power of this new Court, he promised Sir Robert Walpole his protection; and asked in return the assistance of Sir Robert's experience to enlighten him on the present state of affairs, and to instruct him in the future conduct of them.

They went together forthwith to London, and first to the Duke of Devonshire's, who was then President of the Council, but laid up with the gout and not able to attend there. The Duke of Devonshire was a man who had no uncommon portion of understanding; and as his chief skill lay in painting, medals, and horses, he was more able as a virtuoso than a statesman, and a much better jockey than he was a politician. He had a fair character, the dignity of a man of quality, and was justly more considered than most people of the same rank and fortune (who, perhaps, had better abilities), from having been always steady to his party and constant to his friends.

There was nobody present at this meeting but these two knights, the master of the house, my Lord Chancellor King, Lord Trevor, keeper of the Privy Seal, and Sir Paul Methuen, and all that was concerted there was the common forms that were to be observed in the meeting of the Council.

Whilst these things were regulating, Sir Spencer Compton took Sir Robert Walpole aside and desired him, as a speech would be necessary on the occasion to be made in council by the King, and as Sir Robert was so much more accustomed to this sort of composition than himself, that he would be so good to go into another room and make forthwith a draught of what would be proper for the King to say, whilst he went to Leicester Fields[1] to receive His Majesty's commands.

Sir Robert at first seemed to decline this office, but Sir Spencer Compton insisting upon it as a favour to him, Sir Robert Walpole,

[1] The present Leicester Square, where George II, Frederick Prince of Wales and George III successively resided as heirs-apparent.

who was the last man in England he ought to have employed on this occasion, undertook at his request that which, if Sir Spencer Compton had had common sense or foresight, he would have known the better it was done the worse it would be for himself.[1]

That which made this step yet more absurd was that if this precedent-monger had only turned to the old Gazettes published at the beginning of the former reigns he might have copied full as good a declaration from these records as any Sir Robert Walpole could give him.

Sir Robert, retiring into a room by himself, went immediately to work, and Sir Spencer to Leicester Fields, where the King and Queen were already arrived and receiving the compliments of every man of all degrees and all parties in the town. The square was thronged with multitudes of the meaner sort and resounded with huzzas and acclamations, whilst every room in the house was filled with people of higher rank, crowding to kiss their hands and to make the earliest and warmest professions of zeal for their service. But the common face of a Court at this time was quite reversed, for as there was not a creature in office, excepting those who were his servants as Prince, who had not the most sorrowful and dejected countenance of distress and disappointment, so there was not one out of employment who did not already exult with all the insolence of the most absolute power and settled prosperity.

As soon as Sir Spencer Compton had been with the King in his closet, he returned to his coach through a lane of bowers in the ante-chambers and on the stairs, who were all shouldering one another to pay adoration to this new idol, and knocking their heads together to whisper compliments and petitions as he passed.

At his return to Devonshire House he found the declaration for the King already drawn. He approved it, desired Sir Robert's leave to copy it, and begged that he would not, even to the people in the next room, say anything of his having done it. It was first read to the company at Devonshire House, approved of there without any objections, and then carried by Sir Spencer Compton, in his own handwriting, to the King. Sir Robert followed to Leicester Fields, where he found Sir Spencer Compton a good deal embarrassed by

[1] On George III's accession Bute, remembering this incident, was ready with a declaration which he had drawn up long beforehand.

the King's desiring him to alter one passage in the declaration, which Sir Spencer wished should stand, and which if he had not he did not know how to go about to change. He desired Sir Robert to go into the King and persuade him to leave it as it was originally drawn, which office Sir Robert readily accepted, and was thanked by Sir Spencer for the success he ought to have apprehended.

The King stayed in town till the Monday following. During those four days Leicester House, that used to be a desert, was thronged from morning to night, like the 'Change at noon. Nobody but Sir Robert Walpole walked through these rooms as if they had been still empty. His presence, that used to make a crowd wherever he appeared, now emptied every corner he turned to, and the same people who were officiously a week ago clearing the way to flatter his prosperity, were now getting out of it to avoid sharing his disgrace. Everybody looked upon it as sure, and whatever professions of adherence and gratitude for former favours were made him in private, there were none among the many his power had obliged (excepting General Churchill and Lord Hervey[1]) who did not in public as notoriously decline and fear his notice as they used industriously to seek and covet it. These two men constantly attended him, and never paid so much as the compliment of a visit to Sir Spencer Compton, who had already opened a levée and received the solicitations of the whole world as the only channel to the King's ear. Among these herds was Mr. Dodington, one of the lords of the treasury, whose early application and distinguished assiduity at this juncture to the supposed successor of his former patron and benefactor was never forgiven.

Sir Robert Walpole, his brother, Mr. Horace Walpole, ambassador to France, the Duke of Newcastle, and Lord Townshend, the two Secretaries of State, who were, properly speaking, the whole old administration at the death of the late King, expected themselves and were expected by the whole world hourly to be displaced.

The first of these the present King had, in the latter years of his father's reign, called rogue and rascal without much reserve, to several people, upon several occasions; to Horace Walpole he had

---

[1] Hervey usually refers to himself in the third person in order, as he explains, to avoid 'the disagreeable egotisms with which almost all memoir writers so tiresomely abound.'

as liberally and as publicly dispensed the appellations of scoundrel and fool; and for the Duke of Newcastle, the King, when Prince, had been so personally disobliged by him that he had sworn a thousand times he never would forgive him; and, joined to this resentment of the particular injuries he thought he had received from him, he had as to his public character, his parliamentary abilities and knowledge in business, the same just contempt which most other people had contracted for his Grace, either by their own observation or the deference they paid to the opinion of the public. For Lord Townshend, the King looked upon him as no more an honest man than as an able minister, and attributed to the warmth of his temper and his scanty genius, the strength of his passions and weakness of his understanding, all the present intricacy, uncertainty, and confusion in the affairs of Europe.

The whole world knowing this to be His Majesty's opinion of these four governors of this kingdom; that, as I have just related, he used always to speak of the first as a great rogue, of the second as a dirty buffoon, of the third as an impertinent fool, and of the fourth as a choleric blockhead; it was very natural to expect the reins of power would not long be left in their hands. And when Lord Malpas, son-in-law to Sir Robert Walpole, was turned out of the Mastership of the Robes, and not in the softest manner, the day after the King came to the Crown, it was concluded he led a dance which the rest were soon to follow.

If it had not been for the stupidity of Sir Spencer Compton, who did not know his own strength, or what use to make of it, they had all, but certainly at least Sir Robert Walpole, been displaced the very day after the King came to the Crown. But as this awkward statesman was either blind to his own interest or ignorant of his own power, he suffered that opportunity to slip through his hands, which if he had had skill to improve, or resolution to seize, he might indisputably have been what he was equally ambitious of and unfit for.

But as the King was not pressed to the taking of this step, and that his Civil List (which was at present the chief object in his view) was in less than a fortnight to be settled in Parliament, he very naturally deferred any change in the administration till that great and favourite point was determined; and that it might be adjusted to his satisfaction with the unanimous concurrence of all parties, he very prudently chose not to make the one desperate, though he gave the others hopes, and kept the interest of every other body in suspense, that his own might be pursued without opposition; though perhaps, like many other refining historians, I attribute that to prudence which was only owing to accident, two things often mistaken one for the other. But whether it was the effect of policy or the natural consequence of the present juncture of the affairs, whatever was the cause of his conduct, this was certainly the effect—that his postponing thus the gratification of his resentment facilitated the success of his own affairs in Parliament, gave him time to cool, the Queen time to think, and Sir Robert time to work.

On the 19th the Court removed to Kensington, where the King, by the audiences that were asked and the offers that were made to him by the great men of all denominations, found himself set up at auction and every one bidding for his favour at the expense of the public.

On the 27th of June the Parliament met, when the Civil List, unopposed by anybody but Mr. Shippen, the head of the veteran staunch Jacobites, was settled in the following manner. The produce of those funds that had been tied down for the provision of £700,000 a year on the late King, and £100,000 more on the Prince of Wales, was now given entirely to the present King, without a deduction of £100,000 to the present Prince of Wales, but leaving the provision for him to the direction and generosity of his father, and without giving the overplus of £800,000 to the Sinking Fund, which was the use to which the surplus of these funds in the late reign was appropriated after the £700,000 was paid; so that this King had the whole produce of these, which was then computed at an average to amount to £900,000 a year; and if that computation had proved true, the Civil List of this King would have been, by £200,000 a year, a greater revenue than any King of England was ever known to have before. The ridiculous reason given for this exorbitant augmentation of it was the expense of a wife and a great many children—as if no King of England before had ever been married, or to a pregnant wife. And the other sensible argument

was things being so much dearer than they used to be and consequently housekeeping so much more expensive—good excuses for a
farmer's backwardness in paying his rent, but not things that could
be much felt in the manner of living of a king. But unreasonable
as it was thought to settle the Civil List in this extravagant manner,
yet the bill passed the House of Commons without one negative
but Mr. Shippen's. No one thought it reasonable, yet no one opposed
it; no one wished for it, and no one voted against it; and I believe
it is the single instance that can be given, of a question carried
there, without two opponents or well-wishers.

At the same time the Queen's jointure was settled; for the provision of which, in this fit of generosity, these frugal dispensers of
the people's money were pleased to bestow upon her, besides
Somerset House and Richmond Lodge, £100,000 a year, which was
just double what any Queen of England had ever had before. To
such a pitch of extravagance did these contending parliamentary
bidders raise the price of Court favour at this royal auction.

When these two great and laudable works were perfected the
old Parliament was to be dissolved and a new one chosen. It was
at their dismission that the decisive stroke was struck in the con-
tention for power between Sir Robert Walpole and Sir Spencer
Compton. The King had ordered them both to make him a speech,
and when he came to choose shook his head at poor Sir Spencer's
and approved of Sir Robert's.

The only two things that were done, during this short inter-
regnum of Sir Robert Walpole's, contrary to his inclination, were,
first the displacing of his son-in-law, Lord Malpas, which I have
already mentioned; and, secondly, the turning a Sir William
Yonge, a known creature of his, out of the commission of Treasury.

The King used always to call him 'Stinking Yonge,' and had conceived and expressed such an insurmountable dislike to his person
and character that no interest nor influence was potent enough at
this time to prevail with His Majesty to continue him. However,
Sir Robert advised him, upon this disgrace, to be patient, not
clamorous, to submit, not resent or oppose, to be as subservient
to the Court in attendance and give the King his assistance as
constantly and as assiduously in Parliament as if he was paid for
it; telling him and all the world what afterwards proved true, that

whatever people might imagine, Yonge was not sunk, he had only dived, and would yet get up again.[1]

This was the single alteration made after the dissolution of the Parliament contrary to the will and representation of Sir Robert Walpole; and though this was a proof that he was forced to bend in one instance, yet every other change demonstrated his influence.

His son-in-law, Lord Malpas, was put into the Admiralty; his great rival and enemy, Mr. Pulteney,[2] denied leave to stand candidate upon the interest of the Court for Westminster, never consulted in the closet, and always very coldly received in the Drawing-room; a whole race of Chetwynds, Sir Robert Walpole's declared well-wishers, were turned out in a lump; and, what was reckoned the strongest demonstration of his power, Lord Berkeley removed from the head of the Admiralty, and Lord Torrington appointed to succeed him.

This incident, as well as every other material occurrence at this time, proved to all mankind that the little transient interruption that diverted the stream of Sir Robert's power was now borne down and that the current was brought back again and flowed quietly in its former channel. It was now understood by everybody that Sir Robert was the Queen's minister; that whoever he favoured, she distinguished; and whoever she distinguished the King employed. His reputed mistress, Mrs. Howard, and the Speaker his reputed minister, were perceived to be nothing.

But as Sir Spencer Compton had conceived too strong hopes of being Sir Robert's superior ever to serve in the House of Commons quietly under him, and that it might be dangerous, consequently, to suffer him in the chair of a new Parliament, Sir Robert advised the making him a peer. Accordingly he was created Baron of Wilmington; and on this occasion, I think, he might have said, like Agrippina, the mother of Nero, in Racine's *Britannicus*,

> 'Tous ces présens, hélas; irritent mon dépit,
> Je vois mes honneurs croître, et tomber mon crédit.'

It was just his case. But he did not seem to feel the ridicule or the contemptibleness of his situation. That snowball levée of his, which had opened and that gathered so fast, melted away at as quick a

[1] Which he duly did.   [2] The Leader of the Whig Opposition.

pace; his visionary prospects of authority and grandeur vanished into air; and yet he seemed just as well satisfied to be bowing and grinning in the antechamber, possessed of a lucrative employment without credit, and dishonoured by a title which was the mark of his disgrace, as if he had been dictating in the closet, sole fountain of Court favour at home, and regulator of all the national transactions abroad.

Mrs. Howard (afterwards Countess of Suffolk) felt her situation in a very different manner; and though she was too wise and too prudent to have given herself the air of a favourite without feeling she was so, or to have affected the appearance of power without knowing whether she should be able to maintain it, yet, without doubt, she had tried her strength in private, and was mortified to find she had tried it to so little purpose, well knowing that some degree of contempt would attend the not having what in her situation the world would expect her to have, though she had never pretended to be possessed of it, and that a mistress who could not get power was not a much more agreeable or respectable character than a minister who could not keep it.

Mrs. Howard was of a good family, but of so numerous a one, that her fortune originally was a very small one. She was sister to Lord Hobart, and had been married very young to Mr. Howard, a wrong-headed, ill-tempered, obstinate, drunken, extravagant, brutal younger brother of the Earl of Suffolk's family. This ill-matched, unfortunate couple were in a few years reduced to such low circumstances that they could not remain in England, and went, almost in despair, to make their court and seek their fortune, in Queen Anne's time, at Hanover. Mrs. Howard was there taken into the present Queen's service, and laid the foundation of the interest (such as it is) which she is now possessed of. Though the present King was never then said to think of her as a mistress, and when, immediately upon his first coming over, he attached himself to Mrs. Bellenden, a maid of honour to the Princess, Mrs. Howard was always third of that party, and upon a very different foot from that on which her correspondence with the King is now thought to stand. Mrs. Bellenden, who was afterwards married to Colonel Campbell, was incontestably the most agreeable, the most insinuating and the most likeable woman of her time, made up of every ingredient likely to engage or attach a lover. But as she had to do with a man incapable of being engaged by any charm but habit, or attached to any woman but his wife—a man who was better pleased with the air of an intrigue than any other part of it and who did not care to pay a valuable consideration even for that— she began to find out that her situation was only having the scandal of being the Prince's mistress without the pleasure, and the confinement without profit. She, therefore, very wisely, resolved to withdraw her own neck as well as she could, little by little, out of his unpleasant yoke. By this conduct she left Mrs. Howard, who had more steadiness and more perseverance, to try what she could make of a game which the other had found so tedious and so unprofitable that she had no pleasure in playing it and saw little to be won by minding it.

The Prince passed, every evening of his life, three or four hours in Mrs. Howard's lodging, who, as dresser to the Princess, always in waiting, was lodged all the year round in the Court. Mrs. Bellenden continued to be now and then of these parties, till she married, but after that time these visits become uninterrupted tête-à-têtes with Mrs. Howard, that subsist to this hour; and yet I know many of those who are most conversant and best acquainted with the intrigue, anecdotes, and transactions of this Court, who doubt, notwithstanding these appearances, the King's ever having entered into any commerce with her, that he might not innocently have had with his daughter. It is certain that nobody belonging to the Court ever believed he had been happy with Mrs. Bellenden; and though all appearances (the duration of them excepted) were exactly the same with regard to both these ladies, yet there are many people (which seems very unaccountable) who never suspected his lying with the one, and never doubted it with the other.

Mrs. Howard had the misfortune of hearing so ill that the quickness of her apprehension was in mixed companies of little use to her; for, unless the conversation was particularly addressed to her and in a tone of voice much above the common pitch of speaking, she had no share in it; so that by this infirmity she was deprived not only of the pleasure but the advantage of the ordinary commerce of public and general acquaintance, and lost half the benefit of the many qualifications she possessed, so necessary to a thorough good companion, and so rarely united in one person. Good sense, good breeding, and good nature were qualities which even her enemies could not deny her; nor do I know any one good or agreeable quality which those who knew her more intimately would not as readily allow her. She was civil to everybody, friendly to many, and unjust to none: in short, she had a good head and a good heart, but had to do with a man who was incapable of tasting the one or valuing the other, one who seemed to look upon a mistress rather as a necessary appurtenance to his grandeur as a prince than an addition to his pleasures as a man, and thus only pretended to distinguish what it was evident he overlooked and affected to caress what it was manifest he did not love.

When the King came to the Crown, Mrs. Howard was about forty years old,[1] an age not proper to make conquests, though perhaps the most likely to maintain them, as the levity of desiring new ones is by that time generally pretty well over, and the maturity of these qualities requisite to rivet old ones in their fullest perfection; for when the beauty that creates passion begins to decay, women commonly look out for some preservative charms to substitute in its place; they begin to change their notion of their right to being adored, into that of thinking a little complaisance and some good qualities as necessary to attach men as a little beauty and some agreeable qualities are to allure them; and as experience teaches them that the insolence and negligence of security often loses what the humility and circumspection of diffidence helps them to preserve, so they begin to find out that a solicitude to oblige is as essential to a woman as being loved and esteemed, as a capacity of pleasing is to her being liked and admired. Mrs. Howard was so sensible of this truth, that her conduct tallied exactly with these sentiments; but notwithstanding her making use of the proper tools, the stuff she had to work with was so stubborn and so inductile that her labour was in vain, and her situation was such as would have been insupportable to anyone whose pride was less supple, whose passions less governable, and whose sufferance less inexhaustible. For she was forced to live in the constant subjection of a wife with all the reproach of a mistress and to flatter and manage a man whom she must see and feel had as little inclination to her person as regard

[1] She was forty-six; the King was forty-three.

to her advice; and added to this she had the mortification of know-ing the Queen's influence so much superior to hers, that the little show of interest she maintained was only a permitted tenure depen-dent on a rival who could have overturned it any hour she pleased. But the Queen, knowing the vanity of her husband's temper, and that he must have some woman for the world to believe he lay with, wisely suffered one to remain in that situation whom she despised and had got the better of, for fear of making room for a successor whom he might really love, and that might get the better of her. On the other hand Mrs. Howard was in the right to con-tinue there even on this foot, since she could not put herself on any better; for though she had not all the advantages which the sole mistress to a king might expect, yet it enabled her at least to gain that very material point of bettering her fortune; and the exchang-ing indigence and distress for affluence and prosperity was a consideration that no doubt often comforted her in the many mortifications, disappointments, and rebukes which her ambition met with when she endeavoured to join the éclat and power of a king's mistress to those less agreeable appurtenances of that char-acter, the scandal and confinement of it.

However, these quotidian visits which His Majesty when Prince was known to bestow upon her, of so many hours in the four-and-twenty, and for so many years together, had made many superficial courtiers conclude that one who possessed so large a portion of his time must have some share in his heart. This way of reasoning induced many to make their court to her, and choose that channel to recommend themselves to the Prince. The most considerable of those who had done so were the Duke of Argyll, Lord Ilay his brother, the Duke of Dorset, and Lord Wilmington, who none of them could persuade themselves of such inconsistencies and absurdities in any man's character, as to imagine the Prince could give all his leisure hours to a pretty and agreeable woman who had no weight in his counsels and perhaps as small a portion of his person; nor was it more reasonable for them to imagine that any man would be so absolutely governed by his wife who took the liberty of seeming, at least, to keep her chamber-maid under her nose; or to believe that he would receive no impressions in private but from the opinion of a woman whom he took such frequent opportunities to snub, rebuke, and contradict, whenever she delivered it before any standers by.

Whilst the King was Prince there were so few occasions for the Queen to show her credit with him that some were apt to imagine this latent dormant power was much less than it proved itself when the time came that made it worth her while to try, show, and exert it. But as soon as ever the Prince became King the whole world began to find out that her will was the sole spring on which every movement in the Court turned; and though His Majesty lost no opportunity to declare that the Queen never meddled with his business, yet nobody was simple enough to believe it; and few besides himself would have been simple enough to hope or imagine it could be believed, since everybody who knew there was such a woman as the Queen, knew she not only meddled with business, but directed everything that came under that name, either at home or abroad. Her power was unrivalled and unbounded. How dearly she earned it will be the subject of future consideration in these papers.

It was in the summer of 1728 that that coolness, which afterwards ended in a total breach, began to show itself between Lord Townshend and Sir Robert Walpole. It was not yet grown to such a height as to be manifest to those moles of a Court who are always drudging on in their own interested little paths without seeing what passes every day around them; but those few alert courtiers who, like cautious and skilful sailors, see every cloud as soon as it rises and watch every wind as fast as it changes, already perceived the signs of this gathering tempest, prepared for its bursting, and began to set their sails in such a manner as should enable them to shift to the gale that was most favourable, and put them in a readiness to pursue the course they were in or tack about, just as the weather should require, and to that point of the compass where sunshine was most likely to appear.

Posterity will certainly be curious to learn what extraordinary cause there could be for this rupture between two men who, joined to the alliance of brotherhood, had for thirty years together lived in an uninterrupted intimacy on the strictest friendship.

A great mortification to Lord Townshend's pride was the seeing and feeling every day that Sir Robert Walpole, who came into the

world, in a manner, under his protection and inferior to him in
fortune, quality, and credit, was now, by the force of his infinitely
superior talents, as much above him in power, interest, weight,
credit, and reputation. All application was made to him. His house
was crowded like a fair with all sorts of petitioners, whilst Lord
Townshend's was only frequented by the narrow set of a few relations and particular flatterers; and as Lord Townshend in the late
reign had nothing but personal favour at Court to depend upon in
any disputes that might arise between him and Sir Robert, he could
not but grieve to find that resource in the new reign entirely taken
away, the scene quite inverted, and himself as much dependent now
upon Sir Robert's personal interest as Sir Robert had formerly been
upon his. For as the Duchess of Kendal[1] never loved Sir Robert
Walpole, and was weak enough to admire and be fond of Lord
Townshend, so in any nice points that were to be insinuated gently
and carried by favour in the last reign the canal of application to
the royal ear had always been from Lord Townshend to the
Duchess and from the Duchess to the King: whereas now everything that passed to the present King through the Queen (who was
to the son at least what the Duchess of Kendal had been to the
father) was suggested by Sir Robert, and nothing pushed or received
by her from any other hand.

In enumerating the seeds of Lord Townshend's disgust to Sir
Robert Walpole there is another occurs to me, which, trivial as it
may seem, I cannot help mentioning, because I firmly believe it
was a circumstance that operated so powerfully on the weak brain
and strong vanity of this great and noble Lord, that it contributed
more than all the rest put together to settle these little jealousies
and distastes into a fixed insurmountable aversion.

What I mean is, the great house which Sir Robert Walpole built
at Houghton, in Lord Townshend's neighbourhood in Norfolk.

Before Sir Robert Walpole built this house (which was one of
the best, though not of the largest, in England) Lord Townshend
looked upon his own seat at Raynham as the metropolis of Norfolk,
was proud of the superiority, and considered every stone that aug-
mented the splendour of Houghton as a diminution of the grandeur
of Raynham. Had Sir Robert Walpole raised this fabric of fraternal

[1] George I's mistress.

15

discord in any other county in England, it might have escaped the envy of this wise rival; but Sir Robert's partiality to the solum natale, the scene of his youth and the abode of his ancestors, made that neighbourhood, to which the accidental commencement of his friendship with Lord Townshend was first owing, the cause also of its dissolution.

As the misunderstanding between these two ministers increased, Lord Townshend began to think of forming a separate party at Court, and attaching some particular people to himself whom he could look upon as his personal friends, who should go under the denomination of Townshend's men, and on whom he might depend in case these dissensions should come to a total breach. Among these was Lord Trevor, then Privy Seal, and afterwards President of the Council.

There was an occurrence at the latter end of the summer at Windsor, relating to the court Lord Townshend then made to Lord Trevor, which I shall relate, because I think it will give a short but strong sketch both of Lord Townshend's and Sir Robert Walpole's temper; but before I begin my relation I must premise that Sir Robert Walpole at this time kept a very pretty young woman, daughter to a merchant, whose name was Skerret, and for whom he was said to have given (besides an annual allowance) £5,000 by way of entrance-money.[1]

One evening at Windsor the Queen asking Sir Robert Walpole and Lord Townshend where they had dined that day, the latter said he had dined at home with Lord and Lady Trevor; upon which Sir Robert Walpole said to Her Majesty, smiling, 'My Lord, Madam, I think is grown coquet from a long widowhood, and has some design upon my Lady Trevor's virtue, for his assiduity of late in that family is grown to be so much more than common civility, that without this solution I know not how to account for it.' What made this raillery of Sir Robert Walpole's very excusable and impossible to shock my Lord's prudery, let him pique himself ever so much on the chastity of his character, was that my good Lady Trevor, besides her strict life and conversation, was of the most virtuous forbidding countenance that natural ugliness, age, and small-pox ever compounded. However, Lord Townshend,

---

[1] Afterwards the second Lady Walpole.

affecting to take the reproach literally, and to understand what Sir Robert meant to insinuate of the political court he paid to the husband as sensual designs upon the wife, with great warmth replied, 'No, Sir, I am not one of those fine gentlemen who find no time of life, nor any station in the world, preservatives against the follies and immoralities that are hardly excusable when youth and idleness make us most liable to such temptations. They are liberties, Sir, which I can assure you I am as far from taking as from approving; nor have I either a constitution that requires such practices, a purse that can support them, or a conscience that can digest them.' Whilst he uttered these words his voice trembled, his countenance was pale, and every limb shook with passion. But Sir Robert Walpole, always master of his temper, made him no other answer than asking him with a smile, and in a very mild tone of voice, 'What, my Lord, all this for my Lady Trevor?'

The Queen grew uneasy, and to prevent Lord Townshend's replying or the thing being pushed any farther, only laughed, and began immediately to talk on some other subject.

I must now relate the particulars of a more private affair that passed at Court in the first year after His Majesty's accession to the throne. Mr. Howard, having a mind to turn his reputed cuckoldom to the best account, began to give his wife fresh trouble, and in order to make her pay for staying abroad pretended an inclination to have her return home. After, therefore, he had notified his pleasure to her by a summons forthwith to repair to her conjugal habitation, upon her disobedience to his amicable invitation he took out my Lord Chief Justice's warrant to seize her wherever he found her. This step so alarmed Mrs. Howard, who feared nothing so much as falling again into his hands, that for many months she was confined to the narrow limits of the walls of St. James's House, from whence she did not dare to stir one moment or one inch.

Her situation at this juncture was certainly a very odd one and the part she had to act equally extraordinary, difficult, and disagreeable. A husband ordered her home who did not desire to have her there, and a lover was to retain her who seemed already tired of keeping her. On the one side therefore she had authority to combat, and on the other indifference. She was to persuade a man who had power to torment her not to exert it, though it was his greatest pleasure; and to prevail with another who loved money and cared but little for her to part with what he did like in order to keep what he did not.

What was more extraordinary still on this occasion was that the power of her rival, instead of being exerted to disjoin her from her lover, was all employed in contriving means to prevent their separation, Her Majesty very prudently considering that she had nothing to fear from one she had already conquered; that Mrs. Howard's apartment, if she was banished, would not be long empty; and that a new tenant would expose Her Majesty to all these dangers which she had already gone through and surmounted in the time of the old one.

This being the case, a negotiation was set on foot to accommodate matters between Mr. and Mrs. Howard, and upon her obliging herself to pay her husband £1,200 a year during the life of his brother, the Earl of Suffolk (to whom he was next heir), he signed articles on his side by which he bound himself for the future to give her as little trouble in the capacity of a husband as he had ever done pleasure. And so this affair ended, the King paying the £1,200 a year for the possession of what he did not enjoy, and Mr. Howard receiving them, for relinquishing what he would have been sorry to keep.[1]

It was in this winter, just before the Parliament met, that the King was prevailed upon to send for his son from Hanover.[2] His ministers told him that if the Prince's coming was longer delayed an address from Parliament and the voice of a whole nation would certainly oblige His Majesty to send for him and consequently that he would be necessitated to do that with an ill grace which he might now do with a good one. These persuasions prevailed and the King, as children take physic, forced himself to swallow this bitter draught for fear of having it poured down his throat in case he did not take it quietly and voluntarily.

When first the Prince came over he was in great favour with his father, but it lasted not long. The King was pleased with him as a new thing, felt him quite in his power, contemned him as rival, made him no great expense and looked upon his being here with

---

[1] For a fuller account of this incident see pages 87–9.
[2] By George I's orders he had been left at Hanover to be educated there.

so little court paid to him as an escape from a danger which he had dreaded, and yet was obliged to expose himself to. Sir Robert Walpole told me one day that the King, speaking to him of his son soon after his arrival, said with an air of contempt and satisfaction: 'I think this is not a son I need be much afraid of.' But this relation I look upon as apocryphal and give it as such.

The allowance the King made him was two thousand pounds a month, which, with the income of the Duchy of Cornwall, came to about three or four and thirty thousand pounds a year. The opponents, who had a mind to get him, began their attack by telling him how ill his father used him in giving him this short allowance only instead of £100,000, which his father had had when he was Prince of Wales and which was understood by the Parliament, when the Civil List was settled at the beginning of this reign, to be designed now for His Royal Highness.

The Prince, on this occasion, as on all like occasions afterwards, between anger and timidity went just such lengths with those who were against the Court as served to irritate his father and not far enough to attach them to his service.

The Prince's character at his first coming over, though little more respectable, seemed much more amiable than it was upon his opening himself and being better known. For though there appeared nothing in him to be admired, yet there seemed nothing in him to be hated—neither nothing great nor nothing vicious. His behaviour was something that gained one's good wishes, though it gave one no esteem for him. For his best qualities, whilst they prepossessed one the most in his favour, always gave one a degree of contempt for him at the same time, his carriage, whilst it seemed engaging to those who did not examine it, appearing mean to those who did; for though his manners had the show of benevolence from a good deal of natural or habitual civility, yet his cajoling everybody, and almost in an equal degree, made those things which might have been thought favours, if more judiciously or sparingly bestowed, lose all their weight. He carried this affectation of general benevolence so far that he often condescended below the character of a Prince, and as people attributed this familiarity to popular and not particular motives, so it only lessened their respect without increasing their good will, and instead of giving them good impressions of his humanity, only gave them ill ones of his sincerity. He was indeed as false as his capacity would allow him to be, and was more capable in that walk than in any other, never having the least hesitation, from principle or fear of future detection, in telling any lie that served his present purpose. He had a much weaker understanding, and, if possible, a more obstinate temper, than his father; that is, more tenacious of opinions he had once formed, though less capable of ever having right ones. Had he had one grain of merit at the bottom of his heart, one should have had compassion for him in the situation to which his miserable poor head soon reduced him, for his case, in short, was this: he had a father that abhorred him, a mother that despised and neglected him, a sister that betrayed him, a brother set up to pique, and a set of servants that neither were of use to him, nor were capable of being of use to him, nor desirous of being so.

Among the remarkable occurrences of this winter I cannot help relating that of the Duchess of Queensberry being forbid the Court, and the occasion of it. One Gay, a poet, had written a ballad opera, which was thought to reflect a little upon the Court and a good deal upon the Minister. It was called *The Beggars' Opera*, had a prodigious run, and was so extremely pretty in its kind, that even those who were most glanced at in the satire had prudence enough to disguise their resentment by chiming in with the universal applause with which it was performed. Gay, who had attached himself to Mrs. Howard and been disappointed of preferment at Court, finding this couched satire upon those to whom he imputed his disappointment succeed so well, wrote a second part to this opera,[1] less pretty, but more abusive, and so little disguised, that Sir Robert Walpole resolved, rather than suffer himself to be produced for thirty nights together upon the stage in the person of a highwayman, to make use of his friend the Duke of Grafton's authority as Lord Chamberlain to put a stop to the representation of it. Accordingly this theatrical Craftsman[2] was prohibited at every playhouse. Gay, irritated at this bar thrown in the way both of his interest and his revenge, zested the work with some supplemental invectives, and resolved to print it by subscription. The Duchess of Queensberry sat herself at the head of this undertaking,

[1] *Polly.*   [2] The name of the chief opposition paper.

and solicited every mortal that came in her way, or in whose way she could put herself, to subscribe. To a woman of her quality, proverbially beautiful, and at the top of the polite and fashionable world, people were ashamed to refuse a guinea, though they were afraid to give it. Her solicitations were so universal and so pressing, that she came even into the Queen's apartment, went round the drawing-room, and made even the King's servants contribute to the printing of a thing which the King had forbid being recited. The King, when he came into the drawing-room, seeing her Grace very busy in a corner with three or four men, asked her what she had been doing. She answered, what must be agreeable, she was sure, to anybody so humane as His Majesty, for it was an act of charity and a charity to which she did not despair of bringing His Majesty to contribute. Enough was said for each to understand the other, and though the King did not then (as the Duchess of Queensberry reported) appear at all angry, yet this proceeding of her Grace's, when talked over in private between His Majesty and the Queen, was so resented, that Mr. Stanhope, then Vice-Chamberlain, was sent in form to the Duchess of Queensberry to desire her to forbear coming to Court. His message was verbal. Her answer, for fear of mistakes, she desired to send in writing, wrote it on the spot, and this is the literal copy:

Feb. 27, 1728–9.

That the Duchess of Queensberry is surprised and well pleased that the King hath given her so agreeable a command as to stay from Court, where she never came for diversion, but to bestow a great civility on the King and Queen; she hopes by such an unprecedented order as this is, that the King will see as few as he wishes at his Court, particularly such as dare to think or speak truth. I dared not do otherwise, and ought not nor could have imagined that it would not have been in the very highest compliment that I could possibly pay the King to endeavour to support truth and innocence in his house, particularly when the King and Queen both told me that they had not read Mr. Gray's play. I have certainly done right, then, to stand by my own words rather than his Grace of Grafton's, who hath neither made use of truth, judgment, nor honour, through this whole affair, either for himself or his friends.

C. QUEENSBERRY.

When her Grace had finished this paper, drawn with more spirit

21

than accuracy, she gave it to Mr. Stanhope, who desired her to think again, asked pardon for being so impertinent as to offer her any advice, but begged she would give him leave to carry an answer less rough than that she had put into his hands. Upon this she wrote another, but so much more disrespectful, that he desired the first again and delivered it.

Most people blamed the Court upon this occasion. What the Duchess of Queensberry did was certain impertinent; but the manner of resenting it was thought impolitic. The Duke of Queensberry laid down his employment of Admiral of Scotland upon it, though very much and very kindly pressed by the King to remain in his service.

Meanwhile Sir Robert Walpole's distress in the palace kept him still anxious, Lord Townshend's quarrel with him being got to that height that Lord Townshend would neither act on with him nor go out. He talked every day of retiring, but did not stir. The King was brought so far that he had consented to let him go, but would not force him out; the Queen wished him gone, but knew not how to make him go; and Lord Townshend, who, by quarrelling with Sir Robert Walpole and retiring to the country, thought to step quietly out of a sinking ship, when he found the storm subsiding and the ship not likely to sink, began to repent his having turned his eyes to the shore, and had a mind to remain on board. However, it was now too late, and in May 1730 Lord Townshend having positively declared to the King in the winter that he would quit, Sir Robert Walpole had got the King's leave to tell Mr. Stanhope that he should succeed Lord Townshend as Secretary of State. Mr. Stanhope, as a reward for his good services in concluding the Treaty of Seville,[1] had been immediately after created a Peer, by the title of Lord Harrington, and was now at Paris settling at that Court a plan for the execution of the Treaty of Seville by force, in case the Emperor should by force oppose it.

Lord Hervey was to succeed Lord Harrington as Vice-Chamberlain, and because it would have been a great inconvenience to have the borough of Bury[2] lie open all the summer, it was necessary to give Lord Hervey the gold key before the breaking up of the Parlia-

---

[1] A treaty of peace between France, Spain, and England.
[2] Bury St. Edmunds, where Lord Bristol controlled one of the seats.

ment, that he might be rechosen immediately.[1] This enabled Sir Robert Walpole to ask the King's leave to send for the key from Lord Harrington, and to promise him the seals in lieu of it as soon as he came to England, which, of course, pushed Lord Townshend out without Sir Robert seeming to take this step directly to precipitate Lord Townshend's departure. Accordingly, the key was sent for, and given to Lord Hervey.[2]

[1] At that date the Speaker could only issue a warrant for a writ for a by-election in pursuance of an order from the House of Commons, which could only be given when the House was sitting.

[2] The Memoirs of the next two and a half years have been destroyed—see the introductory note.

chapter two

Royal Marriage

1733

TOWARDS THE END of the Session of 1733 the King communicated by a message to both Houses the intended marriage of his eldest daughter, the Princess Royal, to the Prince of Orange, a miserable match both in point of man and fortune, his figure being deformed and his estate not clear £12,000 a year. It was, indeed, nominally double that, but the debts with which it was encumbered and other drawbacks reduced it to what I say. The turn, therefore, which good courtiers gave to this match, and which good subjects believed to be the case, was that the father, for the sake of this country, and the daughter, to ingratiate herself with the people, had consented to take up with this marriage to strengthen on contingencies the Protestant succession to this Crown, and renew an alliance with a family and a name always dear to this nation—an alliance from which this nation had formerly received many benefits, and from which it would not now be liable to incur those disadvantages which, if ever the Crown should be this Princess's inheritance, might attend her being married to a greater prince, who should have larger territories of his own.

This sounded so well that these fictitious merits were most eloquently displayed by all who spoke on this subject, either in the House of Lords or Commons, in order to make the fortune it was expected the Parliament should give, come so much the easier. But the true reason for this match was that there was, indeed, no other for the Princess in all Europe, so that Her Royal Highness's option was not between this Prince and any other, but between a husband and no husband; between an indifferent settlement and no settlement at all; and whether she would go to bed to this piece of

24

deformity in Holland, or die an ancient maid immured in her royal convent at St. James's.

On one side, her pride made her often reflect on the parting with her guards, and several other abatements of state consequential to this match; on the other, she was to consider, whenever her father died, what a disagreeable situation she would be in, dependent on her brother's bounty for a maintenance, and exposed to the mercy of a sister-in-law, who, she knew from her brother's weakness, could not fail of being both his mistress and hers. These considerations led her to that determination, which, grounded on private and personal reasons, was to wear the countenance of national and popular motives, whilst the good people of England were to express their gratitude for what was no obligation, and to extol that conduct as an heroic sacrifice to their interest, which was in reality a well-weighed consultation and prudential concern for her own.

The fortune given her by Parliament was £80,000, which, like her mother's jointure, and not very unlike her father's Civil List, was just double what had ever before been given on the like occasion. There was upwards of that sum at this time lying in the Exchequer, arising from the sale of St. Christopher's[1] and unappropriated by Parliament, which facilitated this generosity; the public on this occasion resembling some particulars, who are much more willing to give out of their stewards' hands than out of their own pockets, and ready enough to assign what they do not see, though they cannot part with what they do.

The Prince of Orange's figure, besides his being almost a dwarf, was as much deformed as it was possible for a human creature to be; his face was not bad, his countenance was sensible, but his breath more offensive than it is possible for those who have not been offended by it to imagine. The personal defects, unrecompensed by the éclat of rank or the more essential comforts of great riches, made the situation of the poor Princess so much more commiserable; for as her youth and an excellent warm animated constitution made her, I believe, now and then remember she was a woman, so I can answer for her that natural and acquired pride seldom or never let her forget she was a Princess, and as this match

[1] £93,000 from the sale of Crown Lands in St. Kitts-Nevis.

gave her little hope of gratifying the one, so it afforded as little prospect of supporting the other.

There is one of two inconveniences that generally attends most marriages; the one is sacrificing all consideration of interest and grandeur for the sake of beauty and an agreeable person; and the other, that of sacrificing all consideration of beauty and person to interest and grandeur. But this match most unfortunately conciliated the inconveniences of both these methods of marrying, and consequently without the advantages of either. However, as she apprehended the consequences of not being married at all must one time or other be worse than even the being so married, she very prudently submitted to the present evil to avoid a greater in futurity.

The Princess Royal's personal beauties were a lively clean look and a very fine complexion, though she was marked a good deal with the small-pox. The faults of her person were that of being very ill made, though not crooked, and a great propensity to fat. She had good parts, a very uncommon quickness in learning, and spoke English, French, German, and Italian, like a native of the four countries; she played on the harpsichord and sung everything at sight, loved needle-work and painting, and did both extremely well. She rose very early, was many hours alone and never unemployed. She had more command of her passions than people generally have whose passions are so strong, so that at the same time that she was by nature as prompt as her father, discretion generally disguised that hereditary fault in her, which, by the want of that discretion, often appeared in him. She was the proudest of all her proud family; and her family the proudest of all their proud nation.

But the valuing herself on her high rank was less excusable in her than in most of her family, because she had really some qualities besides her rank to value herself upon.

But between the strength of her pride, and the strength of her understanding, it is easy to imagine how great the conflict within her must have been on the proposal of this match; and all things considered how uncommon a degree she must have had of the latter for it to have been prevalent over so large a portion of the former.

A little after this intended marriage was made public, and nothing but a few forms remaining to be adjusted for the completion of it, I saw her walking in the garden at Richmond tête-à-tête with her father a considerable time, her hand constantly in his, he speaking with great earnestness and seeming affection, and she listening with great emotion and attention, the tears falling so fast all the while that her other hand went every moment to her cheek to wipe them away. At the conclusion of the conversation he embraced her, whilst she kissed his hand with as much seeming fondness and respect as the Prince of Orange could have kissed hers.

As those who had now the ear of the Prince lost no opportunity to irritate and blow him up against his father, so this marriage gave them occasion to make His Royal Highness think it very hard that the first establishment provided by Parliament for one of the royal progeny should be for any but the heir-apparent to the Crown. He was so very uneasy that to everybody his looks told he was so, and to many his words.

The day the message was brought to both Houses it was whispered about that some friend to the Prince or enemy to the King would take this opportunity of making a proposal in the House of Commons to address His Majesty for the settlement of £100,000 a year to be made on the Prince, which, at the time the Civil List was given, everybody understood and had taken for granted was designed to be done as soon as he should come over; but nobody, when it came to the push, being either zealous enough for the service of the son, or desperate enough with the father, to care to begin it, there was not the least mention made of this measure in public, though it had been so much discoursed of in private. Nor was it in the least to be wondered at that this project should never be brought to execution; in the first place, because the danger everyone ran of being betrayed who entered into any negotiation with His Highness made few people care to begin one; and, in the next place, because the instability of his conduct and the contempt that attended his character made him so little worth getting that no wise or prudent man cared to run any risk for any acquisition that was likely to prove of so small a value and so short a duration.

The coldness between the Prince and his parents at this time increased so much that it furnished conversation to the whole town, though it so far put an end to all that ever used to pass between him and his parents that the King never spoke to him, and the Queen very slightly. Lord Hervey in talking on this subject to Sir Robert Walpole said as natural as people might think it for him to be no personal friend to the Prince, or to wish any disgrace to attend him whilst he was under Mr. Dodington's direction,[1] yet he was really sorry to see the misunderstanding between him and his father drawing to such a height that if something was not done to prevent it nothing less than an open rupture could be expected to be the consequence of it, and that as this was likely to be but a troublesome, turbulent year, he thought those who wished well either to the family in general or even to the present Administration should try to prevent a rupture that must indisputably hurt the interest of the first and could not but create much trouble to the last. He said he was not absolutely of the scripture sentiment, that is, if this were to happen, this House divided against itself could not stand; but that he did think it would weaken its structure, which at this time rather wanted props, than any additional weight to be laid on its foundation. Sir Robert Walpole told Lord Hervey he was so much of his opinion that he had always talked in this strain to the King and Queen, but that they were both so stiff in their resentment and so exasperated against their son that there was no making them bend or temporise with his conduct in the smallest degree.

'I know,' replied Lord Hervey, 'the difficulty there is in persuading either of them to get the better of their pride in most cases. But if you can demonstrate it to be for the pecuniary interest of the other, there is nothing to which he may not be persuaded. Tell the Queen, then, that as Jacobitism is now every day trying all arts to spread itself, and every day gaining ground in the nation, there are those who will infallibly side with the son against his father, not out of love to the first, but out of enmity to the last, and who, knowing this civil contest to be the most favourable circumstance of their main point, will do all they can to foment and encourage it. At the same time you may tell the King that whatever provocations his son may give him, the nation and the Parliament will expect to have him kept, and kept out of the Civil List. What then will be the consequence of turning all the Prince's family in either

[1] Dodington had supplanted Hervey as the Prince's chief political adviser.

House into opponents, but the King's being obliged to pay those for voting against him, whom he now pays for voting for him, and consequently His Majesty's being forced to double the weight of expense in one scale in order to balance what will be taken out of it and thrown into the other?'

'I have often,' said Sir Robert Walpole, 'made these inconveniences stare them in the face, and they are both ready to agree with me that they ought to be prevented; but both differ with me in the means of doing it. For whilst I am always preaching lenity and gentleness the constant answer I receive is that I do not know their son so well as they do; that his understanding is to be influenced and his nature to be wrought upon by nothing but fear; that the more anybody advances towards him the further he retreats; that any step towards softening him would make it more difficult; and that endeavouring to stroke him would only be encouraging him to strike.'

'For my own part,' said Lord Hervey, 'when I was of the Prince's Cabinet Council, I used constantly to be preaching to him that a family quarrel always did a family in general hurt, and most commonly every particular engaged in it; and the greater the family, the greater the misfortune. For this reason I told him all prudent people ever thought it ought always to be avoided, and small inconveniences rather borne with than the great ones that attended such ruptures incurred; that Kings and Princes had much to lose and little to get; and that in disputes of this nature the friends to each side were generally losers; and the common enemies to both the only gainers. This way of reasoning used to have an effect on His Royal Highness, and I fancy if urged home it would not be thrown away on Their Majesties. But the truth of the matter is you do not dare (for what reason I know not) to tell them the ticklish situation they are in; how few friends and how many enemies they have in the kingdom; how unpopular they are to the nation in general, and to how few particulars they are agreeable; that the disaffection to their persons, and the uneasiness under their government increases daily; and that the King, instead of augmenting the number of his enemies by a foolish *fierté*, ought to make use of all those supple insinuating arts which a Prince should put on who wants friends and desires to make them.'

'What you are saying,' interrupted Sir Robert Walpole, 'is certainly true. But who shall tell them all this and expose themselves by such remonstrances to that *fierté*, my dear Lord, which you have described and I want to correct? Who shall tell him the true source of all the difficulties into which he has brought himself; that the affection of those who are called his friends decreases in the same proportion that the inveteracy of his foes augments; that it is as little the fashion to speak well of him in his palace as in the country, and that by his awkward, simple, proud conduct, even among all those whose interest is to be friends to his power, there is not one to be found who is a friend to his person?'

Lord Hervey said it would be very difficult indeed to tell him these things in these words, or all at once; but that he did not think it at all impossible by degrees and gentle means so far to acquaint him with his situation as, by the assistance of the Queen, to make him change his behaviour, and not let it at last prove dangerous to himself in essentials by being so continually disagreeable to other people in trifles as well as essentials. 'People who make their fortunes under a Prince will submit to be snubbed and ill used; and people who are caressed by a Prince, cajoled with good words, and treated with kindness, will serve him without great hire. But our Master endeavours by neither of these ways to attach people to his interest; he has not address enough to win them by flattery, nor has he liberality enough to gain by interest. For in no Court was there ever less to be got, though in no Court was there ever more to be done; never was greater attendance expected, nor ever fewer rewards distributed, and though the servants of no King were ever more punctually paid, yet none were ever less satisfied, nobody making a fortune under him, or getting more than just what defrayed the annual expenses of birthday clothes and the other necessary expenses incurred by dangling after a Court. The true state therefore of his case is (as you very well know) that as he cares for nobody, nobody cares for him; and that even his favours are so awkwardly bestowed that he gives without obliging, is served without being respected, and obeyed without being loved. This being his case I own,' continued Lord Hervey, 'I can by no means find out the good policy of letting him believe he is either popular among his subjects, or beloved by his servants, when the suffering him to continue in that error is the sure way to increase every difficulty in which it has already plunged both him and you. For if nobody is to be brought to serve him, but by the force of money, and more people every day are to be disobliged, the consequence of that must be the price of people every day rising, till the Civil List and the Exchequer will be too little to satisfy them. Besides, as his eyes and ears are both open to the writings and clamours now stirring in the world, if he thinks himself beloved in the nation, to what cause must he ascribe all the discontents he finds there, but to the unpopularity of his Ministers? And if he is to believe that no disaffection reaches him but what rebounds from them, what resolution can be so natural for him to take as that of changing them? You are likewise, in my opinion, all of you playing just the same timid injudicious part with regard to the elections that are coming on, by making him believe they are all in a very good way, and that you cannot fail of a Parliament to your mind; by which means you expose yourselves to two evils, one in present, the other a little more remote; the present evil is the difficulty you will find after such representations to make him give his money freely which you know you must have, and cannot do without. The remoter evil is, that when he shall find at the time of the elections how matters go he must certainly reproach your foresight or your truth and say you were either so ignorant as not to know the situation of the kingdom and the temper of his people, or that you knew both and deceived him.'

This conversation was interrupted by the Duke of Newcastle, who made his entry with as much alacrity and noise as usual, mightily out of breath though mightily in words, and in his hand a bundle of papers as big as his head and with little more in them.

This summer Lord Hervey had more frequent opportunities than any other person about the Court of learning the Queen's sentiments on these affairs, and conveying to her his own. Wednesdays and Saturdays, which were the King's days for hunting, he had her to himself for four or five hours, Her Majesty always hunting in a chaise, and as she neither saw nor cared to see much of the chase, she had undertaken to mount Lord Hervey the whole summer (who loved hunting as little as she did), so that he might ride constantly by the side of her chaise, and entertain her whilst other people were entertaining themselves with hearing dogs bark and seeing crowds gallop.

Sunday and Monday Lord Hervey lay constantly in London; every other morning he used to walk with the Queen and her daughters at Hampton Court. His real business in London was pleasure, but as he always told the King it was to pick up news, to hear what people said, to see how they looked, and to inform Their Majesties what was thought by all parties of the present posture of affairs, he by these means made his pleasure in town and his interest at Court reciprocally conducive to each other.

These excursions put it also in his power to say things as from other people's mouths, which he did not dare to venture from his own, and often to deliver that as the effect of his observation which in reality flowed only from his opinion. However, that he might not draw on others the anger which by this method he diverted from himself, he used, both to the King and the Queen, to say he would willingly let them know everything he heard, but must beg leave always to be excused from telling where he had it or from whom; and as it was of much more use to Their Majesties to know what was said than by whom, so he hoped they would give him leave whilst for their sakes he communicated the one, for his own to be silent upon the other.

On these terms they accepted of his intelligence, and by these preliminaries he was in possession of saying the most disagreeable truths without either being reproved or being called upon for his authors.

The beginning of November the Prince of Orange arrived, and was lodged in Somerset House. Almost all the nobility and people of distinction in England went to wait upon him there; several were of that number who did not come to Court. He came the next morning to St. James's through crowded streets and unceasing acclamations, though the equipage the King sent to fetch him was only one miserable leading coach with only a pair of horses and a pair of footmen.

The palace was so thronged that he could hardly get upstairs or pass from one room to another, most people having a curiosity to see him, and few having yet found out that making their court to him was not making it at all to his future father-in-law.

The maxim the King seemed to have laid down to govern his conduct towards this Prince, and the opinion he seemed to desire tacitly to inculcate, was that the Prince of Orange was a nothing till he had married his daughter, and that being her husband made him everything.

Conformable to this maxim he suffered no sort of public honours to be paid to the Prince on his arrival, and behaved himself with scarce common civility towards him, which the Prince of Orange had sense enough to feel and to seem not to see. The Tower guns were not allowed to salute him, nor was the guard permitted to turn out upon his arrival. Lord Lovelace was sent with one of the King's coaches to receive him at his landing, and with great difficulty the King was persuaded, the night the Prince came first to Somerset House, to send Lord Hervey to him with a compliment.

The Queen desired Lord Hervey the instant he returned to come directly to her apartment, and let her know without disguise what sort of hidden animal she was to prepare herself to see. Lord Hervey, when he came back, assured her he had not found him near to bad as he had imagined; that she must not expect to see an Adonis; that his body was as bad as possible; but that his countenance was far from disagreeable, and his address sensible, engaging, and noble; that he seemed entirely to forget his person, and to have an understanding to make other people forget it too.

Lord Hervey said he fancied the Princess must be in a good deal of anxiety, but the Queen told him he was extremely mistaken; that she was in her own apartment at her harpsichord with some of the Opera people, and that she had been as easy all that afternoon as she had ever seen her in her life. 'For my part,' said the Queen, 'I never said the least word to encourage her to this marriage or to dissuade her from it; the King left her, too, absolutely at liberty to accept or reject it; but as she thought the King looked upon it as a proper match, and one which, if she could bear his person, he should not dislike, she said she was resolved, if it was a monkey, she would marry him.'

From the Queen Lord Hervey went to the Princesses, who were equally impatient for a description of their new brother-in-law, as if they were more likely to have a true one for his being in the

same town than they were from one who had only seen him in
Holland.

The Princess Royal's behaviour next day, and indeed every day,
with the eyes of the whole nation upon her, was something prodigious for propriety, sense, and ease. The Monday following was
the day fixed for the ceremony; but the Prince being taken ill of a
fever the day before, it was put off. He continued ill a long time;
was thought at first in immediate danger, and for a considerable
time in a languishing condition from which it was impossible he
should ever recover.

During this tedious and dangerous illness no one of the Royal
Family went to see him. The King thought it below his dignity,
and the rest, whatever they thought, were not allowed to do it.

The Prince of Orange could not but be extremely concerned at
this treatment; but had, however, the prudence to be silent on a
chapter which his Dutch booby retinue had the imprudence to
preach upon all day and in all companies.

As soon as he was able to go out he went to St. James's, and by
chance dined with the Princesses, who were forbidden to invite him
any more. He removed to Kensington for the air, and was from
thence sent to the Bath. But on his arrival in England, on the day
for the marriage being set, on its being put off, on his illness, on his
recovery, on his being in danger, on his being out of it, the countenance of the Princess Royal to the nicest examiners appeared exactly
the same; which surprised everybody so much the more as she was
known to be of a temper to which nothing was really indifferent,
whatever it appeared.

The Prince of Wales forced himself to be tolerably civil to the
Prince of Orange, though he was hurt at the distinctions paid him
by the nation. Yet the Prince of Wales had at least this satisfaction
in obliging himself to do what he thought right on this occasion,
that he was sure what he was doing was disagreeable to his father.

As to his sister, the Princess Royal, whenever he spoke of her,
it was with as little decency as affection. His mother was not much
more in favour than his sister. He said they were both so interested,
so false, so designing, and so worthless, that it was as impossible
to love or value them, as it was to trust them without being
betrayed, or believe them without being deceived.

The opponents conceived great hopes from these family divisions of strengthening their party this winter in Parliament by the Prince's declaring openly for them. Everybody talked of these quarrels, but the whole family was so little popular that few people justified any of the parties concerned in them or wished them reconciled.

Those in power, fearing they might be hurt by things coming to an extremity, endeavoured for their own interest to palliate and soften matters between the father and the son, but cared no more personally for either of them than they did for one another.

On New Year's Day the Prince of Wales was persuaded by Mr. Dodington to go to the King's levée, where he had not made his appearance for some months, and was now induced to it not from a desire to show respect to his father, but in order (hoping the King would not speak to him) to show the world how ill he was used and what little encouragement he had to pay his father any compliment of that kind. Lord Hervey, who knew from Mr. Hedges (the Prince's treasurer), the night before, that the Prince intended going to the King's levée, told the Queen of it, and desired her to contrive the King's speaking to him, to prevent what they proposed, telling her how useful it would be towards stopping the report of the Prince's ill usage, and what a damp it would cast upon the schemes of those who built their hopes of annoyance this winter upon the expectation of an open rupture in the family.

This intimation had its effect. The Prince was spoken to in the presence of that numerous appearance of bowing nobility and gentry who generally thronged the palace on those days, and the report of no intercourse either of words or visits passing between these two great personages was, of course, contradicted.

Lord Hervey took the opportunity of this interview with the Queen, and the Prince's name being mentioned, to tell her that even the best friends to her, the King, and the Administration were of opinion that the Prince had not money enough allowed him, and that whilst he was so straitened in his circumstances it was impossible he should ever be quiet. 'My God!' said the Queen, 'that people will always be judging and deciding upon what they know nothing of; who are these wise people?' Lord Hervey desired to be excused, and she went on. 'Pray, when you hear them, my Lord, talk their nonsense again, tell them that the Prince costs the King £50,000 a year, which, till he is married, I believe any reasonable body will think a sufficient allowance for him. But, poor creature, with not a bad heart, he is induced by knaves and fools that blow him up to do things that are as unlike an honest man as a wise one. I wonder what length those monsters wish to carry him. But talk to me no more of his usage; I wish he was as right towards the King as the King is towards him.' Lord Hervey said he did not at all dispute the fact of the Prince's costing the King £50,000 a year; but if Her Majesty would give him leave, he would only ask why, instead of the King's being at half that expense invisibly, he would not choose rather to let the Prince keep his own table and give him that allowance in a lump, which everybody would acknowledge to be sufficient, and which, given in this manner, would be at once more useful and satisfactory to the Prince, and more creditable as well as less troublesome to the King. When she was pressed upon this point she had nothing to answer, but that the King did not choose it should be so. But the truth was, they both hated their son to that immoderate degree that they would rather put themselves to inconveniences than make him easy; and whilst she talked of his not having a bad heart, she had (if possible) yet a worse opinion of that than of his head.

This being the Prince's present situation, his debts numerous, his creditors importunate, and his treasury empty, the clandestine correspondence between him and the Opposition continued in full force, he hoping to make some use of their despair, and they of his distress.

I cannot help mentioning two instances of the King's ungiving disposition,[1] which I think such strong proofs of it, that, to people who know not the millions of corroborating testimonies one might bring, they would be alone sufficient to demonstrate it.

The instances I mean are my Lord Lifford, and his sister, Lady Charlotte de Roucy. These two people, born in France, having more religion than sense, left their native country on account of being Protestants; and being of great quality, and not in great circumstances, had, during four reigns, subsisted upon the scanty

[1] See pp. 30–1.

charity of the English Court. They were constantly, every night in the country, and three nights in the week in town, alone with the King and Queen for an hour or two before they went to bed, during which time the King walked about and talked to the brother of armies, or to the sister of genealogies, whilst the Queen knotted and yawned, till from yawning she came to nodding, and from nodding to snoring.

These two poor miserable Court drudges were in more constant waiting than any of the pages of the back stairs, were very simple and very inoffensive, did nobody any hurt, nor gave anybody but His Majesty any pleasure, who paid them so ill for all their assiduity and slavery, that they were not only in affluence, but laboured under the disagreeable burdens of small debts (which a thousand pounds would have paid), and had not an allowance from the Court that enabled them to appear there even in the common decency of clean clothes. The King, nevertheless, was always saying how well he loved them, and calling them the best people in the world. But, though he never forgot their goodness, he never remembered their poverty; and by affording them so much of his time, which nobody but him would have given them, and so little of his money, which everybody but him in his situation would have afforded them, he gave one just as good an opinion of his understanding by what he bestowed, as he did of his generosity by what he withheld. The Queen, whose most glaring merit was not that of giving, was certainly with regard to this poor woman as blameable as the King. For the playthings of princes, let them be ever so trifling, ought always to be gilt, those who contribute to their pleasure having a right to their bounty. To most people, however, it was a matter of wonder how the King and Queen could have such insipid animals constantly with them. The truth of the case was that the King had no taste for better company, and the Queen, though she had a better taste, was forced to mortify her own to please his. Her predominant passion was pride, and the darling pleasure of her soul was power; but she was forced to gratify the one and gain the other, as some people do health, by a strict and painful régime, which few besides herself could have had patience to support, or resolution to adhere to. She was at least seven or eight hours tête-à-tête with the King every day, during which time she was generally saying what she did not think, assenting to what she did not believe, and praising what she did not approve; for they were seldom of the same opinion, and he too fond of his own for her ever at first to dare to controvert it ('consilii quamvis egregii quod ipse non afferret, inimicus'). She used to give him her opinion as jugglers do a card, by changing it imperceptibly, and making him believe he held the same with that he first pitched upon. But that which made these tête-à-têtes seem heaviest was that as he neither liked reading nor being read to (unless it was to sleep) she was forced, like a spider, to spin out of her own bowels all the conversation with which the fly was taken. However, to all this she submitted for the sake of power, and for the reputation of having it; for she was with regard to this as some men are to their amours, the vanity of being thought to possess what she desired was equal to the pleasure of the possession itself. But, either for the appearance or the reality, she knew it was absolutely necessary to have interest in her husband, as she was sensible that interest was the measure by which people would always judge of her power. Her every thought, word, and act therefore tended and was calculated to preserve her influence there; to him she sacrificed her time, for him she mortified every inclination; she looked, spake, and breathed but for him, was a weathercock to every capricious blast of his uncertain temper, and governed him (if influence so gained can bear the name of government) by being as great a slave to him thus ruled, as any other wife could be to a man who ruled her. For all the tedious hours she spent then in watching him whilst he slept, or the heavier task of entertaining him whilst he was awake, her single consolation was in reflecting she had power, and that people in coffee-houses and ruelles[1] were saying she governed this country, without knowing how dear the government of it cost her.

The Queen (who never cared to have Liffords, Miremonts,[2] and Charlotte de Roucys with her but for the King's amusement) loved reading and the conversation of men of wit and learning. But she did not dare to indulge herself as much as she wished to do in this pleasure for fear of the King, who often rebuked her for dabbling in all that lettered nonsense (as he termed it), called her a pedant,

---

[1] 'A circle; assembly at a private house' (*Johnson's Dictionary*).
[2] Another Huguenot refugee.

and said she loved to spend her time more like a schoolmistress than a queen. The King used often to brag of the contempt he had for books and letters; to say how much he hated all that stuff from his infancy; and that he remembered when he was a child he did not hate reading and learning merely as other children do upon account of the confinement, but because he despised it and felt as if he was doing something mean and below him.

The Queen had formerly read a great deal, but after her coming to the throne she had very little time for reading. She understood good writing too in English, the harmony of numbers in verse, the beauty of style in prose, and the force and propriety of terms much better than anybody who had only heard her speak English would ever have thought possible. She had a most incredible memory and was as learned both in ancient and modern history as the most learned men. But as Lord Hervey often used to tell her, she was so profuse of her memory that one could not help grudging her a talent she so often squandered. For there was hardly a romance of ten or twenty volumes ever written of which she was not able to give as good and exact an account as to all the facts, the names of the people concerned in them, and their fictitious genealogies, as she could of any of the most remarkable incidents, or the most celebrated heroes, in the history of Greece and Rome; and was as well versed in pedigrees that were of no more signification than Pantagruel's in Rabelais as she was in those of every reigning prince then in Europe, which I believe she could have traced from the building of Rome or destruction of Troy to the present generation with all their intermarriages and bastards.

There was one sort of study she liked, but did not go near the bottom of it, and that was metaphysics. Those who had heard her talk on that subject and never on any other would have thought she had had as clouded a genius, as superficial a way of thinking, and as inconclusive a way of reasoning, as any head that ever was crowned. This might in part perhaps proceed from some little German prejudices and superstitions contracted by education and strengthened by the unenlightened instructors and companions of her early life, which their wiser successors here could not quite eradicate; and partly, it may be, from her not daring to speak her real opinion but by halves, and choosing rather to let people imagine she thought imperfectly, than to put it in anybody's power to say she talked imprudently. For as she knew she had the reputation of being a little heterodox in her notions, she often (as she has frequently owned) denied herself the pleasure of seeing and conversing with men who lay under that imputation. And it is very probable the same way of reasoning might prevent her giving occasion any other way to the consequences she apprehended from these correspondences.

I must now give an account of the marriage of the Princess Royal. The Prince of Orange returned to Somerset House from the Bath the beginning of March in perfect health, and on the 14th of that month he was married. A covered gallery (through which the procession passed) was built from the King's apartment quite round the palace garden to the little French chapel adjoining to St. James's House (where the ceremony was performed). The gallery held four thousand people, was very finely illuminated, and, by the help of three thousand men who were that day upon guard, the whole was performed with great regularity and order, as well as splendour and magnificence. Lord Hervey had the care of the ceremonial, and drew the plan for the order of the procession.

The hour appointed for all those who were to walk in the procession to assemble was seven at night. The bridegroom, with all the men, was in the Great Council Chamber; the bride, with all the ladies, in the Great Drawing-room; and the King and Queen, with their children and servants, in the King's lesser drawing-room. The Prince of Orange's whole retinue was as magnificent as gold and silver varied in brocade, lace, and embroidery could make them, and the jewels he gave the Princess of immense value, particularly the necklace, which was so large that twenty-two diamonds made the whole round of her neck.

The chapel was fitted up with an extreme good taste, and as much finery as velvets, gold and silver tissue, galloons, fringes, tassels, gilt lustres and sconces could give. The King spared no expense on this occasion; but if he had not loved a show better than his daughter, he would have chosen rather to have given her this money to make her circumstances easy, than to have laid it out in making her wedding splendid.

He behaved himself well during the ceremony; but her mother and sisters were under so much undisguised and unaffected concern the whole time, that the procession to the chapel, and the scene there, looked more like the mournful pomp of a sacrifice than the joyful celebration of a marriage, and put one rather in mind of an Iphigenia leading to the altar than of a bride.

The Prince of Orange was a less shocking and less ridiculous figure in this pompous procession and at supper than one could naturally have expected such an Æsop, in such trappings and such eminence, to have appeared. He had a long peruke like hair that flowed all over his back, and hid the roundness of it; and as his countenance was not bad there was nothing very strikingly disagreeable but his stature.

But when he was undressed, and came in his nightgown and nightcap into the room to go to bed, the appearance he made was as indescribable as the astonished countenances of everybody who beheld him. From the make of his brocaded gown, and the make of his back, he looked behind as if he had no head, and before as if he had no neck and no legs. The Queen, in speaking of the whole ceremony next morning alone with Lord Hervey, when she came to mention this part of it, said, 'Ah! mon Dieu! quand je voyois entrer ce monstre, pour coucher avec me fille, j'ai pensé m'évanouir; je chancelois auparavant, mais ce coup là m'a assommée. Dites-moi, my Lord Hervey, avez-vous bien remarqué et considéré ce monstre dans ce moment? et n'aviez-vous pas bien pitié de la pauvre Anne? Bon Dieu! c'est trop sotte en moi, mais j'en pleure encore.' Lord Hervey turned the discourse as fast as he was able, for this was a circumstance he could not soften and would not exaggerate. He only said, 'Lord! Madam, in half a year all persons are alike. The figure of the body one's married to, like the prospect of the place one lives at, grows so familiar to one's eye, that one looks at it mechanically, without regarding either the beauties or deformities that strike a stranger.' 'One may, and I believe one does (replied the Queen), grow blind at last; but you must allow, my dear Lord Hervey, there is a great difference, as long as one sees, in the manner of one's growing blind.'

The sisters spoke much in the same style as the mother, with horror of his figure, and great commiseration of the fate of his wife.

Princess Emily lied and said nothing upon earth should have induced her to marry the monster. Princess Caroline, in her soft sensible way, spoke truth, and said she must own it was very bad; but that, in her sister's situation, all things considered, she believed she should have come to the same resolution.

What seems most extraordinary was that from the time of their being married till they went out of England, Lord Hervey (who was perpetually with them, and at whose lodgings they passed whole evenings) said that she always behaved to him as if he had been an Adonis, and that he hardly ever took any notice at all of her nor gave her one look (that he had observed) by which one could have guessed that they had ever slept in the same sheets. But she made prodigious court to him, addressed everything she said to him, and applauded everything he said to anybody else.

The Prince of Wales forced himself to be tolerably civil to the Prince of Orange during his stay here; but with the Queen and the Princess Royal he kept so little measure, that the one he never saw but in public, and the other he hardly ever spoke to either in public or private.

One of his wise quarrels with the Princess Royal was her 'daring to be married before him,' and consenting to take a portion from the Parliament, and an establishment from her father, before those honours and favours were conferred upon him. As if her being married prevented his being so, or that the daughter should decline being settled because her father declined the settling of her brother.

Another judicious subject of his enmity was her supporting Handel, a German musician and composer (who had been her singing master, and was now undertaker of one of the operas), against several of the nobility who had a pique to Handel, and had set up another person to ruin him; or, to speak more properly and exactly, the Prince, in the beginning of his enmity to his sister, set himself at the head of the other opera to irritate her, whose pride and passions were as strong as her brother's (though his understanding was so much weaker), and could brook contradiction, where she dared to resent it, as little as her father.

What I have related may seem a trifle, but though the cause was indeed such, the effects of it were no trifles. The King and Queen were as much in earnest upon this subject as their son and daughter, though they had the prudence to disguise it, or to endeavour to disguise it, a little more. They were both Handelists, and sat freezing constantly at his empty Haymarket Opera, whilst the Prince with all the chief of the nobility went as constantly to that of Lincoln's Inn Fields. The affair grew as serious as that of the Greens and the Blues under Justinian at Constantinople. An anti-Handelist was looked upon as an anti-courtier, and voting against the Court in Parliament was hardly a less remissible or more venial sin than speaking against Handel or going to the Lincoln's Inn Fields Opera. The Princess Royal said she expected in a little while to see half the House of Lords playing in the orchestra in their robes and coronets; and the King (though he declared he took no part in this affair than subscribing £1,000 a year to Handel) often added at the same time that he did not think setting oneself at the head of a faction of fiddlers a very honourable occupation for people of quality; or the ruin of one poor fellow so generous or so good-natured a scheme as to do much honour to the undertakers, whether they succeeded or not; but the better they succeeded in it, the more he thought they would have reason to be ashamed of it. The Princess Royal quarrelled with the Lord Chamberlain for affecting his usual neutrality on this occasion, and spoke of Lord Delaware, who was one of the chief managers against Handel, with as much spleen as if he had been at the head of the Dutch faction who opposed the making her husband Stadtholder.

Another cause of the Prince of Wales's wrath to his mother and his sisters was the having Lord Hervey perpetually with them; a gold snuff-box the Queen bespoke, the Arts and Sciences engraved upon it, and gave to Lord Hervey, the Prince said was less in favour to Lord Hervey than to insult and outrage him, and that it was extremely hard a man whom the whole world knew had been so impertinent to him and whom he never spoke to should be picked out by the Queen for her constant companion and her most distinguished favourite.

He told his sisters that the reason of his coming so seldom to the Queen was Lord Hervey's always being there; that they knew he had as lief see the devil as Lord Hervey; that the Queen knew it too, and consequently he supposed kept Lord Hervey there to keep him away.

His sisters told him it was very strange that he should think of making a privilege of choosing his mother's companions one of the conditions of his paying his duty to her. They owned that Lord Hervey had been in the wrong to him once, but that he had behaved with great respect and seeming penitence ever since. They said, too, that this crime was committed two years ago; that the Queen had resented it at first; but when Lord Hervey had done all he could to atone for his fault and was so assiduous a servant in private and so useful to the Court in public, that it would neither be prudent in the Queen with regard to herself, nor just in her with regard to Lord Hervey, still to behave to him as if he was never to be forgiven, and that all his attachment, submission, and services should for ever for the future be to no purpose.

Besides this they said that the King liked to have Lord Hervey with him and made him come to give an account of the proceedings of one House of Parliament or the other every day; in short that he was useful and agreeable both to the King and Queen, and though his crime had been of such a nature that the Prince might expect the Queen not to protect him at first, yet it was not of that sort that no repentance could wipe away the remembrance of it; and that if Lord Hervey's past conduct had deserved the Queen's anger, it must be owned too that by his behaviour ever since he had merited her forgiveness.

The Prince, who never forgot an injury or remembered an obligation, was not convinced by these arguments; nor indeed was the natural and insuperable obstinacy of his temper any more capable of receiving conviction from justice or compassion than his understanding was from the light of truth or the force of reason. The only effect therefore this language had upon him was to exasperate him towards his sisters and not to mollify him in the least towards Lord Hervey. When I speak of the Prince's sisters on this occasion I mean the Princess Royal and Princess Caroline. For the Princess Emily, besides the desire of making her court to her brother, was glad of any back to lash, and the sorer it was the gladder she was to strike. She had much the least sense (except her brother) of the whole family, but had for two years much the prettiest person. She was lively, false, and a great liar; did many ill offices to people and no good ones; and for want of prudence said almost as many shocking things to their faces as for want of a good-nature or truth she said disagreeable ones behind their backs. She had as many enemies as acquaintances, for nobody knew her without disliking her, nor was anybody acquainted with her without knowing her; and everybody in the Court being of the same opinion about her, people spoke their opinion with as little caution as variation. Her sister Caroline's character was just the reverse of hers. She was extremely sensible and not remarkably lively; and as the one would talk very freely of faults in people which she had never discovered, the other's good sense discovered faults which her good-nature prevented her talking of. The Princess Caroline had the finest complexion and the finest bright brown hair that could be seen. She had very pretty limbs too, but her person was rather too fat. She had affability without meanness, dignity without pride, cheerfulness without levity, and prudence without falsehood. She spent her whole time in reading and drawing, was a favourite neither with her mother nor her father, but was passionately fond of her eldest sister, and as well beloved by her as anybody could be that was neither a flatterer of her pride, nor a fool to her ambition. Not that the Princess Royal's pride and ambition were so strong as to get the better of all her passions, though they gave those of tenderness little room to work. Her behaviour to her brother was an instance of her interest, though few other passions made that conquest. For though she had nothing more in point of money perhaps to expect from him, and that she did not care if he went to the devil, or perhaps wished him there, yet in her situation there might be so many contingencies to make the friendship of her brother of use to her hereafter that she ought in prudence to have behaved towards him in a manner that would have made his friendship less irretrievable.

The Princess Royal, with all her good sense, was very imprudent, too, with regard to her manner of talking of her father, and not quite grateful. For her father, as flippant as he was in distributing the shocking effects of his prompt capricious temper to most people, gave so very small a portion of it to the Princess Royal, that he had, I think, a right to have her speak of it at least in the proportion she suffered by it. But she certainly did not love him, and in many occurrences showed it too plainly. She was glad of opportunities to point out his faults, and wherever these were small enough to admit of it she would magnify them and deepen the colours, without caution enough, too, to whom she ventured to communicate herself. After she had quarrelled with her brother she grew very intimate with Lord Hervey, but before that, she had hardly ever been commonly civil to him. For whilst Lord Hervey was well with the Prince she was jealous of his power there and spoke ill of him to weaken it; when he lost power, she spoke ill of him to make her court to her brother, and made a merit to the Prince of behaving to Lord Hervey in a manner which did not proceed from her friendship to the one but a propensity to hurt the other. But notwithstanding she must know that Lord Hervey had seen and felt these disobligations he had to her, yet when she took to having the appearance of being well with him she spoke as freely against her father to him as she had ever done to her brother of him. One day that the King was extremely out of humour and more than ordinarily froward, Lord Hervey, staying tête-à-tête with the Princess Royal in her apartment at Kensington (the King and Queen and her sisters were walking), said he could not imagine what had made the King so abominably cross all that day, for that no letters were come from abroad, and he did not know of anything that had gone ill at home. 'My God!' replied the Princess Royal, 'I am ashamed for you, who have been so long about Papa, to know so little of him as when he is the most peevish and snappish to think it is the most material things that have made him so. When great points go as he would not have them, he frets and is bad to himself; but when he is in his worst humours, and the devil to everybody that comes near him, it is always because one of his pages has powdered his periwig ill, or a housemaid set a chair where it does not use to to stand, or something of that kind.'

His passion, his pride, his vanity, his loving to talk of himself, his military declamations, his giving himself airs about women, the impossibility of being easy with him, his affectation of heroism, his unreasonable, simple, uncertain, disagreeable, and often shocking behaviour to the Queen, the difficulty of entertaining him, his insisting upon people's conversation who were to entertain him being always new, and his own being always the same thing over and over again, in short all his weaknesses, all his errors and all his faults, were the topics upon which at Kensington the summer after she was married (when she was most with Lord Hervey) she was for ever expatiating.

In a few days after the Parliament was up the Princess Royal and Prince of Orange embarked at Greenwich for Holland. Never was there a more melancholy parting than between Her Royal Highness and all her family, except her brother, who took no leave of her at all, and desired the Prince of Orange to let her know his reason for omitting it was the fear of touching her too much. Her father gave her a thousand kisses and a shower of tears, but not one guinea.

Her mother never ceased crying for three days. But after three weeks (excepting post-days) Her Royal Highness seemed as much forgotten as if she had been buried three years. So quick a smoother is absence of the deepest impressions royal minds are capable of receiving. Impressions that are only to be preserved by an effort of memory and reflection are indeed, in all human compositions, like characters written in sand, that, if they are not perpetually retained by our senses, they are seldom of any great duration, and are easily effaced, though ever so strongly marked.

Whilst the Princess lay wind-bound at Gravesend Lord Hervey went, by her desire, to make her a visit: and here it was, by being closeted two or three hours with the Prince of Orange, Lord Hervey found his bride had already made him so well acquainted with this Court, that there was nobody belonging to it whose character, even to the most minute particulars, was not as well known to him as their face. The Prince of Orange had a good deal of drollery, and, whilst Lord Hervey was delivering the compliments of St. James's to him, he asked him, smiling, what messages he had brought from the Prince. Lord Hervey said his departure was so sudden that he had not seen the Prince. 'If you had' (replied the Prince of Orange) 'it would have been all one, since he was not more likely to send his sister a message than he was to make your Lordship his ambassador.' Lord Hervey was a good deal surprised to hear the Prince of Orange speak so freely on this subject, and did not think it very discreet in him; but he was still more surprised when His Highness proceeded to open himself so much on the Prince of Wales's character as made it not hard to discover that his affection to the Prince's person, his opinion of his understanding, his dependence on his truth, and his esteem for his integrity, were all much at the same pitch. He told Lord Hervey what the Prince had said about taking leave of his sister, at which they both smiled. He then acquainted Lord Hervey how often the Prince had entertained him with the recital of his Lordship's ingratitude, a subject on which Lord Hervey begged His Highness to spare him, since it must be extremely disagreeable to anybody to listen to one's own accusation when they were determined never to enter into their defence. The Prince of Orange, however, went on, and talked of Miss Vane,[1] and bade Lord Hervey not to be too proud of that boy, since he had heard from very good authority it was the child of a triumvirate, and that the Prince and Lord Harrington had full as good a title to it as himself. Lord Hervey told the Prince of Orange that his speaking to him in this strain was not only the most effectual, but the most disagreeable method he could take to impose silence upon him, and begged they might either change the topic of their conversation or go to the company below stairs. The Prince of Orange, seeing him really uneasy and embarrassed, began to talk of the affairs of Europe, and showed he was as well informed of the interests of all foreign Courts as he was of the anecdotes of this.

The day the Princess set sail from Gravesend the King and Queen retired to Richmond, where they waited the account of every election under as much anxiety as if their Crown had been at stake. The complexion of the new Parliament was indeed of great moment to them; for never was an opposing party more exasperated against a Court, or a stiffer struggle made to distress it.

Notwithstanding the severe Act passed in the year 1729 to prevent bribery and corruption in elections, yet money, though it had been formerly more openly given, was never more plentifully issued than in these. Every election that went against the Court the King imputed to the fault of those who lost it, and much too frequently, and too publicly, accused the Whigs of negligence; saying at the same time, that if the Tories had had a quarter of the support from the Government that the Whigs had received from it for twenty years together, they would never have suffered the Crown to be

[1] A promiscuous maid of honour, who had been Hervey's mistress but had left him to become the Prince's.

pushed and the Court to be distressed in the manner it now was; and generally added to these declarations, that he would not help saying, for the honour of the Tories, that they were always much firmer united, and much more industrious and circumspect, than the Whigs.

That the King often dropped things of this kind was no secret to either party, and as it piqued the one it animated the other; hurting the cause of those he espoused, and promoting the interest of those he wished to depress.

'This,' said the Queen, in speaking on this subject to Lord Hervey, 'is always the way of your nasty Whigs: though they themselves are supported by the Crown, they are always lukewarm in returning that support to the Crown. They think everything must be done for them and that they are obliged to do nothing themselves in return. Out of place, they are always ready to fall upon the Crown and think in place they have merit enough if they do not join in distressing it, and only stand by and see others tear one in pieces. You other fine Roman and English spirits are so very grateful generally to your Prince, that you grudge him even the power of doing you good, though he employs it only that way, and has no enemies, but such as are so because he employs you and lets you engross all his favour.'

'This is a very heavy charge upon the Whigs,' said Lord Hervey, 'and what, if I thought they deserved, I assure Your Majesty I should be as ready to condemn them [for] as you could be. But give me leave to say, Madam, what I sincerely think, and that is, that if ever any party had merit to a royal family I think they have merit to Your Majesty's. What risks did the Whigs not run, what did they not lose, what fortitude and perseverance did they not show, for your interest and the succession in the House of Hanover during the latter end of Queen Anne's reign? Since the accession of your family in the time of the rebellion, in the time of the Bishop of Rochester's plot, and on many more occasions which do not at this moment occur to my memory, but which I could easily recollect, did not the Whigs exert themselves with the utmost zeal and industry? Have they not pushed prerogative points, maintained the power and honour of the Crown so strenuously and so far, whenever they have thought the interest and security of Your Majesty's family concerned, that they have often been reproached with having not only adopted Tory principles which they used to explode, but even carried those principles higher than ever Tories did? The whole kingdom knows what I say to be true, and if Your Majesty thinks the Tories either would or could do more than the Whigs have done to support you, all I can say is, to repeat what my Lord Sunderland answered to King William when His Majesty told him he would take the Tories in because their principles were more proper to support a King than those of the Whigs. My Lord Sunderland answered: "That is very true, Sir, but you are not their King." '

This discourse passed between my Lord Hervey and the Queen one morning in her closet at Richmond whilst she was at breakfast. During the conversation the King came in, and the Queen telling him what she had been talking of, the whole came over again, the King repeating almost word for word what the Queen had urged before, and Lord Hervey giving much the same answers though in softer terms and a lower voice than he had spoke before, being more in awe of his present disputant than he was of the former.

Sir Robert Walpole was now in Norfolk, pushing the county election there, which the Whigs lost by six or seven voices, to the great triumph of the Opposition. After the election was over he stayed some time at Houghton, solacing himself with his mistress, Miss Skerret, whilst his enemies were working against him at Richmond, and persuading the King and Queen that the majority of the new Parliament would infallibly be chosen against the Court.

Lord Hervey, who was every day and all day at Richmond, saw this working, and found Their Majesties staggering. Upon which he wrote an anonymous letter to Sir Robert Walpole with only these few words in it, quoted out of a play:

> Whilst in her arms at Capua he lay,
> The world fell mouldering from his hand each hour.

Sir Robert knew the hand, understood the meaning and, upon the receipt of this letter, came immediately to Richmond, set everything right, resumed his power, and effaced every impression that had been made either in the mind of the King or Queen to his disadvantage, or in distrust of the new Parliament.

The tumult of the elections being now over, and the King, Queen, and Ministers pretty well satisfied with the complexion of the new-born Parliament, the Court removed for its summer residence to Kensington, and all the conversation of it was turned from domestic to foreign affairs had it not been for an incident I am now going to relate.

One day[1] very abruptly and nobody guessing on what motive, the Prince of Wales sent Lord Carnarvon, his Lord of the Bedchamber in Waiting to the King, to ask an audience and desire to know what time His Majesty would be pleased to allow it him.

The King's answer to his son was that he might come when he would, but, being now near three o'clock, His Majesty went up as usual to the drawing-room and made it impossible for the Prince to see him before the morrow. The news of this audience being asked soon spread, and everyone was conjecturing in what it was likely to terminate. Most people imagined it was to ask the King's leave to go a volunteer to Prince Eugene upon the Rhine. At night the Ministers met to talk of this comet and if they could to ward against the conflagration they expected from it.

Sir Robert Walpole went to the King and Queen and said all he begged of His Majesty was that, if this should prove any extravagant step proposed to his son by the people in opposition, His Majesty would only promise to keep his temper, and not give the advantage which the strongest always give to the weakest when they lose it. The King promised and the next day the Prince after the levée went into the closet.

The substance of what he said was to desire the King would marry him. He then touched slightly on the reserve and sometimes displeasure he had observed and lamented in the King's behaviour towards him and begged to know the cause of it; assuring His Majesty that he had never wilfully done anything to forfeit his favour and would do anything in his power to regain and merit it.

The King told him that his behaviour in general was very childish and silly, but that his particular disregard to his mother and his undutiful conduct towards her was what offended him

---

[1] About the end of June.

more than anything else, and that till he behaved better there he would never find it possible to please him.

As to marrying him he said everybody knew that matches had been proposed, and that it was not his fault these had not taken effect.

Little more passed between them, and the Prince at taking leave said: 'I hope Your Majesty will remember I made this application to you.'

The Prince would have gone immediately from the King's closet to his mother, which she avoided by going into the drawing-room earlier this morning than ordinary, resolving not to see her son, till she had seen the King.

Out of the drawing-room she followed the King so close that though the Prince led her he could say little to her, and to that little he received not one word of answer.

It was quickly known or at least conjectured that Lord Chesterfield had put the Prince upon taking this step, the Prince having rode out with only one groom two mornings before, met Lord Chesterfield in Holland House Walk and there, quitting his horse, walked with him for above two hours.

Everybody saw very plain that this business was not to end in this application to the King, and that it was preparatory to something of the same nature to be moved in Parliament, which was a measure that would wear the face of much greater decency after this previous address to the King, and appear more necessary from this having proved ineffectual.

When the Prince saw the Queen next day, she told him she was very sorry to find that she had been the cause of any coolness between him and his father; that she was sure she had never endeavoured to irritate the King by any complaints, but on the contrary, as she wished nothing so much as their being well together, so she had always sunk circumstances the King had not seen, softened those he had, and taken the Prince's part often against her opinion.

'But what concerns me most,' said she, 'my dear Fretz,[1] is to see you can be so weak as to listen to people who are trying to make a

---

[1] Always spelt thus by Lord Hervey; and as he is the sole authority on the point, his spelling has been retained.

fool of you, who think of nothing but distressing the King at any rate, and would sacrifice not only your interest, but the interest of our whole family, to pursue what they think their own, or to gratify their personal resentment.'

She talked so much to the Prince in this strain, telling him how little those in whom he confided cared for him or considered anything but their present passion; how warily he ought to act; how little he could ever get by exasperating his father; and how unavailing all methods but fair means ever must prove with such a temper as the King's, and power to support it. In short she awakened so much distrust in the Prince on the one hand and alarmed his timidity on the other, that she made him promise to write a submissive letter to the King, told him she would deliver it and do everything she could to set matters right.

Accordingly a letter was written and brought to her to correct. Wherever she thought the submissions too slight, or his compunction not sufficiently explicit, she strengthened the terms till the whole letter was moulded to her own mind. She then delivered it to the King, who commissioned her to give no other answer to his son than that he should judge of the sincerity of his words by the future tenor of his actions.

I shall now recount the different opinions there were on these facts.

When the Queen and Sir Robert Walpole related them severally to me, they were both of opinion that Lord Chesterfield had drawn this scheme originally to create business in the House of Lords upon a point wherein many people would hesitate in standing by the King who would have no scruples upon any other.

As to the letter of recantation, they judged that to have been advised and written by Mr. Dodington, jealous of Lord Chesterfield's growing interest with the Prince and his having had influence enough there to persuade the Prince to ask this audience of the King without Dodington's being either consulted upon it, or acquainted with it. They both told me too that Lord Chesterfield had certainly declared upon the Prince's writing the letter that His Royal Highness was such an unstable creature that there was no trusting him out of one's sight an hour; that Mr. Dodington had told the Prince there never was anything so injudicious as striking this stroke so long before the Parliamentary blow could follow, and that all the Prince could now do towards retrieving this false step was to load the King with submissions and seem to have laid aside all thoughts of prosecuting this design.

When the Queen told Lord Hervey all this, he owned it was seemingly a natural way of accounting for everything that had happened, but that he did not believe it was the true one. In the first place he doubted very much of Lord Chesterfield's having said what was reported of the Prince's levity. In the next place he was very sure Mr. Dodington's credit with the Prince was declining. 'And Madam, besides this,' said Lord Hervey, 'according to Your Majesty's own report of this letter, I see nothing in it that Lord Chesterfield may not have consented to and approved. Why may not he imagine that submission on the side of the Prince upon this occasion will contribute to throw blame upon a refusal on the part of the King? Neither does anything Your Majesty has repeated out of this letter retract in any degree the main purport of the audience, which was a desire of being married. The letter only asks pardon for the manner of making that application, in case it was unfitting, or gave any offence to the King. Contrition and penitence are largely poured out upon that head, but they are confined there, and no fault confessed, nor any receding mentioned with regard to the principal cause of the audience being asked. All these things considered, I should imagine Lord Chesterfield (who might upon reflection think he had rung the alarum-bell too soon) much more likely to have been the author of this letter than Mr. Dodington, especially since the Prince, let him be ever so fluctuating in his measures or changeable in his counsellors, could never in all probability alter so much in both and in so short a time as to commit the whole conduct of this very delicate transaction to the hand of one for whom the day before he had not shown so much regard as even to trust him with any such affair being on the anvil.'

The Queen, who had no great natural propensity to changing an opinion, persisted in believing Dodington the author of the letter and said she did not think the Prince had ever seen Lord Chesterfield between the audience and the recantation as she still called it, though very improperly. Lord Hervey said the Prince possibly had wrote the letter himself. 'Oh my good Lord,' replied the Queen, 'no more than I wrote it. The style of it, the manner in which he had copied it, the tone in which he read it, though he said it was every word his own, and done in haste, plainly showed that it was no more his drawing than drawn without the utmost care and caution.'

'How anybody could work him up to such a step,' Lord Hervey said, 'to me is inconceivable. I am sure when I had the honour of being of his council he used to think very differently; and as I have often told him how little was to be got in present by quarrelling with the King, and how much he would risk in futurity, if ever by intestine divisions he weakened the strength and interest of his family in general, and the advantage he would give by such conduct to those who struck at the whole, he always seemed to feel the force of that reasoning and to be determined never to push things to so dangerous an extremity.' Lord Hervey, knowing by Sir Robert Walpole that the Prince had told the Queen that Lord Hervey had often urged him to resent the usage of his father, took this opportunity to clear himself of that very false charge, and proceeded in this manner.

'I used, Madam, whenever His Royal Highness talked in a high strain of resentment always to tell him: "Sir, I can remember when your father had the misfortune to quarrel with your grandfather, and notwithstanding he had many people of the first rank, quality, understanding, character, and consideration of this kingdom in his party; notwithstanding one of his own servants was in the chair of the House of Commons; and notwithstanding he had a revenue of £120,000 a year independent of the King, I can remember in a very little time how poor a figure his opposition to the Court made, how weary both he and his adherents were of it, what advantage it was to the enemies of this family, and how little it availed him in any one article. And if your father, Sir, in these circumstances grew weary of this quarrel, think what your case would be without these circumstances and with only £10,000 a year instead of £120,000. I make no doubt but that at first Your Royal Highness would find people enough that would lend you money. But in a short time you would find the same people at least as ready to press the payment as they were to make the loan, and your friends, when they had been long your creditors, full as troublesome as your foes. Your Court would be filled with nothing else, for Courts that want support are not thronged like those who can give it, nor is the friendship of Princes much courted when, instead of promoting the interest of those who possess it, it gives umbrage where power threatens and interest calls. But supposing what Your Royal Highness in your most sanguine views can expect should happen; supposing your party should be strong enough to distress the King's measures, and make him bend. What would the consequence of that be? The King would not reconcile himself to you upon condition you would drop your friends, for that (the party still subsisting in opposition, and his distress proceeding from their numbers and force) would do the King no good. In this case therefore his policy must be to buy them to desert you, who by this means would first be their tool and then their sacrifice." ' 'When you talked to him in this manner,' said the Queen, 'how did he used to take it?' 'He always, Madam, used to say I was in the right, to seem to feel the force of such arguments, and to thank me for setting things in their true light before him. Nor did I ever fail to add that, as my situation was such that it was apparently my personal interest, considering his friendship to me and my dependence on the King, that no rupture should happen between them, so it was possible he might think I was either blind to his interest or partial to my own when I reasoned in this manner; therefore I begged him to consider facts and natural consequences only, and put all prejudices, both mine and his own, quite out of the question.' This was a natural and lucky opportunity for Lord Hervey to give the lie, without seeming to know he did so, to several stories, with a thousand particulars, told of him by the Prince to the Queen, most of which tended to persuade the Queen that whilst Lord Hervey had the Prince's ear he was for ever blowing up his resentment, reproaching him for bearing the usage both of his father and his mother, and urging him to let his wrath éclat.

Whether the letter of recantation (very unreasonably so christened) was written by Mr. Dodington or Lord Chesterfield time may perhaps discover; but as I am now writing in the interval between this incident and the meeting of Parliament this truth is as yet dormant; perhaps I may never be able to say who was the author of it, and whether the Queen or Lord Hervey were right in their conjecture, the presumptive evidence of collateral circumstances will only determine; and whether the Prince meant to dupe his father and his ministers at this time by seeming to recede when he did not intend it, or whether he was frightened and intended to sacrifice his own advisers, I am equally as yet at a loss to guess. Perhaps he may be as uncertain which he designs to do as I am, for, as irresolution and falsehood are equally predominant in his composition, it is very probable he may as yet be only determined to deceive somebody, but deliberating whom.

During all this transaction of the audience and the letter, the Princess Emily made her court to her brother by playing the mediative between him and the Queen. As she saw no prospect of being married and reflected that her father was thirty years older than her, she thought it behoved her to keep well with the Prince, upon whom by the course of nature she was to expect she should one day or other find herself dependent. For the Princess Royal (who was come back from Holland), her brother and she were upon worse terms than ever. He was angry at her marrying, but upon her presuming to be with child he was quite outrageous, and though she did not often talk of her brother at this time to the Queen (at least in my hearing), when she did, she cut deep. The Princess Caroline held a sort of silent neutrality, but Lord Hervey was too much distinguished by her, and too well with her, for her to be well with her brother, and her brother was too much the reverse of all the good qualities she possessed for him to be either or loved or liked by one of her worth or discernment.

When Lord Hervey spoke on the Prince's chapter to the Queen (which he never did but when she forced him upon it), he always endeavoured to throw in something or other to prevent his seeming to aim at doing him any ill offices to Her Majesty. Amongst other things at this time he said it always had been his opinion and still was so that the Prince loved Her Majesty on his heart, however he might be persuaded by those about him to hold a conduct as if he did not. 'I believe,' said the Queen, 'he has no inveterate hatred to me, but for love I cannot say I see any great signs of it, though I must own he has really a good heart; and I asked him the other day how he could suffer himself to be persuaded by people who have neither honour, conscience, common honesty, or common good-nature, to act sometimes as if he wanted all those qualities as much as they do.' At the time she said she thought no better of his heart than my Lord Chesterfield ever spoke of hers, and not above two days before she had, in the anguish of her soul, said weeping to Sir Robert Walpole (as he afterward told me), 'My good Sir Robert, I every day more and more think of poor M. Neibourg, my son's old Governor. When he took his leave of me four years ago at Windsor, he said: "Madam, I shall never see you again; but I could not die in peace if I did not discharge my conscience in telling you what I have long seen in the Prince and long endeavoured in vain to correct. He has the most vicious nature and the most false heart that ever man had, nor are his vices the vices of a gentleman, but the mean base tricks of a knavish footman. I do not say this to Your Majesty out of any malice, or with any fear of the Prince being told it again, for I have often said it to him himself and should be glad to say it to him in Your Majesty's presence, that I might if possible make him ashamed to persist in faults and go on in habits which I have tried every other method in vain to cure him of." '

As to Lord Hervey's always speaking of the Prince to the Queen with that seeming partiality, though it may appear extraordinary he should do so, yet upon the examination of his motives it may easily be accounted for. It was from no tenderness towards the Prince, nor any simple affectation of false generosity, but merely from prudence and regard to himself. He knew in family quarrels how natural it was for a suspended affection to revive and how much oftener a mutual interest in the parties had produced a reconciliation between those who had been judged irreconcilable; and in these cases he did not want to be told that the fomentors of the quarrel on either side whilst it subsisted never failed of being the first sacrifices whenever it was made up. Besides, as there are some tempers whose resentment is more irritated by attempts to excuse than by endeavours to aggravate, it is very possible his Lordship *excusando exprobrare* and when he seemed to aim at extenuating the Prince's conduct might not mean to soften the Queen's dislike of it, and knew her too well to imagine it would have that effect. He might be apprised too, it may be, that people frequently rail at those whose part they begin to take the moment they hear them railed at, and therefore chose rather this way to fan the fire he found, than to be catched endeavouring to throw on more fuel, which perhaps like wet wood might have damped the flame it was designed to increase.

Lord Hervey had been too ill used by the Prince to owe him any good turn, or to desire to do him one; and, as he knew him too well to have either love or esteem for him, so whatever his style might be when he spoke of the Prince, it was not feeling any regard to him that made him express himself in so soft a manner. What regard indeed could anybody have for a man who like His Royal Highness had no truth in his words, no justice in his inclination, no integrity in his commerce, no sincerity in his professions, no stability in his attachments, no sense in his conversation, no dignity in his behaviour, and no judgment in his conduct?

One circumstance that happened about this time will in part contribute to justify the likeness of this picture and therefore I will relate it.

When the Prince bought his house[1] in Pall Mall of Lord Chesterfield, which cost £6,000, not having money to pay for it he borrowed this sum of his Treasurer, Mr. Hedges, and obliged himself to repay it at a particular time that expired just as he was grown weary of Mr. Dodington's administration and before Dodington had discovered that he was so. Taking therefore advantage of the favour which he still showed and no longer felt towards Mr. Dodington, he borrowed this £6,000 of him to pay Mr. Hedges, and then, with as little judgment as shame or honesty, bragged to Hedges of having over-reached Dodington, and said: 'With all his parts I have wheedled him out of a sum of money for the payment of which he has no security if I die, and which, God knows, he may wait long enough for if I live.'

This Mr. Hedges, who was really a man of honour as well as a man of sense, told again to Sir Robert Walpole with the utmost indignation and Sir Robert told it to me, saying at the same time, 'You see into what honest and just hands the care and government of this country is like one day to be committed.'

[1] Carlton House.

chapter three

The Queen and Walpole

1734

IN THE AUTUMN of 1733 the war of the Polish Succession had broken out and by the following summer the bad situation of the Emperor's affairs in every quarter gave His Majesty the utmost solicitude to exert himself in the defence of the House of Austria, and to put some stop to the rapid triumphs of the House of Bourbon. For though the King was ready to allow all the personal faults of the Emperor, and was not without resentment for the treatment he himself had met with from the Court of Vienna, yet his hatred to the French was strong, and his leaning to an Imperial cause so prevalent, that he could not help wishing to distress the one and support the other, in spite of all inferior, collateral, or personal considerations.

In all occurrences he could not help remembering that, as Elector of Hanover, he was a part of the Empire, and the Emperor at the head of it; and these prejudices, operating in every consideration where his interest as King of England ought only to have been weighed, gave his Minister, who consulted only the interest of England, perpetual difficulties to surmount, whenever he was persuading His Majesty to adhere solely to that.

The King's love for armies, his contempt for civil affairs, and the great capacity he thought he possessed for military exploits, inclined him still with greater violence to be meddling, and warped him yet more to the side of war. He used almost daily and hourly, during the beginning of this summer, to be telling Sir Robert Walpole with what eagerness he glowed to pull the laurels from the brows of the French generals, to bind his own temples; that it was with his sword alone he desired to keep the balance of Europe; that war and action were his sole pleasures; that age was coming fast upon

60

him; and that, if he lost the opportunity of this bustle, no other occasion possibly might offer in which he should be able to distinguish himself, or gather those glories which were now ready at his hand. He could not bear, he said, the thought of growing old in peace, and rusting in the cabinet, whilst other princes were busied in war and shining in the field. But what provoked him most of all, he confessed, was to reflect that, whilst he was only busied in treaties, letters, and despatches, his booby brother, the brutal and cowardly King of Prussia, should pass his time in camps, and in the midst of arms, neither desirous of the glory nor fit for the employment; whilst he, who coveted the one and was turned for the other, was, for cold prudential reasons, debarred the pleasure of indulging his inclination, and deprived of the advantage of showing his abilities.

This was the language he perpetually held, and in this manner was he for ever declaiming to Sir Robert Walpole, whilst all private business and domestic affairs were at a full stand, and no answer to be got from him to the solicitation of any person whatsoever. Whenever Sir Robert Walpole, with the business of twenty different people taken down in abridgment upon his paper of notes, went into the King's closet to speak to him on those heads, the King always began to harangue on the military topic, and, after a declamation of about an hour long, dismissed Sir Robert without one of the things settled on which he came prepared to speak, and often without giving him opportunity barely to mention them.

This conduct bore every hard way upon Sir Robert Walpole; in the first place, as it pressed him so close to come into the measure of war, which he was determined to keep out of; and in the next, as it forced him to find repeated excuses to put people off who were every day teasing him for answers to their solicitations. For, as everybody is anxious in their own case, and all imagined that decision depended entirely on Sir Robert's will, so whatever pains they felt from suspense were placed to his account. The hopes he gave and the promises he made them were looked upon as ministerial arts to palliate delay, and whatever failed or was postponed from his want of power to prevent it was imputed to him as the effect of negligence or insecurity.

But the circumstances that gave Sir Robert Walpole the most

trouble of all was that with regard to the war he found the Queen as unmanageable and opinionated as the King. There are local prejudices in all people's composition, imbibed from the place of their birth, the seat of their education, and the residence of their youth, that are hardly ever quite eradicated, and operate much stronger than those who are influenced by them are apt to imagine; and the Queen, with all her good sense, was actuated by these prejudices in a degree nothing short of that in which they biased the King. Wherever the interest of Germany and the honour of the Empire were concerned, her thoughts and reasonings were often as German and Imperial as if England had been out of the question; and there were few inconveniences and dangers to which she would not have exposed this country rather than give occasion to its being said that the Empire suffered affronts unretorted, and the House of Austria injuries unrevenged, whilst she, a German by birth, sat upon this throne an idle spectatress, able to assist and not willing to interpose.

Besides her natural propensity to the interest of Germany, she was constantly plied on this side of the question, and warmed as fast as Sir Robert Walpole cooled her, by one Haltorf, the King's sole minister in England for the affairs of his Electorate, a clear-sighted, artful fellow, who was devoted to the interest of Germany and the Court of Vienna, and had more weight with the Queen next to Sir Robert than any man that had access to her. He was a man of great temper, and could reason with decency, and yet was full as hard to be either convinced or persuaded as his master.

The Queen, tired of going between this man and Sir Robert Walpole to report and interpret, and not being so much mistress of their arguments in detail, made M. Haltorf put his system of politics and his plan for the conduct of England at this juncture into writing. In this paper, though the substance of it was little better than treating England as a province to the Empire, yet he reasoned so artfully and so conformably to the Queen's sentiments and inclination, gave up the interest of this country so plausibly, and argued so strongly for the Emperor on the foot of preserving the balance of Europe, that Sir Robert Walpole told Lord Hervey he never saw any memorial better drawn, or more dexterously calculated, by improving the Queen's partiality and piquing her pride, to carry the point he was labouring to bring about.

Haltorf set forth in the most formidable colours the growing power of France and the House of Bourbon. He said all the reasons that induced this country to engage in King William's and Queen Anne's war ought to operate much stronger now, as France was more powerful and in better circumstances, and that, this nation having so cheerfully come into those wars, he could not conceive why Sir Robert Walpole should imagine people would reason so differently now. He insisted upon it that without help from England the Empire was absolutely at the mercy of France; and though the lenity or indolence of the Cardinal had prevented France from the exertion of her power, yet, as the Cardinal was above fourscore years of age, his life was but a bad tenure for the balance of Europe, and that a more active successor would quickly prove how fatally we had neglected to oppose what might then be too strong for us to stop.

This paper, written in French, the Queen gave to Sir Robert Walpole, ordering him to consider it and give her his answer to it in English. Sir Robert Walpole answered it paragraph by paragraph, and in this answer had an opportunity of methodising, recapitulating, and enforcing, every argument he had before made use of either to the King or the Queen to deter them from following their inclination and taking part in this war.

When Sir Robert Walpole gave Lord Hervey an account of these two papers, he said he had at the same time told the Queen that she knew it had been always his opinion ever since this quarrel began in Europe that England ought to have nothing to do with it but to compose it; that if it continued and England took any part in it, her crown would at last as surely come to be fought for as the crown of Poland; and then bade her judge and determine whether the Emperor in justice or in policy ought to receive that support from her that she seemed so desirous to give him.

Lord Hervey approved of everything Sir Robert had written, but still more of what he had said, and told him his last argument, in his opinion, was much the most likely to prevail; for, notwithstanding her partiality to the Empire, if he knew anything of Her Majesty, 'the shadow of the Pretender will beat the whole Germanic body.'

Sir Robert said it was true, and that he had always recourse to that argument whenever he found his others make less impression than he wished. This great minister, besides the interest of England (which I think he had sincerely at heart), was induced by some personal considerations to stick firm to the point of keeping this nation out of the war if possible. In the first place, to avoid the unpopularity of advising war and creating new clamour against his Administration; in the next, he knew the ungrateful task of raising money to support war would all fall to his share, and added to this, I believe he was not without apprehension that more military business might throw the power he now possessed into the hands of military men. Whatever his reasons and motives were, it is certain he was always counsel on the side of peace; and though he pleaded the cause singly against the King, the Queen, and all about them, hitherto he carried his point and kept things quiet.

Lord Hervey was this summer in greater favour with the Queen, and consequently with the King, than ever; they told him everything, and talked of everything before him. The Queen sent for him every morning as soon as the King went from her, and kept him, while she breakfasted, till the King returned, which was generally an hour and a half at least. By her interest, too, she got the King to add a thousand pounds a year to his salary, which was a new subject for complaint to the Prince. She gave him a hunter, and on hunting-days he never stirred from her chaise. She called him always her 'child, her pupil, and her charge'; used to tell him perpetually that his being so impertinent and daring to contradict her so continually, was owing to his knowing she could not live without him; and often said, 'It is well I am so old, or I should be talked of for this creature.'

Lord Hervey made prodigious court to her, and really loved and admired her. He gave up his sole time to her disposal; and always told her he devoted it in winter to her business, and in summer to her amusement. But in the great debate at present on the affairs of Europe, and the part this country ought to act with regard to peace and war, Lord Hervey differed with Her Majesty in opinion *toto cælo*; and, in speaking that opinion to her too freely, often met with very short and very rough answers.

All this summer the Queen used to see Sir Robert Walpole every Monday evening regularly, and at other times casually; but at every conference she had with him (as he told me), though she always said he had convinced her, and that she would give in to the accommodation, yet day after day, for three weeks together, she made him put off the setting on foot those measures which ought to have been taken in consequence of that conviction. And what is very surprising, yet what I know to be true, the arguments of Sir Robert Walpole, conveyed through the Queen to the King, so wrought upon him, that they quite changed the colour of His Majesty's sentiments, though they did not tinge the channel through which they flowed. When Lord Hervey told Sir Robert he had made this observation, Sir Robert said it was true, and agreed with him how extraordinary it was that she should be either able or willing to repeat what he said with energy and force sufficient to convince another without being convinced herself. However, said Sir Robert Walpole, 'I shall carry my point at last; but you, my Lord, are enough acquainted with this Court to know that nothing can be done in it but by degrees; should I tell either the King or the Queen what I propose to bring them to six months hence, I could never succeed. Step by step I can carry them perhaps the road I wish; but if I ever show them at a distance to what end that road leads, they stop short, and all my designs are always defeated. For example, if we cannot make peace and that I can keep this nation out of the war a year longer, I know it is impossible but England must give law to all Europe, yet this I dare not say, since even this consideration would not keep them quiet if they thought peace could not be obtained; and for that reason I graft as yet all my arguments on the supposition that peace will be effected. I told the Queen this morning, "Madam, there are fifty thousand men slain this year in Europe, and not one Englishman, and besides the satisfaction it is to one's good nature to make this reflection, considering they owe their safety and their lives to those under whose care and protection they are, sure, in point of policy, too, it is no immaterial circumstance to be able to say that, whilst all the rest of Europe has paid their share to this diminution of their common strength, England remains in its full and unimpaired vigour. Your Majesty accuses me always (if I may call it an accusation) of partiality to England, and considering nothing else; but whatever motives of partiality sway me, ought they not naturally with double weight to bias you, who have so much more at stake?" '

Lord Hervey asked him if these things made no impression upon her? He said, 'Yes, for a time; but the partiality she has to her own opinions, or to the gratification of her own will, sometimes even against her opinion, turns her again; and if that bias or her inclination can make her own opinion bend, you cannot wonder, my Lord, if it proves too strong sometimes for mine.'

On the 21st October the Princess Royal, who had been paying a visit to her parents, left London to return to Holland. The Queen was most unaffectedly concerned to part with her daughter, and her daughter as unaffectedly concerned to leave England, and exchange the crowds and splendour of this Court for the solitude and obscurity of her own. Lord Hervey was with her in the morning before she set out, the only man (except her favourite, Mr. Schutz) whom she desired to attend her; and, whilst he led her to her coach, she insisted on his writing to her constantly to give her an account how all these hours passed in which she used to have her share. She had Handel and his opera so much at heart that even in these distressing moments she spoke as much upon his chapter as any other, and begged Lord Hervey to assist him with the utmost attention. In an hour after she went Lord Hervey was sent for as usual to the Queen, who was really ill, but was thought to say she was so only from a desire to lay the disorder occasioned by the departure of the Princess on some other cause, and was therefore now as little credited when she said she was sick as she had often been when she was well. Lord Hervey found her and the Princess Caroline together, drinking chocolate, drowned in tears, and choked with sighs. Whilst they were endeavouring to divert their attention by beginning a conversation with Lord Hervey on indifferent subjects, the gallery door opened, upon which the Queen said, 'Is the King here already?' and, Lord Hervey telling her it was the Prince, the Queen, not mistress of herself, and detesting the exchange of the son for the daughter, burst out anew into tears, and cried out, 'Oh! my God, this is too much.' However, she was soon relieved from this irksome company by the arrival of the King, who, finding this unusual and disagreeable guest in the gallery, broke up the breakfast, and took the Queen out to walk. Whenever the Prince was in a room with the King, it put one in mind of stories one has heard of ghosts that appear to part of the company and are invisible to the rest; and in this manner, wherever the Prince stood, though the King passed him ever so often or ever so near, it always seemed as if the King thought the place the Prince filled a void space.

The day before the King's birthday the Court removed from Kensington to London, and the Queen, who had long been out of order with a cough and a little lurking fever, notwithstanding she had been twice blooded, grew every hour worse and worse. However, the King lugged her the night she came from Kensington, the first of Farinelli's performances, to the opera, and made her the next day go through all the tiresome ceremonies of drawing-rooms and balls, the fatigues of heats and crowds, and every other disagreeable appurtenance to the celebration of a birthday. There was a strange affection of an incapacity of being sick that ran through the whole Royal Family which they carried so far that no one of them was willing to own any other of the family ill than to acknowledge themselves to be so. I have known the King get out of his bed, choking with a sore throat, and in a high fever, only to dress and have a levée, and in five minutes undress and return to his bed till the same ridiculous farce of health was to be presented the next day at the same hour. With all his fondness for the Queen, he used to make her in the like circumstances commit the like extravagances, but never with more danger and uneasiness than at this time. In the morning drawing-room she found herself so near swooning that she was forced to send Lord Grantham to the King to beg he would retire, for that she was unable to stand any longer. Notwithstanding which, at night he brought her into still a greater crowd at the ball, and there kept her till eleven o'clock.

On the birthday, Sir Robert Walpole, who had been ill of flying gout for some time, told Lord Hervey he did not care to go to any of the feasts, and would come and dine with him, by which means he should be ready with less trouble to go up to the Queen in the evening, when he could catch her at leisure.

Sir Robert Walpole used always to go into Norfolk twice in a year, for ten days in the summer and twenty in November, and generally set out for his second expedition the day after the King's birthday. He was to do so now, and therefore to take his leave this evening of the Queen. Between six and seven he went up to her from Lord Hervey's lodgings, and stayed there near two hours.

After inquiring much of the state of her health, and finding it very indifferent, he entreated her to take care of herself, and told her: 'Madam, your life is of such consequence to your husband, to your children, to this country, and indeed to many other countries, that any neglect of your health is really the greatest immorality you can be guilty of. When one says these sort of things in general to princes, I know, Madam, they must sound like flattery; but consider particular circumstances, and Your Majesty will quickly find what I say to be strictly true. Your Majesty knows that this country is entirely in your hands, that the fondness the King has for you, the opinion he has of your affection, and the regard he has for your judgment, are the only reins by which it is possible to restrain the natural violences of his temper, or to guide him through any part where he is wanted to go. Should any accident happen to Your Majesty, who can tell into what hands he would fall, who can tell what would become of him, of your children, and of us all? Some woman, Your Majesty knows, would govern him, for the company of men he cannot bear. Who knows who that woman would be, or what she would be? She might be avaricious; she might be profuse; she might be ambitious; she might, instead of extricating him out of many difficulties (like her predecessor), lead him into many, and add those of her own indiscretions to his. Perhaps, from interested views for herself and her own children (if she happened to have any), or from the natural and almost universal hatred that second marriages bear to all the consequences of a first, she might blow up the father against the son, irritate the son against the father, the brothers against one another, and might add to this the ill-treatment and oppression of the sisters, who, with their youth and bloom worn off, without husbands, without fortunes, without friends, and without a mother, might, with all the éclat of their birth and the grandeur of their education, end lives as much objects of pity as they began them objects of envy. To these divisions in the palace the natural consequences would be divisions in the kingdom; and what the consequences of those would be, it is much more terrible to think of than difficult to foresee.'

The Queen wept extremely whilst Sir Robert was speaking to her, and then answered in this manner: 'Your partiality to me, my good Sir Robert, makes you see many more advantages in having me, and apprehend many greater dangers from losing me, than are indeed the effects of the one, or than would be the consequences of the other. That the King would marry again, if I died, I believe is sure, and I have often advised him so to do; but his good sense, and his affection for his family, would put a stop to any such attempts as you speak of in a second wife, or at least would prevent their coming to the height you describe; and as for his political government, he has now such a love for you, and so just a value for your services, as well as such an opinion of your abilities, that, were I removed, everything would go on just as it does. You have saved us from many errors, and this very year have forced us into safety, whether we would or no, against our opinion and against our inclination. The King sees this, and I own it; whilst you have fixed yourself as strongly in favour by an obstinate and wise contradiction to your Prince, as ever any other minister did by the blindest and most servile compliance.'

Sir Robert thanked her extremely for all her goodness and kind thoughts of him: 'But you know, Madam,' said he, 'I can do nothing without you. Whatever my industry and watchfulness for your interest and welfare suggest, it is you must execute. You, Madam, are the sole mover of this Court; whenever your hand stops, everything must stand still, and, whenever that spring is changed, the whole system and every inferior wheel must be changed too. If I can boast of any success in carrying on the King's affairs, it is a success, I am very free to own, I never could have had but by the mediation of Your Majesty; for if I have had the merit of giving any good advice to the King, all the merit of making him take it, Madam, is entirely your own; and so much so that I not only never did do anything without you, but I know I never could; and if this country have the misfortune to lose Your Majesty, I should find it as impossible, divested of your assistance, to persuade the King into any measure he did not like, as, whilst we have the happiness of possessing Your Majesty, any minister would find it to persuade him into a step which you did not approve.'

After this Sir Robert Walpole proposed putting off his journey, which the Queen insisted he should not do. He then said he would desire Lord Hervey to give him every post an exact account of her health, and begged Her Majesty would order Lord Hervey to send it from her own mouth undisguised.

From the Queen's apartment Sir Robert Walpole returned directly to Lord Hervey's, sent for him from his company into a private room, and there told him everything that had passed above; adding at the same time how uneasy he was at the condition in which he had found the Queen, and was obliged to leave her, coughing incessantly, complaining extremely (which in slight indispositions she never did), her head aching and heavy, her eyes half shut, her cheeks flushed, her pulse quick, her flesh hot, her spirits low, her breathing oppressed and in short, all the symptoms upon her of a violent and universal disorder.

He told Lord Hervey he had proposed to the Queen to defer his journey into Norfolk, and said, notwithstanding all she said against, that he would stay, did he not think that, in his own state of health, the air and exercise of this expedition was absolutely necessary to fit him for going through the parliamentary fatigues of the winter.

During this conference Lord Hervey told Sir Robert Walpole that he feared the King had overheard everything that had passed this evening between him and the Queen. Sir Robert started at this, and said: 'If he has, it is impossible he can ever forgive me; but what reason have you, my dear Lord, to think so?' 'I will tell you,' replied Lord Hervey. 'As soon as you left me, having something to say to the Princess Caroline, and knowing she always left the Queen when you came to her, I went up to her apartment to take that opportunity of speaking to her. Not finding her there, I went to the Queen's pages, asked of them where she was, and from them I learned that the King, with his three eldest daughters, when you came to the Queen, went into the bedchamber, which you know is the next room to that where the Queen and you were together. When I heard this, and reflected on what you once told me at Kensington of his shutting himself up in a closet, and leaving the door ajar to listen to a conference between the Queen and you, I immediately concluded that from the same curiosity he had now done the same thing.' 'For God's sake,' said Sir Robert Walpole, 'find out whether it was so or not, and let me know before I set out tomorrow morning for Norfolk.' Accordingly Lord Hervey, going immediately up to the ball, there told Princess Caroline that he had been at her apartment this evening, had not found her at home, and wondered where she had been; upon which she presently told him, that as soon as Sir Robert Walpole came to the Queen, the King, with her and her sisters, went through the Queen's bed-chamber and the younger Princesses' apartment down to their governess's lodgings, my lady Deloraine.

Lord Hervey was not a little pleased to find his conjectures had been false, and quickly made Sir Robert Walpole easy by a short note to tell him what the case had been. The next day Sir Robert set out for Norfolk, and soon after the Princess Royal again for Harwich.[1]

The interest of Lady Suffolk with the King had been long declining. His nightly visits all last winter had been much shorter than they used to be, and not without sometimes a total inter-mission. His morning walks, too, this last summer resembled his nightly visits the preceding winter; and all those who saw them together at the commerce-table in the evening in his private apart-ment plainly perceived they were so ill together that, when he did not neglect her, the notice he took of her was still a stronger mark of his dislike than his taking none. At Richmond, where the house is small, the walls thin, and what is said in one room may be often overheard in the next, I was told by Lady Bristol, mother to Lord Hervey, the lady of the bedchamber then in waiting, whose apart-ment was separated from Lady Suffolk's only by a thin wainscot, that she often heard the King talking there in a morning in an angry and impatient tone; and though generally she could only distinguish here and there a word, yet one morning particularly, whilst Lady Suffolk, who always spoke in a low voice, seemed to be talking a long while together, the King every now and then interrupted her by saying over and over again: 'That is none of your business, madam; you have nothing to do with that.'

Towards the latter end of the summer Lady Suffolk, who had long borne His Majesty's contempt, neglect, snubs, and ill-humour with a resignation that few people who felt so sensibly could have suffered so patiently, at last resolved to withdraw herself from these severe trials, from which no advantage accrued but the conscious pride of her own fortitude in supporting them with prudence.

[1] She had returned to London on hearing from her husband that his arrival at the Hague had been postponed.

On the pretence, therefore, or, more properly speaking, on the plea of ill-health, she asked leave to go for six weeks to drink the Bath waters; from thence she returned the day before the birthday to St. James's, but the King went no more to her apartment, and when he met her in the Queen's dressing-room spoke to her with the same indifference that he would have done to any other lady of the Queen's family, asking her only some slight common drawing-room question.

That the King went no more in an evening to Lady Suffolk was whispered about the Court by all that belonged to it, and was one of those secrets that everybody knows, and everybody avoids publicly to seem to know.

Various were the sentiments of people on this occasion. The Queen was both glad and sorry. Her pride was glad to have even this ghost of a rival removed; and she was sorry to have so much more of her husband's time thrown upon her hands, when she had already enough to make her often heartily weary of his company, and to deprive her of other company which she gladly would have enjoyed.

I am sensible, when I say the Queen was pleased with the removal of Lady Suffolk as a rival, that I seem to contradict what I have formerly said in these papers of her being rather desirous (for fear of a successor) to keep Lady Suffolk about the King, than solicitous to banish her; but, in describing the sentiments of the same people at different times, human creatures are so inconsistent with themselves, that the inconsistency of such descriptions often arises, not from the mistakes or forgetfulness of the describer, but from the instability and changeableness of the person described.

The Prince, I believe, wished Lady Suffolk removed, as he would have wished anybody detached from the King's interest; and, added to this, Lady Suffolk having many friends, it was a step that he hoped would make his father many enemies. Neither was he sorry, perhaps, to have so eminent a precedent for a prince's discarding a mistress he was tired of.

The Princess Emily wished Lady Suffolk's disgrace because she wished misfortune to most people; the Princess Caroline, because she thought it would please her mother; the Princess Royal was violently for having her crushed, and when Lord Hervey said he

wondered she was so desirous to have this lady's disgrace pushed
to such extremity, she replied: 'Lady Suffolk's conduct with regard
to politics has been so impertinent that she cannot be too ill-used';
and when Lord Hervey intimated the danger there might be, from
the King's coquetry, of some more troublesome and powerful
successor, she said (not very judiciously with regard to her mother,
nor very respectfully with regard to her father): 'I wish, with all
my heart, he would take somebody else, then Mamma might be
a little relieved from the ennui of seeing him for ever in her room.'
At the same time the King was always bragging how dearly his
daughter Anne loved him.

Sir Robert Walpole hated Lady Suffolk, and was hated by her,
but did not wish her driven out of St. James's, imagining somebody would come in her place who, from his attachment to the
Queen, must hate him as strongly, and might hate him more
dangerously.

The true reasons of her disgrace were the King's being thoroughly
tired of her; her constant opposition to all his measures; her weary-
ing him with her perpetual contradiction; her intimacy with Mr.
Pope, who had published several satires, with his name to them, in
which the King and all his family were rather more than obliquely
sneered at; the acquaintance she was known to have with many
of the opposing party, and the correspondence she was suspected
to have with many more of them; and, in short, her being no
longer pleasing to the King in her private capacity, and every day
more disagreeable to him in her public conduct.

About a fortnight, therefore, after her return from the Bath,
finding the King persist in withholding his usual visits, she took
the resolution of quitting the Court. She neither had, nor desired
to have (that I ever heard, at least) any *éclaircissement* with the
King, or to take any leave of him, but asked an audience of the
Queen, with whom she was above an hour and a half alone, and
resigned her employment of Mistress of the Robes. The next day
she left the Palace and went to her brother my Lord Hobart's
house in St. James's Square.

What she said to the Queen I never could learn,[1] and, considering all circumstances, it must be very difficult to guess, since I

[1] In the end he did—see p. 87.

cannot imagine the mistress could say to the wife: 'Your husband
not being so kind to me as he used to be, I cannot serve you any
longer.' And for any other reasons Lady Suffolk could allege for
quitting the Queen's service, I am as much at a loss to comprehend what they could be as I believe she was to invent them.

This great Court revolution was for some time the talk of the
whole town. Those who were inclined to make it a topic of in-
vective against the King said it showed the hardness of his nature
that, after Lady Suffolk had undergone twenty years' slavery to his
disagreeable temper and capricious will, after she had sacrificed her
time, her quiet, her reputation, and her health, to his service and
his pleasure, he could use a woman of her merit, prudence, and
understanding so ill as to force her to this step, and for no other
reasons than her having, contrary to the servile conduct of most
courtiers, risked his favour in consulting his interest, and ventured
to tell him those disagreeable truths which few favourites have
honesty and regard enough for their benefactors to impart, and
fewer princes sense enough to bear being informed of, though for
want of such information in time so many princes have been at last
undone.

To have heard Lady Suffolk's friends, or rather the King's
enemies, comment on this transaction, one would have imagined
that the King, instead of dropping a mistress to give himself up
entirely to a wife, had repudiated some virtuous, obedient, and
dutiful wife, in order to abandon himself to the dissolute commerce
and dangerous sway of some new favourite.

Those who justified the King upon this occasion said it was very
natural for a man of so uxorious a turn, and so passionately fond
of his wife, to think little of any other woman, especially at his
time of life; and that nobody surely could imagine there was any
great immorality or any great injustice in his giving those hours to
the Queen which he used to pass with Lady Suffolk; nor was it
very surprising that, in consulting his pleasure only, he should
prefer the conversation of a woman who was all cheerfulness, resignation, and compliance, to that of another who was for ever thwart-
ing his inclinations, reflecting on his conduct, and contradicting
his opinions; that he should like one who was always flattering
him better than one who was always finding fault with him; or be

more pleased with her who was always solving difficulties than with her who was always starting them. It was further added that, since the King intended to continue Lady Suffolk's pension, sure she had no reason to complain, or to think the punishment inflicted on her for censuring his Ministers and condemning all his measures a very severe one, since it was nothing more than his withdrawing himself from hearing what he could not prevent her from uttering.

The malcontents were extremely pleased with this new acquisition to their party, and exulted much in the hopes of this ungrateful conduct of the King's, as they called it, towards Lady Suffolk, occasioning great clamour, and increasing the odium which these industrious anti-courtiers lost no opportunity of propagating against him. But it was a great alloy to their joy, and a great satisfaction to those they opposed, to see this back door to the King's ear (the only way by which any reflections on his Ministers could be conveyed) at last shut up. Nor was it matter of less sorrow to one party than joy to the other to imagine that, after so signal a sacrifice to the Administration, few people in the palace, though ever so well disposed to the Opponents or disaffected to the Minister, would venture, by the same remonstrances to the King, to incur the same fate; everybody, both friends and foes, being equally persuaded that the examples of this wreck would deter any other person from sailing near those rocks on which Lady Suffolk had split.

As to the clamour this event would occasion, they must know very little of the nature of Courts or mankind who flatter themselves that the disgrace of one person, let that person be ever so amiable or considerable, would be anything more than the novel of a fortnight, which everybody would recount and everybody forget; or that an enemy out of the Court would ever be able to give material disturbance to those whom they vainly endeavoured to molest whilst they were in it.

In this manner, then, after twenty years' duration, ended the nominal favour and enervate reign of poor Lady Suffolk, who never had power enough to do good to those to whom she wished well, though, by working on the susceptible passions of him whom she often endeavoured to irritate, she had just influence enough, by watching her opportunities, to distress those sometimes to whom she wished ill.

About the same time of this disgrace there happened another, in the Prince's Court, of a very different nature; I mean that of Mr. Dodington, which began now to be commonly known and publicly talked of, but in a manner very unlike that in which people spoke of Lady Suffolk's. For as, in Lady Suffolk's case, many from political considerations rejoiced at her removal, though none from personal enmity rejoiced at her misfortunes, so with regard to Mr. Dodington it was just the reverse; nobody in a political light thinking it of any consequence whether he was in or out of the Prince's favour, and everybody, from personal dislike of the man, being glad of his meeting with any mortification. Mr. Dodington, whilst some people have the *je ne sais quoi* in pleasing, possessed the *je ne sais quoi* in displeasing, in the strongest and most universal degree that ever any man was blessed with that gift, being, with good parts and a great deal of wit, as far from agreeable in company, as he was, notwithstanding his knowledge and his great fortune, from being esteemed by any party, or making any figure in the State. He was one of those unfortunate people whom it was the fashion to abuse, and ungenteel to be seen with; and many people really despised him, who naturally, one should have imagined, were rather in a situation to envy him. His vanity in company was so overbearing, so insolent, and so insupportable, that he seemed to exact that applause as his due which other people solicit, and to think he had a right to make every auditor his admirer.

The reason the Prince gave for disliking and discarding him was that he hated those trimming dastard souls that had not resolution enough to oppose those whom they were always condemning; and could never think such men honest as were always abetting those measures in public which they were always censuring in private, any more than he could ever approve people's conduct who were perpetually acting openly in concert with the very men that they were for ever secretly abusing and defaming.

Right sentiments these, and pompous expressions; but the Prince's heart was no more capable of giving birth to such sentiments, than his capacity was of clothing them in such words. Lord Chesterfield had repeated these sayings till the Prince had got them by heart, and then gave them as his own reasons for doing from honesty and judgment that which in reality he did from levity and weakness.

The Prince used to say, too, that it was impossible but that there must be something very wrong in a man who not only had no friend, but whom everybody who mentioned him at all spoke of as an enemy.

Mr. Lyttelton, a nephew of Lord Cobham's, whom Dodington had brought about the Prince, had contributed too to this disgrace; for Dodington, from irresolution, or fear of throwing the Prince (as I have said before) into the hand of those who were at the head of the opposing party, had dissuaded the Prince from going those lengths to which Lord Cobham and Lord Chesterfield, who were exasperated to the last degree against the Court, wished to drive him. Lyttelton, therefore, who did and said everything his uncle, Lord Cobham, wished he should, was for ever, by proxy from Lord Cobham suggesting at one ear what Lord Chesterfield at the other was administering in person, both of them inculcating that Dodington's game was so to play the Prince's favour as to keep him in a sort of *équilibre* till he found to which party he could sell His Royal Highness to the best advantage.

Among many other things which Lyttelton suggested to the Prince to depreciate Dodington, he once said to him: 'Though I hate Sir Robert Walpole myself, and think him a bad man and a bad Minister, yet, when I reflect how partial he has formerly been to Dodington, the favours he has conferred upon him, the manner in which he supported him into the world, and the credit in which he supported him there, I own I am shocked when I hear Dodington railing at him; and though all he says may be true, yet the obligations he has to Sir Robert Walpole make me hate the ungrateful man who can forget them; and I feel myself more exasperated against Dodington for publishing and exaggerating Sir Robert Walpole's faults than I am against Sir Robert for committing them.'

Whilst Lyttelton was saying these things to the Prince, he never reflected that it was Dodington who brought him first to that ear into which he was now pouring them; and that he himself was, consequently in a stronger degree, the very thing to Dodington which he was so vehemently reviling Dodington for being to Sir Robert Walpole.

This new favourite, Mr. Lyttelton, was, in his figure, extremely tall and thin. His face was so ugly, his person so ill made, and his

carriage so awkward that every feature was a blemish, every limb
an incumbrance, and every motion a disgrace. But, as disagreeable
as his figure was, his voice was still more so, and his address more
disagreeable than either. He had a great flow of words that were
always uttered in a lulling monotony, and the little meaning they
had to boast of was generally borrowed from the commonplace
maxims and sentiments of moralists, philosophers, patriots, and
poets, crudely imbibed, half digested, ill put together, and con-
fusedly refunded.

Dodington's house in Pall Mall stood close to the garden the
Prince had bought there of Lord Chesterfield, and during Dodington's favour the Prince had suffered him to make a door out of his
house into this garden; which, upon the first decay of his interest,
the Prince shut up, building and planting before Dodington's
house, and changing every lock in his own to which he had formerly given Dodington keys. Dodington, when he found Lord
Chesterfield had supplanted and Lyttelton undermined him, retired
into the country unaccompanied, and as much unpitied in his disgrace as unenvied in his prosperity.

When Lord Hervey told Sir Robert Walpole early in the summer,
when few yet knew it, that Dodington had lost the Prince's favour,
the way he came to know it was by Miss Vane,[1] with whom he was
now privately reconciled, and who ventured to meet him in secret
once or twice a week, and at these meetings entertained him with
the account of everything she learned from the Prince or observed
either in him or the people about him. The manner of her reconciliation to Lord Hervey was from their seeing one another in public
places and there mutually discovering that both had a mind to
forget their past enmity, and renew their past endearments, till
from ogling they came to messages, from messages to letters, from
letters to appointments, and from appointments to all the familiari-
ties in which they had formerly lived, both of them swearing that
there never had been any interruption in the affection they bore to
each other, though the effects of jealousy and rage had often made
them act more like enemies than lovers. The place of their meeting
was an out of the way scrub coffee-house, little frequented, behind
Buckingham House, where neither of them were known. Lord

[1] See note on p. 48.

Hervey used to walk thither from Kensington in a morning after he was dismissed from the Queen, and Miss Vane could easily, under the pretence of walking in St. James's for her health, slip out unobserved to this rendezvous, with a hat over her face, as guarding it from the sun, whilst her chair and servants were left waiting at St. James's. These adventurous intriguers, encouraged by their frequent meetings having hitherto passed unobserved and un-suspected, grew so imprudent and so bold that, Miss Vane being obliged by the Prince's order to take a house at Wimbledon on account of her son's health, she came to town once a week on pur-pose to see Lord Hervey. The place of their meeting upon these occasions was her own house in London, where she herself always opened the door to admit him after it was dark, on foot and wrapped up in a cloak; and having but one servant in town it was easy for her to contrive to send that one out of the way at the hour she was to let her lover in or out. By these means they often passed the whole night together as free from apprehension as if they had been exposed to no danger. This was a great indiscretion in both, but much greater in the one than the other, as Lord Hervey on a discovery would only have been much blamed, whilst Miss Vane would have been absolutely ruined. But when two people have a mutual inclination to meet, I never knew any objection that ought to arise in their own mind prevent their aiming at it, or any foreign obstacle hinder their accomplishing it.

I shall now return to the Princess Royal, who, the day after she came to Harwich, embarked there for Holland. When she had been some time at sea she grew so ill that she either was, or made all those about her say she was, in convulsions; and the wind not being quite fair, she obliged the captain of the yacht, after lying several hours at anchor, to tack about and put her again on shore at Harwich. As soon as she arrived there she despatched a courier to London with letters (written, as it was supposed, by her own absolute command) from her physician, her man-midwife, her surgeon, and her nurse, to say she was so disordered with this expedition that she could not be stirred these ten days from her bed without running the greatest danger of miscarrying, nor put to sea again at all without the hazard both of her child's life and her own. All her train wrote in the same style; and the same judgment was made on these proceedings by the King and Queen, the whole Court, and the whole kingdom—which was, that Her Royal Highness was determined, if possible, to persuade, entreat, or fright her husband and her parents into consenting that she should lie-in in England.

The King and Queen, though she wrote for orders what she should do, declined giving any, but said the Prince of Orange ought to be consulted, and his directions followed. The Prince of Orange was written to by the same people who had written to the King and Queen, and in the same strain. But he, knowing of what prejudice it would be to his affairs to have the Princess Royal lie-in in England, and seeing plainly it was that she drove at, wrote to his wife to propose her coming to Calais, and to the Queen to beg of her not only to oppose this proposal, but to expostulate with her daughter, and forward this expedient, in case she found the Princess averse to it.

These delays made the King, who was always impatient under unavoidable difficulties, but outrageous with those who started any unnecessary ones, so peevish with his daughter that he made the Queen write to say she must and should lie-in in Holland; and, since the Prince of Orange desired she might go by Calais, and that it was thought for her safety she should do so, he consented to it; but this was much against his will, on account of the uncertain terms upon which this Court now was with the Court of France. At the same time that the King ordered the Duke of Newcastle to let M. Chavigny know that the Prince of Orange desired the Princess Royal might go by France into Holland, he charged his Grace to insist on her being received there entirely as a private person; and that there might not at St. James's be all the bustle of a new parting, which must have been the consequence of a new meeting, he ordered the Princess Royal to go across the country the nearest way from Harwich to Dover, without coming by London. But His Majesty being afterwards informed that those roads were impassable at this time of the year in a coach, he said then she might come to London and go over the bridge; but that positively she should not lie in London, nor come to St. James's. Accordingly, after all her tricks and schemes to avoid going to Holland, and to get back to London, she was obliged to comply with these orders, and had the mortification and disgrace to go, without seeing any of her family, over London Bridge, to Dover, from whence, by Calais (where the Prince of Orange met her), she went through Flanders to Holland.

Everybody condemned her conduct in this whole affair, in which her passions and her inclinations entirely got the better of her reason and her understanding. In the first place, everybody wondered she should mistake her own interest, and sacrifice her husband's, so far as to desire to lie-in here; and, in the next place, that she should judge so ill as to imagine, though she was imprudent enough to desire it, that it would be possible for her to compass it; or that she should not be deterred by her love to England from showing there were so many difficulties attended her coming hither. Already the resolution was taken and declared, both by the King and Queen, that upon no account would they ever give her leave to come here again when she was with child. The Queen saw all the false steps her daughter had made, and, as she could not quite disown them, blamed them a little, but repined at them more. The King, teased with the difficulties attending this journey, and not extremely pleased with the expense of it (which amounted to £20,000), said he would positively hear no more about it, and snapped everybody who mentioned the Princess Royal's name. The Princess Emily, as much as she dared, censured and condemned her sister's conduct; the Princess Caroline, as much as she could, excused and softened it.

When Parliament met several election petitions went against the Court.[1] The Marlborough election in particular was lost without a division. And there was one odd circumstance that made the Queen think this affair of much more importance, and more mortifying to Sir Robert Walpole, than it really was; for, after Sir Robert, the next day, had been giving her an account of it, Lord Hervey happening to be with her that evening, she told him she never saw anything so managed as this business had been, nor Sir Robert Walpole ever so much struck and cast down on any occasion in her life. 'He has just been here,' said she, 'and appeared quite confounded and moped, had neither life nor spirit, and seemed more

---

[1] Election petitions were still decided by the House of Commons, on party lines. It was on losing the Chippenham election petition that Walpole resigned in 1742.

shocked (which you know he is not apt to be) than I ever saw any man, and even more than he was at the bustle of the excise.' Lord Hervey, who knew that nothing was so likely to bring Sir Robert into difficulty in the palace as being thought to feel himself in any out of it, told Her Majesty that he believed she had misconstrued Sir Robert's confusion, and imputed it to a cause very different from that which had really occasioned it; and then told Her Majesty that his mistress, Miss Skerret, was extremely ill of a pleuritic fever, in great danger, and that Sir Robert was in the utmost anxiety and affliction for her.

The Queen, who was much less concerned about his private afflictions than his ministerial difficulties, was glad to hear his embarrassment thus accounted for, and began to talk on Sir Robert's attachment to this woman, asking Lord Hervey many questions about Miss Skerret's beauty and understanding, and her lover's fondness and weakness towards her. She said she was very glad he had any amusement for his leisure hours, but could neither comprehend how a man could be very fond of a woman he only got for his money, nor how a man of Sir Robert's age and make, with his dirty mouth and great belly, could ever imagine any woman would suffer him as a lover from any consideration or inducement but his money. 'She must be a clever gentlewoman,' continued the Queen, 'to have made him believe she cares for him on any other score; and to show you what fools we all are in some point or other, she has certainly told him some fine story or other of her love and her passion, and that poor man—avec ce gros corps, ces jambes enflées, et ce vilain ventre—believes her. My God! what is human nature!' While she was saying this, she little reflected in what degree she herself possessed all the impediments and antidotes to desire which she had been enumerating, and that 'My God! what is human nature!' was as applicable to her blindness as to his.

However, her manner of speaking of Sir Robert on this occasion showed at least that he was not just at this time in the same rank of favour with her that he used to be; for though she might not always have been blind to these defects and these weaknesses, at least she had been so indulgent to them as to have been always dumb upon that chapter, and to let these things escape her communicated reflections, if they had not escaped her private observation.

chapter four

Wives and Mistresses

1735

THIS BEING THE third summer since the King's last journey to
Hanover, and this triennial journey one among the many things
which the King continued to do because he had once done them,
His Majesty declared, a little before the Parliament rose, his inten
tion of visiting, as soon as it should rise, his foreign dominions. His
Ministers in England were one and all extremely desirous to divert
His Majesty from this resolution, but did not succeed. It is certain
it would have been much for the despatch as well as for the convenience of foreign negotiations, which were likely to be the chief
business of this summer, that the King should have remained in
England, in order to prevent every paper, which in that case might
be regulated by a short journey only from Sir Robert Walpole's
house at Chelsea to the King's palace at Kensington, being obliged
to make a voyage or two from England to Hanover before it could
be settled. Neither would it have been a very agreeable incident for
the King of Britain, after a month's residence at Hanover, to be
running back again through Westphalia to England with seventy
thousand Prussians at his heels; and yet, considering the terms he
and the King of Prussia were upon at present, this might easily
have happened, and was suggested by Sir Robert Walpole to deter
His Majesty from this expedition. But to their remonstrances His
Majesty always answered, 'Pooh!' and 'Stuff!' or, 'You think to
get the better of me, but you shall not'; and, in short, plainly
showed that all efforts to divert him from this expedition would be
fruitless.

The English Ministers apprehended, too, that if the King went
into Germany, his German Ministers, being all of them Imperialists,
might make the difficulties of keeping His Majesty out of the war,

in case the proposition for peace did not take place, still more troublesome and harder to be surmounted than they had hitherto found them, which might be of fatal consequence when the English Ministers, by experience, knew their influence was barely a match for such difficulties even in their former degree, and combated on this side of the water.

But that which prevented the English Ministers from succeeding in their attempts to prevent His Majesty's intending journey, in my opinion, was the Queen, through whom they chiefly worked, not being heartily desirous they should succeed. Not that Her Majesty could not foresee some inconveniences in his going, but the danger of blowing up his warlike disposition, which was one of the things that alarmed our Ministers the most, disturbed her the least; and to compensate the trouble of transacting all business with him at that distance by letter, she had the pleasure that resulted to her pride from the éclat of the regency, and the convenience and ease of being mistress of all those hours that were not employed in writing, to do what she pleased, which was never her case for two hours together when the King was in England; and besides these *agrémens*, she had the certainty of being, for six months at least, not only free from the conjugal fatigue of being obliged to entertain him twenty hours in the twenty-four, but also from the more irksome office of being set up to receive the quotidian sallies of a temper that, let it be charged by what hand it would, used always to discharge its hottest fire, on some pretence or other, upon her.

But there was one trouble arose on the King's going to Hanover which Her Majesty did not at all foresee, which was his becoming, soon after his arrival, so much attached to one Madame Walmoden, a young married woman of the first fashion at Hanover, that nobody in England talked of anything but the declining power of the Queen, and the growing interest of this new favourite. By what I could perceive of the Queen I think her pride was much more hurt on this occasion than her affections, and that she was much more uneasy from thinking people imagined her interest declining than from apprehending it was so.

It is certain, too, that, from the very beginning of this new engagement, the King acquainted the Queen by letter of every step he took in it, of the growth of his passion, the progress of his applications, and their success, of every word as well as every action that passed—so minute a description of her person, that had the Queen been a painter she might have drawn her rival's picture at six hundred miles' distance. He added, too, the account of his buying her, and what he gave for her, which, considering the rank of the purchaser, and the merits of the purchase as he set them forth, I think he had no great reason to brag of, when the first price, according to his report, was only one thousand ducats—a much greater proof of his economy than his passion.

But notwithstanding all the Queen's philosophy on this occasion, when she found the time for the King's return put off so late in the year that for six weeks together the orders for the yacht were by every post and courier in vain expected, she grew extremely uneasy, and, by the joy she showed when the orders arrived, plainly manifested that she had felt more anxiety than she had suffered to appear whilst they were deferred.

Yet all this while the King, besides his ordinary letters by the post, never failed sending a courier once a week with a letter of sometimes sixty pages, and never less than forty, filled with an hourly account of everything he saw, heard, thought, or did, and crammed with minute trifling circumstances not only unworthy of a man to write, but even of a woman to read,[1] most of which I saw, and almost all of them heard reported by Sir Robert, to whose perusal few were not committed, and many passages in them were transmitted to him by the King's own order, who used to tag several paragraphs with 'Montrez ceci et consultez là-dessus le gros homme.' Among many extraordinary things and expressions these letters contained, there was one in which he desired the Queen to contrive, if she could, that the Prince of Modena, who was to come the latter end of the year to England, might bring his wife with him; and the reason he gave for it was, that he heard Her Majesty was pretty free of her person, and that he had the greatest inclination imaginable to pay his addresses to a daughter of the late Regent of France, the Duke of Orleans—'un plaisir,' ajouta-t'il, for he wrote always in French, 'que je suis sûr, ma chère Caroline, vous serez bien aise de me procurer, quand je vous dis combien je le souhaite.'

---

[1] But see pp. 135 and 165 for a different judgment on the King's letters.

The ridicule of this request to his wife for a woman he never saw, and during his engagement with Madame Walmoden, is a ridicule of that sort that speaks itself much stronger in a bare narrative of the fact than by any comment or reflections; and is as incapable of being heightened as difficult to be credited.

Whilst the King was at Hanover there happened a marriage in England which I believe surprised His Majesty as much as it did many of his subjects; I mean Lady Suffolk's with Mr. George Berkeley. Mr. Berkeley was neither young, handsome, healthy, nor rich, which made people wonder what induced Lady Suffolk's prudence to deviate into this unaccountable piece of folly. Some imagined it was to persuade the world that nothing criminal had ever passed between her and the King; others that it was to pique the King. If this was her reason, she succeeded very ill in her design, for the King, in answer to that letter from the Queen that gave him the first account of the marriage told her: 'J'étois extrêmement surpris de la disposition que vous m'avez mandé que ma vielle maîtresse a fait de son corps en mariage à ce vieux goutteux George Berkeley, et je m'en rejouis fort. Je ne voudrois pas faire de tels présens à mes amis; et quand mes ennemis me volent, plut à Dieu que ce soit toujours de cette façon.'

Those who had a mind to abuse Lady Suffolk the most upon this occasion said she had been so long used to a companion that she could not live without something in that style, and that at her time of life, as there was none to be lost, so she took up with the first engagement that offered. The Queen, who was the first body that told me this marriage was certainly over, and would in a very short time be publicly owned, was extremely peevish with me for saying I did not believe one word of the matter, and that I was sure it was somebody who proposed making their court, by putting Lady Suffolk in this simple light, who had told her this improbable story. 'My God,' said the Queen, 'what an *opiniâtre* devil you are, that you will never believe what one tells you one knows to be true, because you happen not to think it probable! Perhaps,' continued she, 'you are one of those who have so high an opinion of her understanding, that you think it impossible she should do a silly thing; for my part, I have always heard a great deal of her great sense from other people, but I never saw her, in any material great occurrence of her life, take a sensible step since I knew her; her going from Court was the silliest thing she could do at that time, and this match the silliest thing she could do now; all her behaviour to the King whilst she was at Court was as ill-judged as her behaviour to me at leaving it.'

Upon the Queen's mentioning Lady Suffolk's behaviour to her upon her leaving the Court, I said that was a thing that had excited my curiosity more than any incident that had ever happened since my being in it; for that I could not possibly imagine that Lady Suffolk would come to Her Majesty and say: 'Madam, your husband being weary of me, I cannot possibly stay in your house or your service any longer'; and yet, if she did not say that, I could not comprehend what it was she did say. The Queen told me Lady Suffolk had not spoken her sense in those words, but that they differed little in their purport from what I imagined was impossible for her to suggest. 'Then pray, Madam,' said I, 'may I beg to know what was your Majesty's answer?' 'I told her,' said the Queen, 'that she and I were not of an age to think of these sort of things in such a romantic way, and said: "My good Lady Suffolk, you are the best servant in the world, and, as I should be most extremely sorry to lose you, pray take a week to consider of this business, and give me your word not to read any romances in that time, and then I dare say you will lay aside all thought of doing what, believe me, you will repent, and what I am very sure I shall be very sorry for." '

The Queen in this conversation told me many other circumstances relating to Lady Suffolk's affairs, and to her conduct at Court, that till then I was entirely unacquainted with, particularly that she had had £2,000 a year constantly from the King whilst he was Prince, and £3,200 ever since he was King, besides several little dabs of money both before and since he came to the Crown.

She told me the whole history of the bustle Mr. Howard had made to take his wife from the Court which I have in gross related before in these papers[1]; and that, when Mr. Howard came to Her Majesty, and said he would take his wife out of Her Majesty's coach if he met her in it, she had bid him 'do it if he dare; though,' said she, 'I was horribly afraid of him (for we were tête-à-tête)

[1] See pp. 17-8.

all the while I was thus playing the bully. What added to my fear upon this occasion,' said the Queen, 'was that, as I knew him to be so brutal, as well as a little mad, and seldom quite sober, so I did not think it impossible that he might throw me out of that window (for it was in this very room our interview was, and that sash then open just as it is now); but as soon as I got near the door, and thought myself safe from being thrown out of the window, je pris mon grand ton de Reine, et je disois I would be glad to see who should dare to open my coach-door and take out one of my servants; sachant tout le temps qu'il le pouvoit faire s'il le vouloit, et qu'il auroit sa femme, et moi l'affront. Then I told him that my resolution was positively neither to force his wife to go to him if she had no mind to it, nor keep her if she had. He then said he would complain to the King; upon which je prenois encore mon haut ton, and said the King had nothing to do with my servants, and for that reason he might save himself that trouble, as I was sure the King would give him no answer but that it was none of his business to concern himself with my family; and after a good deal more conversation of this kind (I standing close to the door all the while to give me courage), Monsieur Howard et moi nous nous donnions le bonjour, et il se retira.

'After this, that old fool my Lord Trevor came to me from Mrs. Howard, and, after thanking me in her name for what I had done, proposed to me to give £1,200 a year to Mr. Howard to let his wife stay with me; but as I thought I had done full enough, and that it was a little too much not only to keep the King's guenipes' (in English trulls) 'under my roof, but to pay them too, I pleaded poverty to my good Lord Trevor, and said I would do anything to keep so good a servant as Mrs. Howard about me, but that for the £1,200 a year, I really could not afford it.

'But, after all this matter was settled, the first thing this wise, prudent Lady Suffolk did was to pick a quarrel with me about holding a basin in the ceremony of my dressing, and to tell me, with her little fierce eyes, and cheeks as red as your coat, that positively she would not do it; to which I made her no answer then in anger, but calmly, as I would have said to a naughty child: "Yes, my dear Howard, I am sure you will; indeed you will. Go, go! fie for shame! Go, my good Howard; we will talk of this another time."

'About a week after, when upon maturer deliberation she had done everything about the basin that I would have her, I told her I knew we should be good friends again; but could not help adding, in a little more serious voice, that I owned of all my servants I had least expected, as I had least deserved it, such treatment from her, when she knew I had held her up at a time when it was in my power, if I had pleased, any hour of the day, to let her drop through my fingers—thus——'

So much for Lady Suffolk. To return therefore to Germany. During the King's residence there, it was contrived that he should see, as by accident, the Princess of Saxe-Gotha at Herrenhausen. The consequence of this interview was his fixing upon Her Highness for the future bride of the Prince of Wales, and the treaty was immediately set on foot.

Soon after he came to this resolution he wrote to the Queen to give her leave to communicate it to her son; and upon her doing so she told him that it would certainly be proper for him to take leave of a mistress whom he kept in so open a manner as he did Miss Vane.

The Prince's attachment to Lady Archibald Hamilton growing every day stronger than the other, made him listen to this advice from the Queen with more willingness than compliance with her counsel, or decency in his own conduct, without this additional motive, would in all probability have produced.

Lady Archibald Hamilton was not young, had never been very pretty, and had lost at least as much of that small share of beauty she once possessed as it is usual for women to do at five-and-thirty, and after having lain many years by a man old enough to be her father and being the mother of ten children.

Her husband, Lord Archibald Hamilton, was a Scotchman, uncle to the Duke of Hamilton, a Lord of the Admiralty, and of so quiet, so secure, and contented a temper, that he seemed cut out to play the passive character his wife and the Prince had graciously allotted him.

His wife was cunning, and had just sense enough to make that cunning useful to her, when employed to work on such a husband as Lord Archibald Hamilton, and such a lover as the Prince of Wales; and succeeded perfectly well in flattering the first into an opinion of her virtue, and the latter into an admiration of her beauty and understanding, which she facilitated by the much easier task of making the Prince believe she was entirely captivated by his.

But as there always are some people who doubt of the most notorious intrigues, as well as others who make no doubt of what only themselves believe, so there were some few who thought, or, I rather believe, affected to think, that this commerce between Lady Archibald Hamilton and the Prince was merely platonic, though stronger symptoms of an *affaire faite* never appeared on any pair than were to be seen between this couple. He saw her often at her own house, where he seemed as welcome to the master as the mistress; he met her often, too, at her sister's; walked with her day after day for hours together tête-à-tête in a morning in St. James's Park; and whenever she was at the drawing-room (which was pretty frequently), his behaviour was so remarkable that his nose and her ear were inseparable, whilst, without discontinuing, he would talk to her as if he had rather been relating than conversing from the time he came into the room to the moment he left it, and then seemed to be rather interrupted than to have finished.

Her jealousy of Miss Vane made her not satisfied with the Prince's only taking a public leave of her; she feared, notwithstanding that step was taken to amuse the world, and as a necessary preliminary to his future marriage, that His Royal Highness would still continue to see her in private, and perhaps with more pleasure when it would be with less liberty.

The Prince, therefore, to please Lady Archibald Hamilton and quiet these apprehensions, not only sent Lord Baltimore, one of his Lords of the Bedchamber, to Miss Vane to say how necessary it was, on his marriage being now so near concluded, for him to take his leave of her, but ordered Lord Baltimore to propose to her, as the most proper manner of parting both for him and her, that she should go immediately for two or three years into Holland or France, or any other place she would choose out of England. And in case Miss Vane did not seem to relish this proposal, Lord Baltimore was ordered to add, that though the Prince would for her life continue the £1,600 a year he had allowed her ever since she left the Court in case she complied with this proposal, that he would not allow her one farthing if she rejected it. As for her son, Lord

Baltimore was to tell her that the Prince would take care of his education here in England; and his Lordship was fully instructed not only to press the journey on Miss Vane in point of interest, but to represent to her how much more agreeable it would certainly be for her to go out of the way for some time, and avoid seeing and hearing all the little malicious triumphs of those who would not fail to repay themselves on this occasion for all that their envy had made them suffer on her account during her prosperity and her possession of the Prince's favour.

When Lord Baltimore brought this proposal to Miss Vane, she was extremely shocked not only at the purport of his message but this manner of delivering it. For though Mr. Lyttelton had attached himself to Lady Archibald Hamilton, and Dodington she knew had a mind to attach the Prince to a mistress of his own providing, one Miss Bowyer, an intimate friend to his own mistress, Miss Bean, yet Miss Vane had always, and with great reason, looked on Lord Baltimore, who during her favour had made great court to her, as entirely attached to her interest. Her answer therefore to Lord Baltimore was that she would send none to the Prince through a hand from which she found she was to expect so little friendship, and by a man whom she perceived too late she had very injudiciously hitherto taken for her well-wisher.

Lord Hervey and Miss Vane met constantly all this summer once or twice a week. The Prince had taken her a house at Wimbledon where all her servants were, except one old fellow and a maid, who were left in her house in town. This made it easy for her to let Lord Hervey into her house in town unperceived and thither once or twice a week she constantly came to meet him, who used to be admitted as soon as it was dark and go away before it was light.

But the difficulty of getting tea, fruit, and supper, at her house made them soon change the scene of their meeting to his lodgings at St. James's, and his wife being gone into France with the Duke and Duchess of Richmond for three months, this coast was quite clear. Miss Vane used to walk thither, Lord Hervey himself letting her in and out; and in this manner they used to pass whole nights together, as little apprehensive of danger as if no eyes had been upon them and that at this juncture it would not have been as convenient to the Prince as destructive to her to have traced this commerce and proved it upon her.

Miss Vane, who had for several years been subject to fits, was at this time extremely ill, and one night when she was in bed at St. James's was taken suddenly with so violent a fit of the cholic that in a quarter of an hour she fell into convulsions. Lord Hervey in vain to recover her crammed cordials and gold powder down her throat; her convulsions grew stronger and at last she fell into a swoon that lasted so long he thought her absolutely dead.

What confusion and distress this put his Lordship into is easier to be imagined than described. He did not dare to send for any assistance, nor even to call a servant into the room, for not one was trusted with the secret. What to do he could not tell, nor what would or would not be said when it should come out, and to conceal it was impossible, that Miss Vane was found dead in his lodgings. Whilst he was agitated with these thoughts and apprehensions, she came to herself, and by the help of more cordials, more gold powder, and hot napkins to her stomach, he got her up, dressed her, and led her to a chair in Pall-Mall, not daring to have one brought to take her up at his lodgings.

But even this accident did not prevent these indiscreet people from exposing themselves in the same manner to the same dangers, or from meeting as frequently as they had formerly done.

As soon as Miss Vane had received this message by Lord Baltimore, she wrote to Lord Hervey to tell him that she must speak to him the next day, though it was not their usual day for meeting, on business of the utmost consequence, in which she stood in need of his immediate advice. Curiosity as well as compliance made him obey this summons, and as soon as they met she related all the particulars of what had passed between her and Lord Baltimore, abusing him much, the Prince more, and telling Lord Hervey that she wished nothing so much as to be disembarrassed of the Prince, except the being at liberty to see his Lordship with more ease, so this proposal of separation from H.R.H. would have given her much more pleasure than ever she found in his acquaintance had it not been for this conditional article of going out of England, which she was determined for his Lordship's sake not to comply with, though she was entirely at a loss how she should go about to avoid it. She said she had no friend left about the Prince, now she had found out Lord Baltimore to be no longer such, who had common sense, and was resolved therefore to send her answer to the Prince in writing. What that answer must be, she said, she depended entirely on Lord Hervey to determine, and begged him therefore to write her a copy of such a letter as he thought it proper on this occasion she should send.

Lord Hervey, who had a mind to keep Miss Vane in England, and was not a little pleased to have an opportunity of fretting the Prince, undertook this commission very willingly, and wrote immediately the following copy of the letter she was to send.

SIR,

Considering the manner in which I have lived with Your Royal Highness, I think I might, without being thought very impertinent, begin this letter with complaining that, when you have anything to say to me, Your Royal Highness should think an ambassador necessary to go between us; and though a harsh or unkind thing, I must own, would always be little consistent with what I think I have deserved from Your Royal Highness, yet it would sure want no such additional weight as the letting another convey it, and consequently be acquainted with the little regard or concern you retain for me.

That Your Royal Highness is going to be married I may repine at; but I appeal to you if ever I was so unreasonable as to reproach you with it, or to imagine that my interest was to be put in competition with the interest of England, or that what was right for your affairs was not to outweigh every consideration of mine.

But that Your Royal Highness should break with me in the most shocking way; that you should not be content to abandon me without banishing me, nor take yourself from me without depriving me from every other friend, relation, and acquaintance, and depriving me of those comforts at a time when I shall want them most; is sure an aggravation to my bad fortune and unhappy situation which you are as much in the wrong to ask me as I should be myself to comply with.

Your Royal Highness need not be put in mind who I am, nor from whence you took me. That I acted not like what I was born, others may reproach me; but if you took me from happiness and brought me to misery, that I might reproach you. That I have long lost your heart I have long seen and long mourned. To gain it, or rather to reward the gift you made me of it, I sacrificed my time, my youth, my character, the world, my family, and everything that a woman can sacrifice to a man she loves. How little I considered my interest, you must know by my never naming my interest to you when I made this sacrifice, and by my trusting to your honour when I showed so little regard, when put in balance with my love, to my own. I have resigned everything for your sake but my life; and, had you loved me still, I would have risked even that too to please you; but as it is, I cannot think in my state of health of going out of England, far from all friends and all physicians I can trust, and of whom I stand in so much need. My child is the only consolation I have left. I cannot leave him, nor shall anything but death ever make me quit the country he is in. Your Royal Highness may do with me what you please; but a Prince who is one day to rule this country will sure, for his own sake, never show he will make use of power to distress undeservedly; and that one who has put herself without conditions into his hands has the hardest terms imposed upon her, though she never in her life did one action that deserved anything but your favour, your compassion, and your friendship; and it is for these reasons I doubt not but Your Royal Highness will on this occasion, for your own sake if not for mine, do everything that will hinder you from being blamed and me from being more miserable than the reflection of what is past must necessarily make one who has known what it was to be happy, and can never expect to taste that font again.

I know how vain it would be to think reproaches could ever regain a heart which kindness could not keep, and for that reason I will add nothing more than to assure Your Royal Highness I shall ever wish you health, prosperity, and happiness, and shall ever be, with unalterable affection, etc.

Miss Vane was extremely pleased with every part of this letter except that which professed any regard for His Royal Highness, and would fain have had those expressions more of a piece with the rest. She would also have carried this letter away with her to have copied it at home, but Lord Hervey insisted on its not going out of his lodgings in his handwriting, and, notwithstanding all the opposition she made to it, and her reproaches to him for his distrusting her conduct on an occasion where she was as much or more concerned than he to keep the secret, he made her write it out in her own hand before he let her stir out of the lodgings.

And that her brother Harry Vane might not disavow her in this proceeding, Lord Hervey advised her, before she sent the letter to the Prince, to send a copy of it to her brother for his approbation. Harry Vane, knowing by the style of the letter that it was none of her own, and guessing it (as she told Lord Hervey) to be Mr. Pulteney's, readily gave in to her sending what he thought had been advised by one whose understanding and friendship for his sister he had so great an opinion of.

Accordingly the letter was sent through one Vreid's hands, a *valet de chambre* of His Royal Highness who used always to convey all the letters that passed between them. As soon as the Prince received it he flew into a violent passion, said he knew the letter was not of her writing, and that he would be revenged not only of the villain who had given her this advice, but of her for following it. The letter was shown by him to his mother, his sisters, his servants, and everybody that he could get to read it, in order to justify the rigour with which he said he was determined to treat her if she did not produce the rascal that had put her upon taking this step. On the other hand, Miss Vane showed the letter to all her friends, and told the story of Lord Baltimore's embassy that occasioned it; and Lord Hervey had the secret satisfaction of exposing and fretting the Prince; whilst everybody who pretended the least regard for Miss Vane, or for Mr. Pulteney, who was generally thought the author, justified that which they would have been the first people to condemn, had they known out of what quiver this arrow had been shot.

Miss Vane stuck to it that she had written every word of the letter herself, and justified the substance of it on the provocation of Lord Baltimore's having told her from the Prince that, if she would not live abroad, she might for him starve in England.

The Prince, finding everybody condemned the brutality of this rough message, determined to deny he had ever sent it; and Lord Baltimore not being much fonder of the credit of delivering it, the Prince and he agreed together to say the proposal was made to her as a thing His Royal Highness thought would be agreeable to her, from what Miss Janssen, sister to Lord Baltimore's wife (a very dexterous lady) had reported from a conference she had had with Miss Vane on this subject, in which she had been commissioned to feel Miss Vane's pulse on this point, and, if she could, to lead her to it.

As the Prince therefore denied the having sent, and Lord Baltimore the having delivered, the rough message Miss Vane said she had received, and that she could make no proof of it, as she had been alone with Lord Baltimore when this interview happened, her brother, Mr. Pulteney, Mr. Mansel, and all those who pretended any remains of friendship for her, advised her to write a second letter to the Prince, in which she should only justify the former on the supposition of her having understood Lord Baltimore in the manner I have already related.

She had recourse for the second letter to the same hand that worked the first, and these were the contents of it:

It is so easy to remove the appearance of a fault when one is conscious of not meaning to commit one, that I make no doubt but Your Royal Highness will think me thoroughly justified for writing my last letter when I tell you nothing could have induced me to such an expostulation but the harsh message which I thought I had received by Your Royal Highness's order through Lord Baltimore.

In that confusion, shame, and vexation, I wrote just what I felt, but resolved (how ill I might execute my resolution I know not) to urge my own request, and to represent what I thought your ill usage of me, in the most respectful terms that such complaints would admit of. If I said anything I ought not to say, or in a manner I ought not to say it, I am heartily sorry, and ask your pardon, and appeal now to your justice to tell me whether I ever did or said anything in my life that was not consistent with what I owed to you, though I am very ready to own I have for your sake done things very inconsistent with what I owed to myself.

That I received such a message by Lord Baltimore is certain; whether he was authorised to deliver it I know not; it is certain, too, that all the messages I ever sent by him were answers to others, and not any that came originally from me. It is hard Your Royal Highness will not allow me an opportunity to clear myself; but, deal with me as you please, I shall ever pray for your happiness and prosperity, even whilst I reflect it at least to your love, if not to your hate, that I owe the loss of my own. I am, with the greatest respect and truth, etc.

In consequence of all these transactions, it was at last settled that she should have her house in Grosvenor Street for ever, £1,600 a year for life, that her son should not be taken from her, and that she should be at liberty to live where she pleased.

But soon after this, her cholics, loss of appetite, and general decay, growing fast upon her, she was advised to go to Bath, where, in about two months, she finished a life that, at her going to Bath, she said was, from the circumstances she was now in, likely to prove the happiest she had ever had.

Her son, who was left with her brother when she went to Bath, died about a week before her of convulsion fits. The Queen and the Princess Caroline told Lord Hervey that they thought the Prince more afflicted for the loss of this child than they had ever seen him on any occasion, or thought him capable of being.

But to go back to the King. The time being now come that His Majesty was obliged to undergo the mortification of returning to his British dominions, in order to keep his birthday there, he at last sent the long-expected orders for the yachts; and hearing they were at Helvoetsluys, he set out from Hanover on Wednesday morning, the 22nd of October, and arrived at Kensington the Sunday following, before dinner, just as the Queen returned from chapel. Her Majesty, attended by all the Court, met him at the great gate as he alighted from his coach. She kissed his hand before she presumed to touch his lips, mutual embraces followed, and this kissing ceremony at the door of the coach ended as it began, by Her Majesty again glueing her mouth to the King's hand, which he was graciously pleased to offer afterwards to lead her upstairs. This was a sort of triennial honour bestowed upon the Queen by His Majesty, for I never knew him to confer it on any other occasion than a return from Hanover. As soon as they got upstairs they went directly into the Queen's gallery, where the King ordered all the company, both men and women, to be let in and presented to him.

He stayed there near half an hour, talked to most people but the Queen, and it was by her order, not his, that the company was at last dismissed.

But by unreasonably hurrying himself to arrive in England, though he was as unreasonably sorry to return thither at all, he had made himself extremely ill; for whilst he travelled in this violent manner, day and night, and almost without any rest, only for the pleasure of bragging how quick he moved, he had so heated his blood that he was feverish for several days after he returned; and by sitting so long in his coach had brought upon himself such a severe fit of the piles, to which he was extremely subject, that he was in great pain, lost a great quantity of blood, and had so violent an inflammation and swelling attending this complaint, that for a fortnight together his surgeon was forced to attend him with alternate applications of lancets and fomentations.

This disorder was kept a great secret to all the Court, but the consequences of it were no secret. Everybody shared the warm and frequent sallies of his abominable temper, and everybody imputed them to what was the joint though not the sole cause of these eruptions, which was the affliction he felt for the change of a German life to an English one, with the society of a stale wife instead of a new mistress; and, what grated more than all the rest, the transition to limited from unlimited power.

Whilst the late King lived, everybody imagined this Prince loved England and hated Germany; but from the time of his first journey, after he was King, to Hanover, people began to find, if they had not been deceived in their former opinion, at least they would be so in their expectations; and that his thoughts, whatever they might have been, were no longer turned either with contempt or dislike to his Electoral dominions. But after this last journey Hanover had so completed the conquest of his affections that there was nothing English ever commended in his presence that he did not always show, or pretend to show, was surpassed by something of the same kind in Germany. No English or even French cook could dress a dinner; no English confectioner set out a dessert; no English player could act; no English coachman could drive, or English jockey ride, nor were any English horses fit to be drove or fit to be ridden; no Englishman knew how to come into a room, nor any Englishwoman how to dress herself, nor were there any diversions in England, public or private, nor any man or woman in England whose conversation was to be borne—the one, as he said, talked of nothing but their dull politics, and the others of nothing but their ugly clothes. Whereas at Hanover all these things were in the utmost perfection. The men were patterns of politeness, bravery, and gallantry; the women of beauty, wit, and entertainment; his troops there were the bravest in the world, his counsellors the wisest, his manufacturers the most ingenious, his subjects the happiest; and at Hanover, in short, plenty reigned, magnificence resided, arts flourished, diversions abounded, riches flowed, and everything was in the utmost perfection that contributes to make a prince great or a people blessed.

Forced from that magnificent delightful dwelling to return again to this mean dull island, it was no wonder, since these were his notions of them, that he felt as great a change in his humour as in his enjoyments; and that frowns should take the place of smiles upon his countenance, when regret had taken that of pleasure in his heart. But as everybody who came near him, in any calling (except just that of a common courtier in his public circle at the levée or the drawing-room), had some share of his bilious temper at this time, so what everybody knew and everybody felt, everybody talked of and everybody confessed; for, by a practice very uncommon in courts, people, instead of hiding with shame the snubs they received from their master, bragged of them in mirth; and, by finding these distinctions so general, revealed in sport those affronts which, had they been more particular, the objects of them would have concealed in sorrow.

In truth, he hated the English, looked upon them all as king-killers and republicans, grudged them their riches as well as their liberty, thought them all overpaid, and said to Lady Sundon[1] one day as she was waiting at dinner, just after he returned from Germany, that he was forced to distribute his favours here very differently from the manner in which he bestowed them at Hanover; that there he rewarded people for doing their duty and serving him well, but that here he was obliged to enrich people for being rascals, and buy them not to cut his throat.

The Queen did not always think in a different style of the English, though she kept her thoughts more to herself than the King, as being more prudent, more sensible, and more mistress of her passions; yet even she could not entirely disguise these sentiments to the observation of those who were perpetually about her, and put her upon subjects that betrayed her into revealing them.

I have heard her at different times speak with great indignation against assertors of the people's rights; have heard her call the King, not without some despite, the humble servant of the Parliament, the pensioner of his people and a puppet of sovereignty, that was forced to go to them for every shilling he wanted, that was obliged to court those who were always abusing him, and could do nothing of himself. And once added, that a good deal of that liberty that made them so insolent, if she could do it, should be much abridged; nor was it possible for the best prince in the world to be very solicitous to procure benefits for subjects that never cared to trust him. At other times she was more upon her guard: I have heard her say she wondered how the English could imagine that

[1] One of the Queen's women of the Bedchamber.

99

any sensible prince would take away their liberty if he could. 'My God!' she cried, 'what a figure would this poor island make in Europe if it were not for its government! It is its excellent free government that makes all its inhabitants industrious, as they know that what they get nobody can take from them; it is its free government, too, that makes foreigners send their money hither, because they know it is secure, and that the prince cannot touch it; and since it is its freedom to which this kingdom owes everything that makes it great, what prince, who had his senses, and knew that his own greatness depended on the greatness of the country over which he reigned, would wish to take away what made both him and them considerable? I had as lief,' added she, 'be Elector of Hanover as King of England, if the government was the same. Who the devil would take you all, or think you worth having, that had anything else, if you had not your liberties? Your island might be a very pretty thing in that case for Bridgeman and Kent to cut out into gardens; but, for the figure it would make in Europe, it would be of no more consequence here in the West than Madagascar is in the East: and for this reason, your princes, if they are sensible, as impudent and as insolent as you all are with your troublesome liberty, will rather bear with your impertinences than cure them, a way that would lessen their influence in Europe full as much as it would increase their power at home.'

But, at the very moment Her Majesty was uttering these truths, the love of rule, the thirst of dominion, and the jealousy of prerogative were so strongly implanted in her, the German and the Queen so rooted in her mind, that the King himself had not more at heart all the trappings and pageantry of sovereignty than she the essential parts of it; nor could she more easily brook any checks to the authority of the Crown than he any contradiction to his opinion.

His Majesty stayed but two days after his arrival at Kensington, and then removed to London, to keep his birthday and settle there for the winter; but during this short stay at Kensington most of the inhabitants of the Court spoke of his behaviour to the Queen as quite different from what it had formerly been, some of them from seeing instances of the change, and others from fancying they saw them because they expected to see them.

The accumulated trifles that contribute to forming opinions of this kind are much easier observed than related, and depend upon the combination of so many little circumstances that to try to describe them would be a task as tedious as imperfect. One example, however, I will give. In the absence of the King, the Queen had taken several very bad pictures out of the great drawing-room at Kensington, and put very good ones in their places. The King, affecting, for the sake of contradiction, to dislike this change, or, from his extreme ignorance in painting, really disapproving it, told Lord Hervey, as Vice-Chamberlain, that he would have every new picture taken away, and every old one replaced. Lord Hervey, who had a mind to make his court to the Queen by opposing this order, asked if His Majesty would not give leave for the two Vandykes, at least, on each side of the chimney to remain, instead of those two sign-posts, done by nobody knew who, that had been removed to make way for them. To which the King answered, 'My Lord, I have a great respect for your taste in what you understand, but in pictures I beg leave to follow my own. I suppose you assisted the Queen with your fine advice when she was pulling my house to pieces and spoiling all my furniture. Thank God, at least she has left the walls standing! As for the Vandykes, I do not care whether they are changed or no; but for the picture with the dirty frame over the door, and the three nasty little children,[1] I will have them taken away, and the old ones restored; I will have it done too tomorrow morning before I go to London, or else I know it will not be done at all.' 'Would Your Majesty,' said Lord Hervey, 'have the gigantic fat Venus restored too?' 'Yes, my lord; I am not so nice as your Lordship. I like my fat Venus much better than anything you have given me instead of her.' Lord Hervey thought, though he did not dare to say, that, if His Majesty had liked his fat Venus as well as he used to do, there would have been none of these disputations. However, finding his jokes on this occasion were as little tasted as his reasonings approved, and that the King, as usual, grew more warm and more peremptory on everything that was said to cool and alter him, his Lordship was forced to make a serious bow; and though he knew the fat Venus was at Windsor, some of the other pictures at Hampton Court, and all the frames of the

[1] No doubt the Vandyke of Charles I's children, now at Windsor Castle.

removed pictures cut or enlarged to fit their successors, he assured His Majesty that everything should be done without fail, next morning, just as he had ordered.

Lord Hervey told the Queen, next morning at breakfast, what had passed the night before, who affected to laugh, but was a good deal displeased, and more ashamed. She said the King, to be sure, was master of his own furniture; and asked Lord Hervey if the pictures were changed; who told her 'No,' and why it was impossible they should. She charged him not to tell the King why, but to find out some other reason. Whilst they were speaking the King came in, but, by good luck, said not one word of the pictures. His Majesty stayed about five minutes in the gallery; snubbed the Queen, who was drinking chocolate, for being always stuffing, the Princess Emily for not hearing him, the Princess Caroline for being grown fat, the Duke for standing awkwardly, Lord Hervey for not knowing what relation the Prince of Sultzbach was to the Elector Palatine, and then carried the Queen to walk, and be resnubbed, in the garden. The pictures were altered according to the King's direction soon after; and the excuse Lord Hervey made for their not being done that morning was the man's being out of the way who was always employed on those occasions.

When Lord Hervey told Sir Robert Walpole how ill it went with the Queen, Sir Robert said it was impossible, since the King had tasted better things, it should be otherwise; and that he had told the Queen she must not expect after thirty years' acquaintance, to have the same influence that she had formerly; that three-and-fifty and three-and-twenty could no more resemble one another in their effects than in their looks; and that, if he might advise, she should no longer depend upon her person, but her head, for her influence, as the one would now be of little use to her, and the other could never fail her. He added another piece of advice to this, which I believe was as little tasted as that which introduced it. It was to send for Lady Tankerville, a handsome, good-natured, simple woman (to whom the King had formerly been coquet), out of the country, and place her every evening at commerce or quadrille in the King's way. He told the Queen it was impossible the King should long bear to pass his evenings with his own daughters after having tasted the sweets of passing them with other people's, and that, if the King would have somebody else, it would be better to have that somebody chosen by her than by him; that Lady Tankerville was a very safe fool, and would give the King some amusement without giving Her Majesty any trouble. Lady Deloraine, who was very handsome, and the only woman that ever played with him in his daughters' apartment, Sir Robert said was a very dangerous one; a weak head, a pretty face, a lying tongue, and a false heart, making always sad work with the smallest degree of power or interest to help them forward; and that some degree of power or interest must always follow frequent opportunities given to a very coquette pretty woman with a very coquet idle man, especially without a rival to disturb or share with her. I must observe here, by the by, that Sir Robert Walpole told Lord Hervey, whilst he was relating this conference, that the King had bragged he had last winter lain with Lady Deloraine, which I must also observe I do not believe, I mean that the King had lain with her and not that he would not have told it if he had, nor that the scruple of making one daughter's governess his whore and the other daughter's apartment his bawdy house prevented him; yet that must have been the case had he lain with Lady Deloraine, for he never saw her anywhere else.

Lord Hervey asked Sir Robert Walpole how the Queen behaved upon giving her this counsel, and was answered, that she laughed, took it extremely well, and seemed mightily pleased with all he said; which I dare say was not the case. That the Queen laughed, I can easily believe; but imagine the laugh was rather a sign of her having a mind to disguise her not being pleased, than any mark that she was so; and I have the more reason to believe so, as I have been an eye-witness to the manner in which she has received ill-understood jokes of that kind from the same hand, particularly one this year at the King's birthday, when, pointing to some jewels in her hair, she said, 'I think I am extremely fine, too, though' (alluding to the manner of putting them on) 'un peu à la Moïse; I think they have given me horns.' Upon which Sir Robert Walpole burst out into a laugh and said he believed Mrs. Purcel (the woman who usually dressed the Queen's head) was a wag. The Queen laughed on this occasion too; but, if I know anything of her countenance, without being pleased, and not without blushing.

This style of joking was every way so ill understood in Sir Robert Walpole, that it was astonishing one of his extreme penetration could be guilty of it once, but it was much more surprising that with all his observation he could be guilty of it twice.

For, in the first place, when he told the Queen that the hold she used to have of the King by the charms of her person was quite lost, it was not true; it was weakened but not broken, and the charms of a younger person pulled him strongly perhaps another way, but they had not dissolved her influence, though they balanced it. In the next place, had it been true that the Queen's person could no longer charm any man, I have a notion that would be a piece of intelligence which no woman would love or like any man the better for giving her. It is a sort of thing which every woman is so reluctant to believe, that she may feel the effects of it long without being convinced that those effects can proceed from no other cause; and even after she is convinced of it herself, she still hopes other people have not found it out, and cannot help disliking anybody who lets her know he sees what she wishes everybody should be blind to.

In the midst of all this ill-humour shown by the King to the Queen at his first arrival, he made her a present of some fine coach-horses he brought from Hanover, which those who knew not his manner of thinking, and his usual motives for making presents of this sort to the Queen, took to be a mark of his kindness; but the truth was, he brought the horses over because he had a vanity in showing them here, and gave them to the Queen as he had done Richmond, and several sets of horses before, which he used as much as she, that Her Majesty, having the nominal property of them, might be at the expense of keeping them.

When he came to London his humour was not much mended by the circumstances of an empty town, a very thin appearance on his birthday, and the reason some fools near his person gave for people not being more richly dressed, which was, that they kept their fine clothes for the Prince's wedding. Sir Robert Walpole being to go to Norfolk with a great deal of company for three weeks, as he used to do at this time of the year, to the hunting congress (as it was called), was another circumstance which, as it contributed to thin the town, and particularly the levées and drawing-rooms, contributed too to sharpen His Majesty's temper, whose edge, whenever it was whetted, was seldom put in a sheath.

Sir Robert Walpole was at present in such high favour, on things going so well abroad, that he had only now and then his skin a little razed by this edge when it was sharpest, whilst others were sliced and scarified all over. Sir Robert Walpole, too, the King said, speaking on this present epidemical rural madness, he could forgive going into the country. His mind, His Majesty said, wanted relaxation, and his body exercise; and it was very reasonable that he should have a month in the year to look after his own private business, when all the rest of the year he was doing that of the public and his Prince. But what the other puppies and fools had to do to be running out of town now, when they had had the whole summer to do their silly business in, he could not conceive.

When the Duke of Newcastle, among the rest, asked his leave to go into the country, His Majesty pretended to take it upon another foot and said: 'With all my heart, my Lord, since Walpole is going, I wish you would all go and leave me a little in quiet, that I might not hear of a letter, or a despatch, or any business, till he comes back again.'

When the Duke of Grafton notified his design to go into the country, the King told him it was a pretty occupation for a man of quality, and at his age, to be spending all his time in tormenting a poor fox, that was generally a much better beast than any of those that pursued him; for the fox hurts no other animal but for his subsistence, whilst those brutes who hurt him did it only for the pleasure they took in hurting. The Duke of Grafton said he did it for his health. The King asked him why he could not as well walk or ride post for his health; and said, if there was any pleasure in the chase, he was sure the Duke of Grafton could know nothing of it; 'for, with your great corps of twenty stone weight, no horse, I am sure,' added His Majesty, 'can carry you within hearing, much less within sight, of your hounds.' This last dialogue I was present at. The Duke of Newcastle's was from Sir Robert Walpole.

The King, who never used to be civil to the Queen, even when he was kind, was now abominably and perpetually so harsh and rough, that she could never speak one word uncontradicted, nor do any one act unreproved; and though the Queen, whilst she knew the King's heart was as warm to her as his temper, could, for the sake of the agreeable advantages she reaped from the one, support and forgive the irksome inconveniences she was exposed to from the other, yet now the case was altered for, as his heart grew cooler and his temper warmer, so her sufferings were increased, and the usual recompense for them lessened. In the midst of this his disagreeable behaviour towards her, she one morning, smiling, to conceal her real concern, and to avoid seriously reproaching him, said to him, just as he was going out of her apartment to his own side, that, as Sir Robert Walpole had always been her friend, and that he was the single person in the Court who seemed at present in any degree of favour with His Majesty, she would apply to him to speak a word in her behalf, and try if he could get the rigour of her present treatment a little softened. The King was so far from taking or returning this joke that, with eyes which always swelled and widened with eagerness and grew as red as other people's cheeks when he was angry, he said he did not know what she meant by these complaints, nor what rigour he had exercised towards her. 'I am very ill, and I believe nobody is in the same good-humour sick as well; and in the next place, if I was well, do you think I should not feel and show some uneasiness for having left a place where I was pleased and happy all day long, and being come to one where I am as incessantly crossed and plagued?' To which the Queen, changing the tone of voice in which she had begun this expostulation, and answering in his own, asked him, if he was so happy at Hanover, why he did not stay there. 'I see no reason,' she said, 'that made your coming to England necessary; you might have continued there, without coming to torment yourself and us, since your pleasure did not call you; I am sure your business did not, for we could have done that just as well without you as you could have pleased yourself without us.' Upon which the King, in a great huff, trembling with passion, and without a word in reply, went out of the room.

I relate this conversation just as Sir Robert Walpole told it to me, and as he said the Queen told it to him; but I am apt to believe either he embellished in repeating this incident, or she bragged in reporting it. At least I am sure the smartness of her last speech, thus represented, was very little of a piece with the rest of her conduct during these turbulent times, since whenever, in public or private, I have seen her with the King, she has always behaved with the obsequiousness of the most patient slave to the most intemperate master; returned every injury with flattery, and every contradiction with acquiescences; crouched when he spurned, and, with the implicit resignation of the most rigid Christian, whenever he smote one cheek turned the other.

I cannot resist giving here, by way of specimen, an account of one conversation between her and him and Lord Hervey, whilst the circumstances of it are yet fresh in his memory.

About nine o'clock every night the King used to return to the Queen's apartment from that of his daughters, where, from the time of Lady Suffolk's disgrace, he used to pass those evenings he did not go to the opera or play at quadrille, constraining them, tiring himself, and talking a little bawdry to Lady Deloraine, who was always of the party.

At his return to the Queen's side the Queen used often to send for Lord Hervey to entertain them till they retired, which was generally at eleven. One evening among the rest, as soon as Lord Hervey came into the room, the Queen, who was knotting whilst the King walked backwards and forwards, began jocosely to attack Lord Hervey upon an answer just published to a book[1] of his friend Bishop Hoadly's on the Sacrament, in which the Bishop was very ill-treated; but before she had uttered half what she had a mind to say, the King interrupted her, and told her she always loved talking of such nonsense and things she knew nothing of; adding that if it were not for such foolish people loving to talk of those things when they were written, the fools who wrote upon them would never think of publishing their nonsense, and disturbing the Government with impertinent disputes that nobody of any sense ever troubled himself about. The Queen bowed, and said, 'Sir, I only did it to let Lord Hervey know that his friend's book had not met with that general approbation he had pretended.' 'A pretty fellow for a friend!' said the King, turning to Lord Hervey. 'Pray what is it that charms you in him? His pretty limping gait' (and

[1] *A plain Account of the Nature and End of the Sacrament of the Lord's Supper.*

then he acted the Bishop's lameness), 'or his nasty stinking breath?
—plaugh!—or his silly laugh, when he grins in your face for
nothing, and shows his nasty rotten teeth? Or is it his great honesty
that charms your Lordship? His asking a thing of me for one man
and, when he came to have it in his power to bestow, refusing the
Queen to give it to the very man for whom he had asked it? Or
do you admire his conscience that makes him now put out a book
that, till he was Bishop of Winchester, for fear his conscience might
hurt his preferment, he kept locked up in his chest? Is his conscience so much improved beyond what it was when he was Bishop
of Bangor, or Hereford, or Salisbury, for this book, I hear, was
written so long ago? Or was it that he would not risk losing a
shilling a year more whilst there was anything better to be got than
what he had? My Lord, I am very sorry you choose your friends so
ill; but I cannot help saying, if the Bishop of Winchester is your
friend, you have a great puppy and a very dull fellow and a great
rascal for your friend. It is a very pretty thing for such scoundrels,
when they are raised by favour so much above their desert, to be
talking and writing their stuff, to give trouble to the Government
that has showed them that favour; and very modest in a canting
hypocritical knave to be crying, "The kingdom of Christ is not of
this world," at the same time that he, as Christ's ambassador,
receives £6,000 or £7,000 a year. But he is just the same thing in
the Church that he is in the Government, and as ready to receive
the best pay for preaching the Bible, though he does not believe a
word of it, as he is to take favours from the Crown, though, by his
republican spirit and doctrine, he would be glad to abolish the
power of it.'

During the whole time the King was speaking, the Queen, by
smiling and nodding in proper places, endeavoured all she could,
but in vain, to make her court by seeming to approve everything
he said; and well, indeed, might she approve it, for it was almost
word for word what she had said to Lord Hervey on this subject
in the summer when the book first came out, which Lord Hervey,
to flatter her, whilst she flattered the King, gave her to understand
he remembered, by telling her very emphatically, when she asked
him what he had to say to all this, 'Your Majesty knows already
all I have to say on this subject'; and then added (to sweeten the

King), 'but how partial soever I may be to my friend, I assure Your Majesty I am not so partial to myself as to imagine, let his cause be ever so good, that I should be able to plead it with success against the very able counsel that I have just now heard draw up the charge on the other side.'

He then, in order to turn the conversation, told the King that he had that day been with a Bishop of a very different stamp, who would never, he dared to answer for him, disturb His Majesty's Government with writing. The man he meant was one Wilcocks, Bishop of Rochester, the dullest branch of episcopacy, and the most ignorant piece of orthodoxy, in the whole kingdom. 'As soon,' continued Lord Hervey, 'as Lord Wilmington, Lord Chancellor, and I, had to-day discharged Your Majesty's commission in proroguing the Parliament, my Lord of Rochester carried us to Westminster Abbey to show us a pair of old brass gates to Henry VII's Chapel, which were formerly overrun with rust and turned quite black, but are now new-cleaned, as bright as when they were first made, and the finest things of the kind I ever saw in my life.' Whilst Lord Hervey was going on with a particular detail and encomium on these gates, the Queen asking many questions about them, and seeming extremely pleased with the description, the King stopped the conversation short by saying: 'My Lord, you are always putting some of these fine things in the Queen's head, and then I am to be plagued with a thousand plans and workmen.' Then turning to the Queen, he said, 'I suppose I shall see a pair of these gates to Merlin's Cave, to complete your nonsense there.' (This Merlin's Cave was a little building so christened, which the Queen had lately finished at Richmond.[1]) The Queen smiled, and said Merlin's Cave was complete already; and Lord Hervey, to remove the King's fear of this expense, said that it was a sort of work that if His Majesty would give all the money in his exchequer he could not have now. 'A propos,' said the Queen, 'I hear the Craftsman has abused Merlin's Cave.' 'I am very glad of it,' interrupted the King: 'you deserve to be abused for such childish silly stuff, and it is the first time I ever knew the scoundrel in the right.'

This the Queen swallowed too, and began to talk on something

---

[1] A library, designed by Kent, containing a number of wax-work figures, including one of Merlin.

else, till the conversation (I know not by what transition) fell on the ridiculous expense it was to people, by the money given to servants, to go and stay two or three days with their acquaintance in the country; upon which the Queen said she had found it a pretty large expense this summer to visit her friends even in town. 'That is your own fault,' said the King; 'for my father, when he went to people's houses in town, never was fool enough to be giving away his money.' The Queen pleaded for her excuse that she had only done what Lord Grantham had told her she was to do; to which His Majesty replied, that my Lord Grantham was a pretty director; that she was always asking some fool or other what she was to do; and that none but a fool would ask another fool's advice. The Queen then appealed to Lord Hervey whether it was not now as customary to give money in town as in the country. He knew it was not, but said it was. He added, too, that to be sure, were it not so for particulars, it would certainly be expected from Her Majesty. To which the King said, 'Then she may stay at home, as I do. You do not see me running into every puppy's home, to see his new chairs and stools. Nor is it for you,' said he, addressing himself to the Queen, 'to be running your nose everywhere, and trotting about the town to every fellow that will give you some bread and butter, like an old girl that loves to go abroad, no matter where, or whether it be proper or no.' The Queen coloured, and knotted a good deal faster during this speech than she did before, whilst the tears came into her eyes, but she said not one word. Lord Hervey (who cared not whether he provoked the King's wrath himself or not, provided he could have the merit to the Queen of diverting His Majesty's ill-humour from her) said to the King, that, as the Queen loved pictures, there was no way of seeing a collection but by going to people's houses. 'And what matter whether she sees a collection or not?' replied the King. 'The matter is, Sir, that she satisfies her own curiosity, and obliges the people whose houses she honours with her presence.' 'Supposing,' said the King, 'she had a curiosity to see a bawdy house or a tavern, would it be fit for her to satisfy it? and yet the bawd or the innkeeper would be very glad to see her.' 'If the bawd and the innkeeper,' replied Lord Hervey, 'were used to be well received by Her Majesty in her palace, I should think the Queen's seeing them at their own houses would give no additional scandal.' The King, instead of answering Lord Hervey, then turned to the Queen, and, with a good deal of vehemence, poured out an unintelligible torrent of German, to which the Queen made not one word of reply, but knotted on till she tangled her thread, then snuffed the candles that stood on the table before her, and snuffed one of them out; upon which the King, in English, began a new dissertation upon Her Majesty, and took her awkwardness for his text.

The account of this conversation upon paper swells into so great a length that I shall enumerate no more particulars; what I have said will suffice for a sample of this conference, and this conference for a sample of many more of the same kind.

The Queen commended Lord Hervey's behaviour extremely to the Princess Caroline, who told him of it again; and next morning, when the Queen saw him, she told him, smiling: 'Our conversation last night was admirable; but I think you looked at me once as if you thought I was ready to cry.' Lord Hervey, who knew the Queen had no mind he should think she was much hurt at what had passed, said Her Majesty did not use to interpret looks so ill; and that he was so far from looking towards her and thinking her ready to cry, that he looked a contrary way, concluding her ready to laugh, and for fear, if he had met her eyes, that they might both have misbehaved.

In short, at this time the Prince, who was not upon a foot of being spoken to by his father, was the only person who did not taste of his ill-humour, and, though he was most of all in his displeasure, he least of all felt the effects of it. As the King hated, too, to talk of him almost as much as to talk to him, and disliked to have him the subject of his conversation almost as much as he did to have him the object of his sight, so he was as little apt to rail at him directly when he was absent as to snub him when he was present; though by a side-wind sometimes he took the pleasure of laying it on him pretty thick. The Queen one night speaking of a man that had been ill-used and behaved ill in a fray at the playhouse, the King said: 'I suppose nobody knows such a scoundrel.' To which the Queen replied, his name was Bray, and that the King knew his father very well. 'His father,' said the King, 'might be a very worthy man, though his son a puppy. One very often sees fathers and sons very little alike; a wise father has very often a fool for his son. One sees a father a very brave man, and his son a scoundrel; a father very honest, and his son a great knave; a father a man of truth, and his son a great liar; in short, a father that has all sorts of good qualities, and a son that is good for nothing.' But His Majesty drew this picture of a father and a son with so much eagerness, complimenting the one so strongly, and inveighing against the other so vehemently, that the Queen, though a good deal mistress of her countenance, looking towards Lord Hervey, betrayed that she took the parallel as it was meant; and the King himself, feeling he had pushed it too far, turned off the ridicule he thought he had incurred with quickness enough, by saying that sometimes it was just the reverse, and that very disagreeable fathers had very agreeable men for their sons. I suppose in this case he thought of his own father, as in the other he did of his own son.

One morning whilst he was dressing, before the company was let in, and when nobody but those who had the privilege of the bedchamber were present, he indulged himself in another sally of this kind against his son, by saying, whilst he was talking of the actors that he had seen in the play of Harry the Fourth the night before, that there were some really very good ones, but for the Prince of Wales, he must own he never saw so awkward a fellow and so mean a looking scoundrel in his life. Everybody who was present, I believe, had the same thought, but all very properly pretended to understand His Majesty literally, joined in the censure, and abused the theatrical Prince of Wales for a quarter of an hour together.

But there was a circumstance at this juncture known to but few people, which gave the Queen and Sir Robert Walpole, and those who wished well to either of them, more trouble than all the other effects of His Majesty's ill-humour put together, though the Queen always denied believing it. This circumstance was His Majesty's having given his word to Madame Walmoden to return to Hanover by the 29th of May next summer; which promise being known to all her friends, the night before His Majesty left Hanover, Madame Walmoden, at supper, in a mixture of tears and smiles, toasted the 29th of May, which all the rest of the company pledged in a bumper.

The King had never yet, that I could learn, given the least hint of this intention to anybody on this side of the water; I am sure he had not to the Queen or Sir Robert Walpole; and Lord Harrington, I believe, had been as close upon this subject as his master. It was told to Lord Hervey by Mr. Poyntz, who I guess had it from one Weston, a great friend of his, a sensible fellow, and *commis* to Lord Harrington. When Lord Hervey told it to Sir Robert Walpole, Sir Robert seemed at first much surprised and concerned; and afterwards said: 'But he shan't go for all that. His Majesty imagines frequently he shall do many things, which, because he is not at first contradicted, he fancies he shall be let to do at last. He thinks he is devilish stout, and never gives up his will or his opinion; but he never acts in anything material according to either of them but when I have a mind he should. I am going, my Lord, to make an odd declaration for a minister, for generally it is the policy of ministers to throw the blame of everything wrong done on their master; but I am willing to own, whenever our master does wrong, it is the fault of his ministers, who must either want resolution enough to oppose him, or sense enough to do it with success. Our master, like most people's masters, wishes himself absolute, and fancies he has courage enough to attempt making himself so; but if I know anything of him he is, with all his personal bravery, as great a political coward as ever wore a crown, and as much afraid to lose it.'

How Sir Robert could reconcile this speech with his keeping up such an army in England, and in the present circumstances of England, I know not; or how he would be able to justify this measure in private without disavowing in some degree the other assertion, I am quite at a loss to guess. However, Lord Hervey knew too well how little anybody likes to have such puzzling questions put to them to desire Sir Robert to clear up this matter.

The King gave other very strong marks at this time of his fondness for Madame Walmoden, which were as little known here as the promise he had made of returning to Hanover; one of which the Queen knew, but was ashamed to tell even to Sir Robert Walpole. This was that His Majesty, who till this year always used to stay with the Queen in a morning till after he had had the military amusement of peeping through the cane-blinds of the windows to see the guard relieved, which was hardly ever finished till eleven o'clock, did now forego that joy as well as the pleasures of his wife's conversation, and went every morning to his own side by nine o'clock or a little after, where he constantly wrote for two or three hours to Madame Walmoden, who never failed sending and receiving a letter every post.

The suppers, the balls, the shows and masquerades, with which this son of Mars entertained his new Venus were not only the frequent topics of his private conversation with the Queen at this time, but added to this he had the goodness to bring over pictures in fine gilt frames, to adorn the Queen's dressing-room; and was often so gracious to Lord Hervey when he was with Their Majesties in this dressing-room for an hour or two in the evening, to take a candle in his own royal hand, and tell him the story of these pictures, running through the names and characters of all the persons represented in them, and what they had said and done the whole night these entertainments had been exhibited; during which lecture Lord Hervey, whilst he was peeping over His Majesty's shoulder at these pictures, was shrugging up his own, and now and then stealing a look to make faces at the Queen, who, a little angry, a little peevish, and a little tired, with her husband's absurdity, and a little entertained with his Lordship's grimaces, used to sit and knot in a corner of the room, sometimes yawning and sometimes smiling, and equally afraid of betraying those signs either of her lassitude or her mirth.

The King, about a month before the session concluded, began to break the ice in hinting his intention to go again this year to Hanover; and as Madame Walmoden's being with child before he left Hanover had extremely increased his fondness for her before they parted, so the birth of a son this spring had very much whetted his impatience to return to her. A child, in most correspondences of this kind, is a cement that binds them faster, and the silly vanity old men have in getting one was an additional circumstance that made the King's fondness for Madame Walmoden increase much more on this incident than it would have done from the same cause twenty years ago. This being His Majesty's present situation, as the Church debates in Parliament had a little protracted the session beyond what was expected and, of course, postponed His Majesty's departure, he grew so inordinately peevish that everybody about him wished him gone almost as much as he wished to leave them.

It was generally reported, and as generally believed, that he one day said to the Queen on this subject, in one of his fretful transports, when she was talking of what had passed in the House, and that the Bishops should not be suffered by the Court to be so irritated by the present run against them as to be made desperate and irreconcilable, that he did not care a farthing how it ended, provided it did but end some way or other; and, upon her attempting to reply, that he stopped her short, by saying: 'I am sick to death of all this foolish stuff, and wish with all my heart that the devil may take all your Bishops, and the devil take your minister, and the devil take the Parliament, and the devil take the whole island, provided I can get out of it and go to Hanover.' But the truth of this speech I cannot pretend to authenticate.

I must now go a little back to give an account of the Prince's marriage, which was another principal event of this winter. It had been so longed talked of without anything being done to forward it, that everybody began to think it was not designed, when a step was taken that showed at last the King was in earnest. This step was His Majesty's sending a message in form to the Prince by five of the Cabinet Council—Lord Chancellor Talbot, Lord Wilmington, President of the Council; Lord Godolphin, Privy Seal; Duke of Grafton, Chamberlain; and Duke of Devonshire, Steward—to acquaint the Prince that His Majesty, if His Royal Highness liked it, would demand the Princess of Saxe-Gotha for him in marriage. The Prince made answer with great decency, duty, and propriety, that whoever His Majesty thought a proper match for his son would be agreeable to him.

In consequence of this message to the Prince, Lord Delaware, Treasurer of the King's Household, was nominated for the embassy to Saxe-Gotha to demand the Princess of her brother the Duke in marriage for the Princes of Wales. Lord Delaware, if the King chose him to prevent the Prince's having any jealousy of his future bride's affections being purloined on the way by him who was sent to attend her to England, was the properest man His Majesty could have pitched upon; for, except his white staff and red riband, as

Knight of the Bath, I know of nothing belonging to the long, lank, awkward person of Lord Delaware that could attract her eyes; nor do I believe there could be found in any of the Goth or Vandal Courts of Germany a more unpolished ambassador for such an occasion.

The necessary precautions for this embassy taking up some little time, the King, being very impatient to return to Hanover to the arms of Madame Walmoden, declared to his Queen and his Ministers, that if matters could not be so managed as to bring the Princess of Saxe-Gotha into England before the expiration of the month of April the marriage should either be put off till the winter or solemnised without him, for that he would positively set out for Germany as soon as ever the Parliament was up.

This declaration obliged the Ministers to hurry on this affair, and on Sunday morning, the 25th of April, whilst the King was at chapel, news was brought him that the Princess of Saxe-Gotha was landed at Greenwich. On the Tuesday following, about two o'clock, she came to St. James's; and, the marriage being to be performed that evening, the whole Court, and almost indeed the whole town, resorted to St. James's in their wedding-clothes to see her arrival.

She came from Greenwich in one of the King's coaches to Lambeth, was conveyed from thence to Whitehall in one of his barges, and from Whitehall came through St. James's Park and Garden in the King's chair to the foot of the steps that go out of the King's apartment into the garden, where the Prince, who had been often at Greenwich in these two days, received her and led her up to the King, who had been waiting (not very patiently) above an hour with the Queen and the whole Court in the great drawing-room to receive her. As soon as she came she threw herself all along on the floor first at the King's and then at the Queen's feet, who both took her up and embraced her. This prostration was known to be so acceptable an accosting to His Majesty's pride that, joined to the propriety of her whole behaviour on this occasion, it gave the spectators great prejudices in favour of her understanding, which on better acquaintance afterwards soon mouldered away.

This Princess was but seventeen years old when she came to England, knew not a mortal here, and was suffered to bring nobody but one single man with her, so that in this situation, and brought from the solitude of her mother's country-house in Saxe-Gotha at once into the crowd, intrigues, and pomp of this Court, the bare negatively good conduct of doing nothing absurd might reasonably prejudice sensible people in her favour. Sir Robert Walpole was one of this number, who said to me the morning after the wedding that her gaining upon the King last year in one interview enough to make him fond of the match and her behaving at Greenwich to the Prince in such a manner as to put him in good-humour with it, after all His Royal Highness had uttered against her before he had seen her, were circumstances that spoke strongly in favour of brains that had but seventeen years to ripen.

She could speak not one word of English, and few of French; and when it was proposed the year before to her mother, when this match was resolved upon, that she should be taught one of these languages, her mother said it must be quite unnecessary, for the Hanover Family having been above twenty years on the throne, to be sure most people in England spoke German (and especially at Court) as often and as well as English. A conjecture so well founded that I believe there were not three natives in England that understood one word of it better than in the reign of Queen Anne.

The Princess was rather tall, and had health and youth enough in her face, joined to a very modest and good-natured face, to make her countenance not disagreeable; but her person, from being very ill-made, a good deal awry, her arms long, and her motions awkward, had, in spite of all the finery of jewels and brocade, an ordinary air, which no trappings could cover or exalt.

She did not appear at all embarrassed on this occasion, which most people gave as an instance of sense; but Lady Stafford, an old French lady, daughter of the famous Count de Gramont, who had a pension from this Court, and had lived for many years in England, and had as much wit, humour, and entertainment in her as any man or woman I ever knew, with a great justness in her way of thinking, and very little reserve in her manner of giving her opinion of things and people, said: 'Pour moi, je trouve qu'on juge très mal car si cette pauvre Princesse avait le sens commun, elle doit être embarrassée dans sa situation; quand on a un tel rôle à jouer, qu'on doit épouser un sot Prince et vivre avec un désagréable animal toute sa vie, on doit sentir ses malheurs, et je suis sûre qu'elle est sotte, et même très sotte, puis qu'elle n'est pas embarrassée et qu'elle ne paraît point confondue dans toutes les nouveautés parmi lesquelles elle se trouve.'

The King and Queen dined this day as usual in their own apartment, but the Duke and the Princesses were ordered to dine with the Prince and his bride in the Prince's apartment, where the King, to avoid all difficulties about ceremony, had ordered them to go undressed. Notwithstanding which the Prince wisely contrived to raise a thousand disputes, pretending first that his brother and sisters should sit upon stools whilst he and his bride sat in armed chairs at the head of the table; next, that they should not be served on the knee, though neither of these things had ever entered before into his head since he came into England, and that he had ate with them constantly every day.

However, in both these things and several others, the Princesses having had their directions from the King and Queen what they were to do, His Royal Highness was overruled; the Princesses would not go into his eating-room, but stayed in his ante-chamber, till the stools were taken away and chairs carried in and being to be served by their own servants at table, they ordered their servants to do everything for them, just as the Prince and Princess's did for them; only after dinner, the Princess Caroline told me, they were forced to go without their coffee, for fear that being poured out by a servant of the Princess's, they might have met with some disgrace had they accepted of any in the manner of giving it.

I mention these occurrences to show from what wise motives the irreconcilable differences in princely families often proceed, and by what important circumstances they are prudently and sensibly on both sides generally widened and kept up, and what right people of their age and rank have either to reprehend or despise children in a nursery that are scratching and pinching one another for tops and shuttlecocks, when these purpled children are running the risk of losing the advantages they have over the rest of the world, by squabbling and contesting with one another for trifles of as little moment—for chairs, and stools, and the posture in which they are to receive a little wine and water.

At night about nine o'clock the ceremony of the wedding was performed in much the same manner as that of the Princess Royal had been, only there was no gallery built. Consequently there could be no procession in form, and they were married in that Chapel to which the King constantly goes on a Sunday.

At supper nothing remarkable happened but the Prince's eating several glasses of jelly, and every time he took one turning about, laughing, and winking on some of his servants.

The King went after supper to the Princess's apartment whilst the Queen undressed the Princess, and when they were in bed everybody passed through their bed-chamber to see them, where there was nothing remarkable but the Prince's nightcap, which was some inches higher than any grenadier's cap in the whole army.

There were various reports on what did and did not pass this night after the company was retired. The Queen and Lord Hervey agreed that the bride looked extremely tired with the fatigues of the day, and so well refreshed next morning, that they concluded she had slept very sound; and Her Majesty did not forget to descant at the same time with her usual enjoyment on the glasses of jelly and the nightcap, saying the one made her sick, and the other, if it had not been her son, would have made her laugh.

The two Houses of Parliament addressed the King on this occasion, and in the House of Commons three very remarkable speeches were made by Mr. Grenville and Mr. Lyttelton, two of Lord Cobham's nephews, and Cornet Pitt, who got up one after another in the House of Commons to compliment the Prince's character and the Princess's family and to insinuate, not in very covert terms, that the King had very little merit to the nation in making this match, since it had been owing to the Prince demanding it of his father, and the voice of the people calling for it too strongly not to be complied with.

At the end of the session Cornet Pitt was broke for this, which was a measure at least ill-timed, if not ill-taken; since the breaking him at the end of the session looked as if it had been done on account of the general tenor of his conduct during the session, to avoid which interpretation, if the Court did not think him too inconsiderable an object to be distinguished by such a mark of its resentment, he ought certainly to have been turned out the night after he made this speech, to mark out the crime that drew the King's indignation upon him.

Before the King went abroad he sent a message by the Duke of Grafton to the Prince to let him know that wherever the Queen resided there would always be apartments provided for him and the Princess. This message being verbal, when the Prince complained that it was to tell him he was to be prisoner wherever the Queen resided, that explanation of it was denied, and on the King's side of the house it was said that it was rather a civility shown to the Prince; though in reality everybody knew how it was meant, and the design was certainly to prevent either Prince or Princess having a separate court, and so afterwards explained.

I forgot to mention one thing in its proper place, which was the dispute between the Queen and the Prince, when she nominated the Princess's servants before her coming over, about Lady Archibald Hamilton's being one of the Ladies of the Bedchamber. The Prince insisted much upon it; but the Queen said whether she believed Lady Archibald innocent or not, the Prince's behaviour to her had been so particular, and had caused her to be so generally talked of as being his mistress, that it was impossible for her to put Lady Archibald about the Princess without incurring the censure of the whole world; and therefore all she could do to oblige him in this particular was, as the Princess was designed to have four Ladies, to nominate but three, leaving a vacancy in case the Princess liked to have Lady Archibald about her, to add her afterwards. But Mrs. Townshend, wife of his Groom of the Bedchamber, whom the Prince also solicited to have one of the Women of the Bedchamber, the King peremptorily refused, not on account of prudery, for the Prince was never talked of for Mrs. Townshend, but for political reasons, His Majesty bidding the Queen say to her son that as Mr. Townshend was the most impertinent puppy in the Prince's whole family, he was determined not to reward him for being so; and that it was more favour than either the servant or master deserved that he himself was not turned out.

Upon the Prince's marriage the King increased his allowance from £24,000 to £50,000 a year, which the Prince said was robbing him of £50,000 as the Parliament when it gave the Civil List at the King's accession designed him £100,000, which the King had had in the former reign when he was Prince of Wales; and most people were of the same opinion.

The breach between these two parts of the family grew wider every day, and this circumstance of the £100,000, as it was one of the principal causes of their disagreement, and indeed the most material point in dispute between them, it was not likely the breach would ever be healed, as the one would never cease to think the withholding half of this income a wrong done to him, and the other would never be prevailed upon, right or wrong, to give it.

chapter five

The Queen's Last Regency

1736

IN THE MIDDLE of May the King left England, and the same morning he left St. James's to embark at Gravesend the Queen went to Richmond, taking with her her children, her Lady and Woman of the Bedchamber in Waiting, and Lord Hervey. The Prince pretended that he designed to follow her next day and stay at his house at Kew till the Queen returned to Kensington to open her commission of Regent, which she never used to do till the news was brought of the King's being landed in Holland. But the Princess being taken ill the night before they were to remove to Kew, or being ordered to say she was so, the Prince sent to let the Queen know he was prevented by the indisposition of his wife from coming to Kew as he had intended, and ordered all the things and servants which had been sent thither to be brought back to London.

The Prince first said the Princess had the measles, but as he could not get Dr. Hollings, who attended her, to confirm this report, he brought the measles down to a rash, and at last compounded for a great cold.

The Queen having a mind to be satisfied of the truth of the case, whilst she thought the Princess in perfect health, as she herself told me, pretended to believe her ill, and with great civility and maternal kindness went with her two eldest daughters to London to see her. But the Princess keeping her bed, and the room being made (on purpose, as the Queen imagined) very dark, she returned as little informed of the true state of her daughter-in-law's health as she went.

However, most people were of opinion this illness, if not entirely feigned, was much aggravated by the Prince's report of it, partly because he liked better to stay in town and divert himself there, but chiefly to take the first opportunity of evading, if not disobeying, the order he had received from the King by the Duke of Grafton.

When the Queen went to Kensington to open her commission of Regent, His Royal Highness did not think fit to appear at Council, but contrived to come to Kensington just after the Council was over, and pretending he had designed to be present, though he was too late.

Lord Harrington's ill state of health was made the pretence for Horace Walpole's being sent in his stead this year to Hanover with the King. But had his health been better, his interest at Court was so much worse that some other reason would have been found and given for his not going; for it was a resolution to my knowledge taken the year before by the Queen and Sir Robert, that Lord Harrington should never be suffered to go thither with the King again.

There were a great number of commissions in the army vacant, which the King, from a natural dilatoriness in his temper, joined to a particular backwardness in giving, had postponed filling up all the winter, not withstanding the frequent and pressing instances made to him by Sir Robert Walpole, who never received any other answer on these occasions from His Majesty, than 'My God! It is time enough. I will fill them up at the end of the session.'

Most people thought the King's reason for keeping commissions in the army vacant in this manner was because the pay during their being vacant went into his pocket, and had that been the case his conduct would not have been so wonderful in this particular. But it was not his avarice that operated in this point, for he got little or nothing by it, the intermediate pay not coming to him, but being accounted for to the public. It was therefore owing merely to his reluctance to oblige, and his loving nobody well enough to have any pleasure in preferring them that this vast number of posts in the army was unfilled.

At the end of the session, when Sir Robert came with these numerous solicitations, the King said it was impossible for him in the hurry of his departure to answer them all; so signed only some few before he went, and a few more after he got to Hanover, which was an illegal practice, the regal power being not divisible, and the instrument that constituted the Queen Regent having of course delegated all the regal power to, and vested it in, her.

His Majesty's happiness with Madame Walmoden at Hanover did not last long without alloy or interruption, an unlucky accident happening, that gave occasion to His Majesty to fret, as much as it gave occasion to those who were less concerned in it to laugh.

The fact was this. Whilst the King was at Herrenhausen, and Madame Walmoden at her lodgings in the palace at Hanover, one night the gardener found a ladder, which did not belong to the garden, set up against Madame Walmoden's window; and concluding it was with a design to rob her, this poor, innocent, careful servant made diligent search in the garden, and found a man lurking behind an espalier, whom he concluded to be the thief; accordingly, by the assistance of his fellow-servants, he seized and carried him to the captain of the guard then upon duty. When the prisoner was brought to the light, it proved to be one Monsieur Schulenburg, a relation of the Duchess of Kendal's and an officer in the Imperial service. He complaining to the captain of the guard of this violence, and the captain of the guard, like the gardener, thinking nothing but a design of robbery could be at the bottom of this affair and that a man of that rank was certainly no robber, ordered him to be released.

This affair made a great noise immediately, and Madame Walmoden, thinking it would be for her advantage to tell the story herself first to the King, ordered her coach at six o'clock in the morning, drove to Herrenhausen, and went directly to the King's bedside, threw herself on her knees, drowned in tears, and begged of His Majesty either to protect her from being insulted or to give her leave to retire. She said she doted on him as her lover and her friend, and never when she gave him her heart considered him as a King; but that she found too late, that no woman could live with a King as with a man of inferior rank; but that a thousand people, for political reasons, and with whom she was too weak to struggle were studying every day new tricks to ruin her; and therefore as she foresaw sooner or later she must be undone, though she preferred the King's love to every other pleasure or happiness in the world, yet as her cowardice made her prefer security and quiet even to that, she begged His Majesty would give her timorous innocence leave to retire out of a world and a Court she was unfit to live in.

The King, surprised at this unexpected visit and this long preface, asked what all this meant. She then told the story just as I have related it, and said she was sure this was a trick of the Schulenburg family, and perhaps a contrivance of Madame d'Elitz to ruin her.

This Madame d'Elitz was a Schulenburg, sister to my Lady Chesterfield, a very handsome lady, though now a little in her decline, with a great deal of wit, who had had a thousand lovers, and had been catched in bed with a man twenty years ago and been divorced from her husband upon it. She was said to have been mistress to three generations of the Hanover family; the late King, the present, and the Prince of Wales before he came to England, which was one generation more than the Duchess of Valentinois, who had been mistress to Henry II, could boast of in France.

The present King had quitted Madame d'Elitz for Madame Walmoden, upon which a quarrel ensued between the two ladies, and the King thereupon had turned Madame d'Elitz out of the palace the year before. Just, therefore, when the King set out for Hanover this year, Madame d'Elitz set out for England, where she now was with her aunt and sister, the Duchess of Kendal and Lady Chesterfield.

Madame Walmoden affected to the King to believe that all this had happened the night before from a plot laid by Madame d'Elitz and her family to be revenged of her for the victory she had got over them in the King's favour.

The King was extremely incensed, and ordered the captain of the guard at Hanover to be put under arrest immediately for having released Monsieur Schulenburg, and Monsieur Schulenburg to be again apprehended.

The King's letter to the Queen about this affair was a very extraordinary one, asking her, as he would have done a man-friend, what she thought of all this business; saying perhaps his passion for Madame Walmoden might make him see it in a partial light for her, and desiring the Queen to 'consulter le gros homme' (meaning Sir Robert), 'qui a plus d'expérience, ma chère Caroline, que vous dans ces affaires, et moins de préjugé que moi dans celle-ci.'

In the meantime, in England there happened several disturbances of a family and public nature, which I must not pass over in silence.

The Princess of Wales took it into her head to have some scruples about receiving the sacrament according to the manner of the Church of England, and went to the communion at a Lutheran German chapel.

The Queen, at the desire of Sir Robert Walpole, spoke to the Prince on this subject, and told him he ought to interpose, representing to him, when this thing came to take air, how ill it would be received not only by the bishops and clergy, but by the people of England in general, and what bad consequences it might have, by giving the whole nation prejudices against his wife.

The Prince assured the Queen he had already said everything he could think of on this subject to his wife to no purpose; that in answer, she only wept and talked of her conscience.

Lord Hervey advised the Queen at her next conference to tell the Prince that this might grow a very serious affair; for as the Act of Succession enjoined the heirs to the Crown, on no less a penalty than the forfeiture of the Crown, to receive the sacrament according to the manner of the Church of England as by law established, it was impossible to say how that law might be construed to extend to the wife of the Prince of Wales, and whether she might not possibly be sent back to Saxe-Gotha.

All these arguments and conferences had their effect at last so well that the Princess dried her tears, lulled her conscience, and went no more to the Lutheran Church, but received the sacrament like the rest of the royal family.

An old woman called Madame Rixleiven, who had been the Princess's governess at Saxe-Gotha and was sent for to England at her request, was thought to have put this conscientious nonsense into the Princess's head; but talking to her too freely also on conjugal points, the Prince soon grew to dislike her, and sent her back from whence she came.

There was another thing which happened soon after, relating to going to church; which, though an affair not of devotion and religion, but of pride and ceremonial, yet as it is of the number of royal trifles that had like to have been of serious consequence, I must insert.

The Prince and Princess, whether from an air of grandeur or by chance I know not, used generally to come to chapel at Kensington after the service had been some time begun; and the Princess, when she did so, being obliged to crowd by the Queen, and to pass before her, between the Queen and where her book lay, the Queen, who really found it troublesome, the passage being very narrow, and, besides the trouble, thinking it had not a very respectful or decent air, after suffering it two or three Sundays, sent and ordered Sir William Irby, the Princess's chamberlain (Her Majesty being already in the chapel), to bring the Princess in at another door where the Ladies of the Bedchamber came in, and through which the Princess might come to her place without crowding by the Queen if she was standing, or being obliged to stay at the door, if the Queen was kneeling, till Her Majesty rose up. But notwithstanding these orders the Prince, who was present when the Queen's Vice-Chamberlain delivered them to the Princess's, commanded Sir William Irby to carry the Princess into chapel at the same door he used to do, and accordingly he did so.

The Queen, as it is natural to believe, did not much approve of this disobedience to her orders; and, speaking of it the next morning to Lord Hervey, said she believed nobody was ever treated so impertinently as to be told one should not be mistress in one's own house, nor be able to order what doors should or should not be opened.

Lord Hervey said she was certainly in the right; but that it was very plain by this, and many other particulars in the Prince's conduct since the King went, that he endeavoured to force her to quarrel with him during his father's absence, that he might have it to say that the one was as hard to be lived with as the other; for which reason, if he were to advise Her Majesty, he would wish, if the Prince was to sit down in her lap, that she would only say she hoped he found it easy. He added that if she ordered her servants to stand at the chapel-door where she went in, and not suffer it to be opened after she was once seated, to be sure she might keep the Princess from coming in and make Her Royal Highness go round to the other door or back again to her own apartment. But then it would make an éclat, and the Prince would carry a point he had more at heart than the door, which was that of a public dispute.

After this, the Prince, being told, I believe, by some of his own people that he was in the wrong, ordered the Princess, whenever she was not ready to go into chapel with the Queen, not to go at all, and by this means avoided either persisting or yielding.

The Prince had contrived to put Lady Archibald Hamilton so well into the Princess's good graces that she was her first favourite, and always with her; and to obviate any alarms that might be given to her jealousy, he told the Princess himself that malicious people had set it about that she was his mistress; and that the Queen, who was glad of any pretence to cross him, had laid hold of this excuse to refuse making her one of the ladies of the Princess's Bedchamber, though he had pressed it extremely; and that the Queen had owned she never believed there was the least foundation for any such report. At the same time he extolled Lady Archibald's merit and virtue, and said, though she was married very young to an old man, and had been very pretty, that not the least blemish had ever been thrown upon her character till some of the King and Queen's Court, to vex him and to please them, who grudge him the friendship of every man and woman that ever attached themselves to him, made this malicious insinuation.

This had its effect so well that the Princess made it her request to the Queen that she would write to Hanover to the King, to ask his leave for her to take Lady Archibald Hamilton into her service; to which the King consenting, Lady Archibald was immediately made Lady of the Bedchamber, Privy Purse, and Mistress of the Robes to the Princess, with a salary, for all three together, of nine hundred pounds a year.

It would be endless if I were to tell how many hints the Prince gave of the Princess being with child this summer; but one foolish circumstance in Her Royal Highness's manner of passing her time I must relate, which was her playing every day with a great jointed baby, and dressing and undressing it two or three times every day. Princess Caroline, who had heard that the sentinels and footmen used to stand and stare and laugh during this performance, desired her sister-in-law one day not to stand at her window during these operations on her baby; for though there was nothing ridiculous in the thing itself, yet the lower sort of people thinking everything so that was not customary, it would draw a mob about her and make *la canaille* talk disagreeably.

Notwithstanding the little *démêlées* that happened between the

Queen and the Prince, Her Majesty, being determined not to quarrel with him during the King's absence, never failed asking him and the Princess to dine with her (which they often did during the summer) whenever they came in the morning to her drawing-room. The Princess, too, came sometimes to music, and play in the Queen's gallery at night, but the Prince never. The Queen was always very easy with her, and used to acknowledge she should be the weakest creature in the world, as well as the most unjust, if she took anything ill of the Princess; for that she knew the Princess did nothing without the Prince's order, and must do everything he did order her. For which reason I once heard the Queen add: 'Poor creature, if she were to spit in my face, I should only pity her for being under such a fool's direction, and wipe it off.' And to give the Queen her due, she was always remarkably and industriously civil to her and has often said to me she thought there was no sort of harm in her, that she never meant to offend, was very modest and very respectful, and that for her want of understanding it was what to be sure fatigued one when one was obliged to be with her, but what one must want understanding oneself to be angry with her for not having. When Lord Hervey used to come to the Queen in the afternoon, those days the Prince and Princess had dined with her, the Queen used generally to accost him with yawning and complaining of the vapours; telling him often at the same time, that the silly gaiety and *fade railleries* of her son, joined to the silent stupidity of her *ennuyante* daughter-in-law, had oppressed her to that degree that she was ready to cry with the fatigue of their company, and felt herself more tired than she believed she should have done if she had carried them round the garden on her back.

During this whole summer the Queen was in as good-humour, health, and spirits as I ever saw her. Her pride was shocked, and she seemed a good deal hurt, for some time after the King went; but this cloud soon dispersed, and the being freed from his ill-humour seemed to be a full compensation for all his good-humour being bestowed elsewhere.

Lord Hervey was with her this summer at Kensington every day, and almost all day, Saturdays excepted, which she always passed at Kew, and he in London.

The Queen's temper and patience under the King's neglect held out tolerably well till it came to be sure that his stay at Hanover would be protracted beyond his birthday.[1] But this being a mark of his indifference to her, and the strength of his attachment to another, with which she had never been more mortified, she began to deviate a little from the general resolution she before seemed to have taken, of submitting to every slight her husband thought fit to put upon her, not only without resenting or murmuring, but even without seeming to feel or see it. She began to slacken in her assiduity towards His Majesty in her letters and the length of them; the thirty or forty pages, which used to be their usual length, were shrunk to seven or eight; and it is probable that the style (though this is only conjecture) abated as much of its cordiality as the bulk of its quantity. Lord Hervey had observed these alterations and disapproved them; but as the Queen had always spoken of this amour of the King's with Madame Walmoden as a thing she despised, and that Lord Hervey back again had talked of it as a thing below her regard, and often turned every circumstance of it into ridicule, his Lordship did not now care to risk the taking it on a more serious tone, or to seem to observe that Her Majesty had done so, when she had not thought fit to give the least hint of this alteration either in her way of acting or thinking; nor was there perhaps any in the latter, though there was in the former.

However, as he apprehended such a change would weaken her interest yet more with the King rather than retrieve it, Lord Hervey told Sir Robert Walpole what he had remarked, and begged him somehow or other to prevent her going on in a way that would certainly destroy her. Sir Robert Walpole said nothing could ever quite destroy her power with the King, though several things might happen temporarily to weaken her influence or to make the exercise of it more difficult. Lord Hervey replied that he knew but two ways any woman had of keeping her power with any man, which were by the man's fondness for her person or by habit; that, as to the first, it was very plain that cement no longer subsisted to unite the King and Queen; and that, for the other, these frequent absences, he feared, would bring habit to operate with no more force than inclination, especially when the King found whenever he

[1] October 30.

broke into this habit of being with his wife, it was for his pleasure, and whenever he returned to it, that it proved for his mortification. Sir Robert Walpole allowed all this to be very true, but insisted still that the Queen had by a long course of years, and by the King's opinion of her understanding, as well as security in her truth to him, got such an ascendant over His Majesty's mind that it was impossible for anything to dissolve it. However, he said he was entirely of Lord Hervey's opinion that her taking the *fière* turn would hurt her, and that he had observed she was going into that method before Lord Hervey had told him of it; that he had already spoken slightly on the subject to the Queen, and resolved, if he saw hints had no effect, to give her his opinion more plainly. Accordingly he did so, and gave Lord Hervey, some time after, an account of what had passed between him and the Queen on this subject. He said he had told Her Majesty that if he had a mind to flatter her into her ruin, he might talk to her as if she was now five-and-twenty years old, and try to make her imagine that to alarm the King with apprehensions of losing her affection might awaken his fear and bring him back. But as this was not the case, he said he should be unpardonable if, in order to talk in a style that might please her, he should give her counsel that would ruin her. He said it was too late in her life to try new methods, and that she must never hope now to keep her power with the King by reversing those methods by which she had gained it, that nothing but soothing, complying, softening, bending, and submitting, could do any good; but that she must persist in those arts, must press the King to bring this woman to England; and that if Her Majesty would do this, trust to him, and take his advice, he would engage she should get the better of her. He taught her this hard lesson till she wept; and Her Majesty, instead of reproaching him for the liberty he had taken, promised to do everything he had desired her, and thanked him for the friendship he had shown towards her. When Sir Robert Walpole related this passage to Lord Hervey, he added: 'My Lord, she laid her thanks on so thick, and made such professions of friendship and gratitude, that I found I had gone too far; for I am never so much afraid of her rebukes as her commendations. I know how to justify myself against the first, but not against the latter, as I know them often to be false, and dare not receive them but as if I thought they were true.'

However, Sir Robert Walpole did not disguise his suspicions so well but that the Queen perceived them; for, two or three days afterwards, walking with Sir Robert Walpole in her gardens at Richmond, where she passed every Saturday all this summer, she told him: 'I saw you did not believe me the other day, nor imagine, though I promised to take your advice, that I intended to keep my word: own the truth, am I not in the right?' Sir Robert Walpole (who was certainly a very ill-bred man), yet by the force of his understanding, made an answer to this question that if one had known no other stroke of his character in point of breeding, one should have concluded him as polite a courtier as dexterous states-man. 'Madam (said he), Your Majesty, in asking if I disbelieve you, would put a word into my mouth so coarse that I could not even give it place in my thoughts; but, if you oblige me to answer this question, I confess I feared.' 'Well,' replied the Queen, 'I under-stand what "I feared" means upon this occasion; but to show you your fears are ill-founded I have considered what you said to me, and am determined this very day to write to the King just as you would have me; and on Monday, when we meet at Kensington, you shall see the letter.' Accordingly, a most submissive, kind, and tender letter was written by Her Majesty to the King, assuring him she had nothing but his interest and his pleasure at heart; that she had long known such was her duty, and that she hoped he had long known such was her practice; that she hoped the uninter-rupted series of her conduct ever since he had known her would make his recollection convince him of this truth more fully than all she could say; and the letter ended with making it her earnest request to the King that he would bring Madame Walmoden to England, and giving him repeated assurances that his wife's con-duct to his mistress should be everything he desired when he told his pleasure, and everything she imagined he wished when she was left to guess it.

The Queen never showed Lord Hervey this letter, nor ever gave him the least hint of her having written one to this effect further than always agreeing with him when he said he wished this new favourite to be brought over; and frequently, when he talked to her on this subject, she would begin to sing or repeat these words: 'Se mai più saro gelosa mi punisca il sacro nume,' etc., which was the beginning of a song in one of Handel's operas called Porus: and always spoke of these conjugal infidelities as things about which only girls and fools ever made themselves uneasy; acknowledging at the same time, as she knew the discontent the King's annual journeys to Hanover created here, that there was nothing she wished so much as that he would bring Madame Walmoden over. She would often say at the same time how much she had wished to keep Lady Suffolk at Court, and though the generality of the world, who always made false judgments on these occasions for want of seeing *le dessous des cartes*, had imagined Lady Suffolk's disgrace was the effect of Her Majesty's intrigues and a proof of her influence over the King, that it was so much the contrary that she had done all she could to persuade her to stay in that audience Lady Suffolk asked of her; and that when she told the King she had done so, the King snubbed her for it, and said: 'What the devil did you mean by trying to make an old, dull, deaf, peevish beast stay and plague me when I had so good an opportunity of getting rid of her.'

But notwithstanding all the reasonable things the Queen could say on these two subjects, of having formerly desired to keep Lady Suffolk at St. James's, and now desiring to bring Madame Walmoden thither, she neither felt all she said, nor was willing even in her own mind to reflect on all she felt, but often deceived even herself as well as others, and (from wishing she could think as her pride and her interest would dictate to her) would not permit herself to see that the wife in her breast was perpetually combating the Queen, and the woman revolting against the politician.

When Sir Robert Walpole told Lord Hervey of this letter that the Queen had written to the King to solicit his bringing Madame Walmoden over, he gave the manner of cooking it the greatest encomiums in which it was possible to speak of such a performance; he said she had not pared away the least part of his meaning, but had clothed his sentiments in so pretty a dress, had mixed so many tender turns in every paragraph, and spoke with such decent concern of her own situation as well as consideration of the King's, had covered all her own passions so artfully, and applied so pathetically to his, that Sir Robert Walpole said he did not believe anybody but a woman could have written a letter of that sort, nor any women but the Queen so good a one.

Lord Hervey said he was quite satisfied with this report of the letter; and had only one question more to ask, which was, if Sir Robert thought the letter went? Sir Robert said he really believed it did; for though upon his first reading it he thought it was so good that it was never designed to go, yet the Queen's whole behaviour that morning had such an air of openness and sincerity that he really believed the letter would be sent that night to Hanover. 'Her behaviour was very different this morning,' continued he, 'from what it was when first I spoke to her on this subject. She acknowledged I had before made her half angry with me; and the anger she owns is never dangerous; it is only her commendations alarm me, for whenever she daubs I fear.

'But this day,' continued Sir Robert, 'she went even further than I desired, by telling me she intended to make the King the offer of taking Madame Walmoden into her service, which I advised her against, telling her if the King should accept that offer it could have no good air in the world, as it must either draw contempt upon her from being thought too mean a condescension in her if it should be judged merely her own doing, or would bring an odium upon the King if it should be concluded that Madame Walmoden had been forced upon her.' The Queen then gave the example of Lady Suffolk's situation, which had made no clamour at all of this kind; to which Sir Robert Walpole replied that he could not help thinking the world would judge very differently of the two cases, as the King's making one of the Queen's servants his mistress, or his mistress one of the Queen's servants, were two things which nobody would see in the same light.

Soon after all apprehensions of this letter not having been sent were totally dissipated, for an answer to it came from the King, which the Queen showed to Sir Robert Walpole. This letter wanted no marks of kindness but those that men express to women they love; had it been written to a man, nothing could have been added to strengthen its tenderness, friendship, and affection. He extolled the Queen's merit towards him in the strongest expression of his sense of all her goodness to him and the gratitude he felt towards her. He recommended her understanding, her temper, and in short left nothing unsaid that could demonstrate the opinion he had of her head and the value he set upon her heart. He told her too she knew him to be just in his nature, and how much he wished he could be everything she would have him. 'Mais vous voyez mes passions, ma chère Caroline! Vous connaissez mes foiblesses, il n'y a rien de caché dans mon cœur pour vous, et plût à Dieu que vous pourriez me corriger avec la même facilité que vous m'approfondissez! Plût à Dieu que je pourrais vous imiter autant que je sais vous admirer, et que je pourrais apprendre de vous toutes les vertus que vous me faites voir, sentir, et aimer!' His Majesty then came to the point of Madame Walmoden's coming to England, and said she told him she would do anything he would have her, that she relied on the Queen's goodness, and would give herself up to whatever Their Majesties thought fit, and to be disposed of implicitly as they should direct. Sir Robert Walpole, who gave Lord Hervey an account of this letter merely by memory (but said he had read it several times), assured Lord Hervey it was so well written, that if the King was only to write to women, and never to strut and talk to them, he believed His Majesty would get the better of all the men in world with them.

The King in this letter gave a full description to the Queen of Madame Walmoden's person, understanding, and temper. He said she was far from being a regular beauty, but had a very agreeable countenance; was rather genteelly than exactly made. 'Qu'elle n'avait pas un esprit éclatant, mais enjoué et amusant; mais à l'égard du cœur elle est sûrement la meilleure créature du monde.' This was the conclusion of her corporal and mental picture. In this letter, too, the King having desired the Queen to prepare Lady Suffolk's lodgings for Madame Walmoden, Her Majesty, when she had shown the letter to Sir Robert, said, 'Well now, Sir Robert I hope you are satisfied. You see this mignonne is coming to England.' Upon which Sir Robert shook his head. 'What do you mean by that?' said the Queen. 'I mean,' said Sir Robert, 'that Your Majesty is not pleased with me when you think she is coming, and that you imagine by this letter that she will do what she no more designs than you wish. Madam, it is very plain to me that she won't come, and that—I wish I could speak Latin to you—I would tell Your Majesty that when the King assured her she might depend on Your Majesty's goodness to her, I believe her answer was—sic notus Ulysses?' 'Pray, explain that to me,' replied the Queen. 'The explanation, Madam,' said Sir Robert, 'is that she has a character of Your Majesty only from your enemies; that she mistrusts when she pretends to confide, that she fears your goodness when she says she relies upon it, and never intends to trust to what—I soften her thoughts when I only say—she doubts. I must add too, Madam, though the King tells you more than I believe any man from the beginning of the world ever told his wife of his mistress, yet depend upon it he does not tell you all, and there are some things pass between them—as communicative as you think him and as he really is—unreported. However, Madam, get him here and be ruled by me. We will notwithstanding all this bring her here and humble her too. Lord Hervey said to me the other day, in speaking of the subject, "If you can but once get this favourite to St. James's she will in three months be everything Lady Suffolk was, but deaf"; and it is really, Madam, the true state of the case, and your only option is whether you will fear her at a distance or despise her near.' 'Well,' said the Queen, 'we shall soon see; for I have this very day wrote the King word that I will get Lady Suffolk's lodgings ready immediately, and enlarge them by adding the two rooms where my books now are which join to Lady Suffolk's lodgings, and I will hire some rooms for my books in the meantime till my library that is building[1] in the Park shall be fit to receive them.'

When Sir Robert Walpole told all this again to Lord Hervey, he added that it was those bitches Lady Pomfret and Lady Sundon, who were always bemoaning the Queen on this occasion, and making their court by saying they hoped never to see this saucy whore brought under Her Majesty's nose here, who made it so difficult to bring the Queen to do what was right and sensible for her to do.

Lord Hervey did not say he guessed who had told him this, but was as sure as if he had heard her that it was Mrs. Selwyn, a Bedchamber Woman of the Queen, and the only woman about the Court who loved Sir Robert Walpole, as he himself knew and often would say. Mrs. Selwyn was a simple, cunning woman, who hated Lady Sundon, and to make her court to Sir Robert had told him

[1] In the Green Park, on the site of Stafford House, now the London Museum.

this story. Lord Hervey, who really loved Lady Sundon, and looked upon her as a woman deserving to be loved and esteemed, as she had very great, good, and noble qualities, said he firmly believed Sir Robert was as much mistaken about Lady Sundon as about Lady Pomfret; for as to the latter, the Queen, he was sure, never permitted her to talk on these subjects to her at all; and as to Lady Sundon she was certainly no fool, and had been long enough about the Queen to know that nobody could make their court so ill as those who affected pitying her; neither did he imagine Lady Sundon judged so ill of the Queen's interest as to think it better for her that Madame Walmoden should continue where she was, beckoning the King every summer to Hanover, to risk his life and irritate his subjects. 'My Lord,' says Sir Robert, 'you have a sneaking kindness for Lady Sundon, and therefore pretend to think better of her than you do, or than she deserves; but as to what I have now told you, I know it to be true—I say I know it—and at the same time I know too she has given hints, as if I wished to bring this woman over only to play the wife upon the mistress and the mistress upon the wife, as my own interest should occasionally prompt me, without caring a farthing what became of either, provided I could keep my power; and what I now tell you, you may depend upon I know to be truth.' His peremptory repetition of his knowing all this to be true, obliged Lord Hervey in common decency and good breeding to give up the dispute, but did not make him alter his opinion. 'À propos,' said Lord Hervey, 'to playing the mistress and the wife upon one another, has the report so current about town of your brother's having made a great feast at Hanover on Madame Walmoden's birthday any foundation?' Sir Robert Walpole said that his brother's conduct was so different from what was insinuated by a report of this kind, that he was very confident nothing had ever passed between him and Madame Walmoden that looked as if he knew she was the King's mistress, and that Horace thought himself so much in the Queen's favour that he was sure if anybody was to ask him who had the best interest with the Queen of the two brothers, Horace would answer himself. Sir Robert's jealousy of anybody pretending to have interest with the Queen but himself never appeared so strongly as on this occasion, for he could not help saying what I have repeated even of his own brother without at the same time showing such dislike as surprised Lord Hervey a good deal, considering the situation of Horace, but alarmed him much more considering his own.

A little while after this conversation Lord Hervey, having a mind to be satisfied whether he was in the right in his opinion of Lady Sundon's never having spoken to the Queen against Madame Walmoden's coming to England, talked with her upon the subject, told her how right he thought it, and asked her opinion about it; but before he began the conversation insisted on Lady Sundon giving her honour she would never give the least hint to anybody whatever that he had ever asked her this question, or spoken to her upon this chapter; and Lady Sundon was one of the few courtiers whose honour, so solemnly given, Lord Hervey would have thought any security on such an occasion. Lady Sundon assured Lord Hervey that directly or indirectly she had never mentioned this to the Queen in her life, nor heard the Queen speak upon the subject; that as to her private opinion, as she was no Minister, she would wish Madame Walmoden here; for that she foresaw nobody but a Minister that would be distressed by her being here. Lord Hervey then asked if she had never talked of this to any other lady. Lady Sundon assured him she had always avoided not only talking but hearing anything relating to Madame Walmoden; and added that Mrs. Selwyn the other day in the Queen's antechamber, where they were together alone, had quite astonished her by the free manner in which she had spoke of these things; 'but favourites you know, my Lord, may venture anything.' 'She told me,' continued Lady Sundon, 'that she believed if the King should go again next summer to Hanover, it would be for good and all, for that the people would be so exasperated they would never let him come back.' 'To which,' said Lady Sundon, 'I replied as cautiously as I could (for I know Madam Selwyn), to be sure the disposition of the people towards the King was not so good as one wished it, but I hoped it was not as bad neither as she seemed to apprehend it.' Mrs. Selwyn (Lady Sundon said) then asked her whether she did not think it would be better to have Madame Walmoden in England? To which she replied she believed there would be difficulties both ways. 'And this,' said Lady Sundon, 'is all I would say, though she tried me make me more open, and would really have distressed me had not Lord Grantham come into the room, whom for the first time in my life I was glad to see.'

This was enough to convince Lord Hervey that he had conjectured well; and though Sir Robert Walpole several times after spoke to him of Lady Sundon's talking in this strain to the Queen, Lord Hervey only said (as he had done at first), without letting Sir Robert know he had ever spoken to Lady Sundon about it, that he did not think it probable; and would venture his head that the Queen had never let anybody but Sir Robert and himself talk to her on the chapter of Madame Walmoden at all. Lord Hervey, by way of softening his flat contradiction of Sir Robert in this fact, added: 'If you, Sir, had told me anything that you had seen or heard, perhaps I might believe one of your senses against my own five; but as you had this from intelligence, you will give me leave to say I think my observation on this point as good as theirs; and I'll be hanged if 'tis true.' Sir Robert said: 'Ask the Queen; I do not believe she will deny it.' Lord Hervey, who knew Sir Robert's reason for bidding him ask the Queen, replied: 'You and I, Sir, are well enough acquainted with the Queen to know that when she lets a sentiment escape her which she is ashamed of, that she had rather one should think it was planted in her, than that it grew there; and though she would not lay it upon anybody herself, she will suffer you uncontradicted to lay it on whom you please, provided you take it off her. But, believe me, the greatest obstacle in this kingdom to Madame Walmoden's coming here is the Queen's own heart, that recoils whenever her head proposes it.'

In October the King wrote to the Queen to desire her to remove from Kensington to London, saying the season of the year being so far advanced, and that house where she was having the reputation of being damp, he fancied the Queen would find it better for her health, as well as easier to the Ministers that were to attend her,[1] to go now and settle for the winter at St. James's; but as the

---

[1] Croker quotes, in illustration of this passage, from a letter of Lord Hervey's to his mother, dated 27th Nov. 1736: 'The road between this place (Kensington) and London is grown so infamously bad, that we live here in the same solitude as we should do if cast on a rock in the middle of the ocean, and all the Londoners tell us there is between them and us a great impassable gulf of mud. There are two roads through the park, but the new one is so convex and the old one so concave, that by this extreme of faults they agree in the common one of being, like the high road, impassable.'

Queen understood this to be an offer which he thought himself obliged to make, and one which he had rather she did not accept, Her Majesty determined to stay at Kensington till the King should set out from Hanover, and only go to London time enough to receive him there. She knew the King and his way of thinking thoroughly; and certainly imagined this air of retirement, and her seeming to decline all state and parade during his absence, would be most agreeable to His Majesty; and that her choosing this part when he had pressed her to take the other would make the choice doubly meritorious.

In the meantime the people of all ranks grew every day more discontented at the King's stay in Germany. The people belonging to the Court were uneasy at it, as it made the Court so much more unpopular; and those who were attached to the Queen were yet more so from the apprehension of these long absences being both the means and signs of her altered power. The tradesmen were all uneasy, as they thought the King's absence prevented people coming to town, and particularly for the birthday; the citizens made this preference he seemed to give to his German dominions a pretence to show their disaffection, but were before so thoroughly disaffected that it made no great addition to what they felt, though it opened the sluices of their clamorous mouths. The ordinary and the godly people took the turn of pitying the poor Queen, and railing at His Majesty for using so good a wife, who had brought him so many fine children, so abominably ill. Some of them (and those who, if he had heard all this, would have fretted him most) used to talk of his age, and say, for a man at his time of day to be playing these youthful pranks, and fancying himself in love, was quite ridiculous, as well as inexcusable. Others, in very coarse terms, would ask if he must have a mistress whether England could furnish never a one good enough to serve his turn; and if he thought Parliament had given him a greater Civil List than any of his predecessors only to defray the extraordinary expenses of his travelling charges, to support his Hanover bawdy-houses in magnificence, and enrich his German pimps and whores.

To this familiar manner of talking were added several little ingenious manuscripts. Pasquinades were stuck up in several quarters of the town, and some practical jokes and satires (that no marks of dissatisfaction might be omitted) were likewise exhibited. An old lean, lame, blind horse was turned into the streets, with a broken saddle on his back and a pillion behind it, and on the horse's forehead this inscription was fixed:

'Let nobody stop me—I am the King's Hanover Equipage going to fetch His Majesty and his whore to England.'

At the Royal Exchange, a paper with these words was stuck up:

'It is reported that his Hanoverian Majesty designs to visit his British dominions for three months in the spring.'

On St. James's gate this advertisement was pasted:

'Lost or strayed out of this house, a man who has left a wife and six children on the parish; whoever will give any tidings of him to the churchwardens of St. James's Parish, so as he may be got again, shall receive four shillings and sixpence reward.

N.B.—This reward will not be increased, nobody judging him to deserve a Crown.'

It would be too tedious to enumerate half the things of this nature that were put in practice on this occasion; but Dion Cassius and Suetonius do not inform us of more jokes, verbal or practical, put upon Cæsar on his return to Rome than were exhibited against our Augustus for not returning to England; nor was Nicomedes oftener objected to the one than Madame Walmoden to the other. But most of these things lost the effect they were designed to have on the King so much, that instead of mortifying his pride, irritating his wrath, and covering him with shame, many of them only served to flatter his vanity; for as the two characters he most affected were the brave warrior and the tender lover, so he looked on all these satires and lampoons as so many proofs of his eminence in the last of these callings.

When the Queen declared she intended to stay at Kensington till the King came, the Prince, who had a mind to go to London for the same reason that the Queen avoided it—which was because he thought His Majesty would dislike it—told the Queen his expenses at Kensington were so great, and his lodgings there were so damp, that he intended to remove to London, and would fain have drawn her in either to consent to this design or to lay her commands upon him not to put it into execution, but he could bring neither of these things about; she declined both. And for fear His Royal Highness might misreport the conversation, she repeated the substance of it next morning to him in the following letter:

Je suis fâchée, mon cher fils, quand vous me consultez, que je ne puis pas toujours vous donner le conseil qui vous plairoit le plus, même dans les bagatelles: mais considérant les ordres que vous avez reçues du Roi, par le Duc de Grafton, il est impossible que je puise approuver votre dessein d'aller vous établir à Londres pendant que je resterais encore à Kensington. Quant à la proposition que je vous ai faite, que la Dame de la Princesse sera toujours reçue à la table de ma Dame ici, je ne l'aurois jamais faite si je ne m'étois pas souvenue que dans le tems du feu Roi à Hampton Court ma Dame étoit reçue les jours publiques, de même, par son ordre, à la table de son gentil-homme de la chambre; et je puis vous assurer, mon cher fils, que comme amie et comme mère, vous me trouverez toujours prête à faire toute chose non seulement pour votre intérêt, mais aussi pour votre plaisir, dans toutes les occasions.

The Prince made no answer in writing immediately to this letter, but told the Queen, when he saw her that day at dinner, that as she had ordered him to send any answer in writing he did not care to give her the trouble of one; and now again renewed his importunity to desire her to declare her pleasure what he should do, adding, that if she would lay her commands upon him to stay at Kensington, he would certainly obey them. The Queen said she had desired no answer to her letter, because she never insisted upon anything from him merely as point of form, and that as his going or staying was the only subject of her letter, his conduct would be the answer; that as to her pleasure in it, there never could be any exception to the general desire she had for the Prince in all things to obey the King and that for adding her commands upon any occasion to the King's, she could not help thinking it quite unnecessary with regard to the Prince, and not right to the King, to imagine that the addition of her orders could give force to his.

Here ended this conversation; and the next morning the Prince wrote the Queen the following letter:

MADAME,

Après avoir considéré tout ce que votre Majesté m'a dit sur ma proposition d'aller à Londres, j'ai résolu de faire le palais de Kensington, pendant que vous y resterez, mon principal séjour, malgré tous les inconvéniens que j'y trouve; et je me soumets en cette occasion, non pas de peur des conséquences qui pourroient en arriver si je ne le faisois pas, ni par espérance d'aucun avantage que je pourrois tirer en le faisant, mais par le principe de cette soumission qu'un fils doit à ses parens.

Etant avec beaucoup de respect, Madame,
De votre Majesté, etc.,
FREDERICK.

The copies of these two letters cannot be very exact, as the Queen showed them to me but once; but, as I wrote them down from memory immediately after I came from the Queen, the difference between them and the originals I believe is only verbal, and very minute; for the main substance of them, I am sure, was just as I have given it.

The next time the Queen saw the Prince after his sending her this letter, she told him it was very well written, and asked him if he had written it himself? The Prince coloured from a mixture of shame and anger, and asked her why she thought him incapable of writing it. She said she did not think him at all incapable of writing everything in it that was well; but that the expression of 'un fils à ses parens' was not French, but a translation from English, which had made her imagine it was written by some Englishman.

When she showed Lord Hervey these letters, she asked him who he thought had written His Royal Highness's? Lord Hervey said the Prince was not now well enough with Lord Chesterfield to have consulted him; and, besides that, Lord Chesterfield would have written better French, as well as with more turns and points; that Mr. Lyttelton would have been more verbose; and therefore that he should imagine it was the work of young Pitt, who was now perpetually with the Prince, and at present in the first rank of his favour.

Pursuant to the purport of this letter the Prince made Kensington his *séjour principal* (as he called it) for the rest of the time the Court stayed at Kensington, that is, he left the Princess's maids of honour and some of the under servants constantly there; but the Princess and he seldom lay there above one night or two in the week. She kept her drawing-room and he his levée there constantly every Monday morning; sometimes too they came on a Thursday; but for the rest of the week they were either at Kew or London, and seldom two days together in the same place, which gave the Queen occasion to say to him once, pleasantly enough, that they did not seem to lead the lives of Princes, but gipsies, who generally lie under a different hedge or in a different barn every night. She told me, too, that the King had chid her in his letters for letting them ramble about in that manner, to which she said she had sent the King word that they neither asked her leave to go out, nor were of an age to be locked up.

The Prince had at this time a great mind to intimate to the people about him that the Princess was breeding. Orders were frequently issued from his own royal mouth to his coachman, as he was stepping into the coach, to drive softly whenever the Princess was with him, and several little hints of the like nature were often thrown out. But a very different opinion of this matter reigned on the Queen's side of the house. Her Majesty did not only doubt of her daughter-in-law's being with child but made it a question whether the Prince's marriage had ever been consummated. She had heard so many stories of different kinds relating to this affair, and even from the Prince's own mouth, who, as she said, spoke sometimes of himself in those matters as a Hercules, and at other times as if he was fourscore, that she told Lord Hervey she did not know what to think about it, and begged him seriously to tell her whether he thought the Prince was capable of having a child or not. 'As for those of little Vane, you know, my dear Lord, I have a thousand times told you that I was always sure they were yours; and if I had wanted further proof of their being so, your son William whom you so reluctantly brought to me this summer would have convinced me of it, because if he had been twin-brother to little Fitzfrederick, he could not have been more like him. Put all affectation therefore out of the question, look upon me as your friend, and answer me seriously on this point, as one that I am most extremely anxious to be satisfied in.'

Lord Hervey said Her Majesty had put this question to him in such a manner that it was impossible for him to decline answering it. 'And though there are several things, Madam, that I would refuse speaking upon, yet whenever I do speak, you may depend upon it, it will be without any deceit, and that I will always either say I won't tell or tell the truth. In the first place, then, Your

Majesty must know that the chief intelligence that I can have on this subject must have been from Miss Vane, who I do not tell Your Majesty always adhered to truth. She used to describe the Prince in these matters ignorant to a degree inconceivable, but not impotent, and my firm belief is that he is as capable of having children as any man in England.'

The Queen said that there was as little dependence to be had on the Prince's truth as Miss Vane's. 'For you know,' said she, 'how apt we are to embroider; but with regard to this particular business, less is to be collected from him than on any other subject. Sometimes he speaks of himself as if he was the late King of Poland, at other with a despondency of having children, and in so pathetic a tone, that he is ready to cry, and seems to think it impossible. The other day he took me aside to tell me in my ear of an operation that was performed upon him by his Surgeon Valet de chambre Vreid, which I was as far from understanding as believing, and begged him to talk of something else, because he only made me sick and ashamed without comprehending what he meant. He has told me that he has often got nasty distempers by women, dont je ne crois pas un mot.' Lord Hervey said he did not believe it neither, but supposing he had, that his being able to get those distempers would be no proof of his being able to get children, as he believed Farinelli might have the pox, though he could not have heirs.

The Queen asked Lord Hervey if he could not get some intelligence from Lady Dudley. 'You know,' said she, 'that woman has lain with half the town as well as Fretz and consequently must know whether he is like other men or not.' Lord Hervey replied that he did not doubt but that there was one way in his power of knowing all Lady Dudley could tell him; but that his curiosity was not strong enough to make him risk his nose to satisfy it.

The Queen said she was excessively anxious upon this head, and added: 'I know his rage to have children is such that there is nothing he is not capable of to gain the point of the Princess being with child. I know he was so solicitous for the reputation of having a child by Vane that, though you have perjured yourself a thousand times by swearing it was not so, yet I am as sure as if I had heard him do it that he asked you to get one for him—hold your tongue,

I will not hear you tell any more lies upon that head.' 'I am not going,' interrupted Lord Hervey, 'to speak upon that head, but I beg leave to say, even supposing that to be true, there would sure be a great difference between asking a man to lie with one's mistress and asking him to lie with one's wife; besides, Your Majesty must suppose the Princess in the secret for this project to be brought to bear.' 'I am sure,' replied the Queen, 'if you were to undertake it, you could contrive, though I know not how you would go about it, to do it without her knowledge.' 'Supposing the Prince has ever consummated his marriage with her, I believe I could,' said Lord Hervey, 'but if he never has, it would be impossible; for though I believe I could contrive to put one man upon her for another, I could not put a man upon her for a woman, and the novelty of a consummator could never pass upon her for the quiet of her former bedfellow.'

The Queen said she was sure the Princess looked upon herself to be as much married to the Prince as any woman is married to any man. Lord Hervey said that was not proof of her being so unless she had been married before. 'But supposing,' replied the Queen, 'that he is actually married to her and yet despairs of getting children himself, do you think then you could contrive, if he and you were both willing, without her knowledge to go to bed to her instead of him?' 'Nothing so easy,' replied Lord Hervey. 'My God, how is it possible?' said the Queen. 'Why, for a month before and after the time of putting this design in execution I would advise the Prince to go to bed several hours after his wife, and to pretend to get up for a flux several times in the night, to perfume himself always with some predominant smell, and by the help of these tricks it would be very easy, not using himself to talk to her in bed, to put the change of any man near his own size upon her that he pleased.' 'I love you mightily, my dear Lord Hervey,' said the Queen, 'but if I thought you would get a little Hervey by the Princess of Saxe-Gotha to disinherit my dear William, I could not bear it, nor I do not know, what I should not be capable of doing.' 'As for me,' said Lord Hervey, 'Your Majesty must know upon the foot I am with the Prince I am quite out of the question; and to speak seriously my great, good, and amiable Queen, it is impossible you can have any fear on this score. For what in the Prince's situation could be so contemptible as to make such a request to another? Or what other, all circumstances considered, if the Prince did make the request, would risk complying with it?' 'As for Fretz being capable of making the request,' replied the Queen, 'I believe it as much as I believe myself incapable of assisting him in such a design. He has a notion, no matter how well or ill founded, that if the Princess was to have no children he should have no respect paid him, that it would hurt his reputation as a man and his interest as a prince, that he should be looked upon as nothing, and in short I am sure he had rather die than not have her to be with child. Then as to getting anybody to do him this favour, he would give them money enough to make it their interest; and besides that, there are few men who would not find their vanity extremely flattered in placing a child of theirs upon the throne.' 'As to money,' said Lord Hervey, 'the risk any man must run from the danger of being discovered, or of being assassinated by the Prince's own contrivance afterward to prevent a discovery, would make it very difficult for anybody to think it their interest for any sum of money the Prince could give them to excuse this project; and as to the food it would be to their vanity, vanity feeds but very slightly when it feeds in private; and this is a diet it could never feed upon in public. Supposing I had had the honour to be born Your Majesty's son,'—'I wish to God you had,' interrupted the Queen,—'that is very kind,' replied Lord Hervey, 'but supposing I had, does Your Majesty imagine, though I believed any other man than the King my father, that I should ever act as if I believed it; or that filial piety would get so far the better of resentment in my mind that I should not wish the man murdered, whoever gave a hint to me of my being his son?' 'Au bout du conte,' said the Queen, 'I know not what to think, but altogether I know it makes me very uneasy.'

Lord Hervey had several conversations on this subject with the Queen and with the Princess Caroline, who were both so prepossessed with the notion of the Prince's being incapable of having a child of his own, and his being capable of persuading somebody else to get one for him, that there was no possibility of making them change either of these opinions or of curing the fears or removing the suspicions consequential to these two odd points of faith.

Neither the Queen nor Princess Caroline loved the Prince, and yet both of them had by fits a rest of management for his character, which made them, though they were very ready to allow all his bad qualities, mix now and then some good ones, which he had very little pretence to. They used to say that he was not such a fool as one took him for; that he was not wise neither; that he could sometimes be very amusing, though often very *ennuyant*; and that in everything he was made up of such odd contradictions, that he would do the meanest, the lowest, and the dirtiest things about money, and at other times the most generous; that his heart was like his head, both bad and good; and that he very often seemed to have a worse heart than he really had, by being a knave when he thought he was only avoiding the character of being a dupe, and by doing things to people without reflecting enough on what he was doing, to know he was hurting them so much as he really did. Lord Hervey said that was an excuse one might make at any time, without a possibility of being disproved, for any action in anybody; but that if he saw anyone of thirty years old picking out people's eyes with a pair of scissors, it would be very difficult for a stander-by to persuade him that the person who was performing that operation thought he was paring their nails. The Queen said that would indeed, she believed, be something difficult; but if, in paring their nails, he only cut into the finger a little, one might sure imagine that wounding the flesh was accident, and that in reality he only thought of cutting their nails too close to scratch him; 'and this I firmly believe was sometimes the case. When he betrayed you, laughed at Dodington, and gave up Lord Chesterfield, he was certainly very false to every one of you, one after another; but when he was so, he thought of nothing more than clearing himself of the suspicion one might have of his being weak enough to be governed.'

Lord Hervey told the Queen she was the best apologist he knew in the world, but said the consequences of the Prince's conduct were equally prejudicial to His Royal Highness's character, let the motive be what it would; and that it could never be so fatal to any Prince to have it thought he was to be governed as to have it known he was not to be trusted, which was certainly the Prince's case, and said of him by everybody that ever spoke of him, and thought even by many who did not speak of him. 'This will certainly, too, Madam, as well as his inconstancy, make anybody who shall get a temporary possession of him when he comes to be King think of nothing but their own interest, and pushing it as fast as they can, without any view of what becomes of him, or any remorse for any inconveniences they may draw him into.' 'This, my dear Lord,' said the Queen, 'is what I have often told him; and, as I hope the King will live yet a great while, experience and growing wiser will, I hope, make this poor young man feel the truth of what he imagines now one always tells him with some view to one's own advantage, and not with any regard to his. I believe, too, what I dare say you do not, that there is nothing he dreads more at present than the King's death.'—'I am so far from believing it,' said Lord Hervey, 'that I cannot comprehend your being serious when you say it is your opinion, and am firmly persuaded there is nothing he wishes so much; and that he does not esteem himself less capable of ruling wisely than Cæsar.'—'You are mistaken,' said the Queen. 'Besides, the great debts he has contracted, payable at that time, make him apprehend this period still more.'—'If that were any reason,' said Lord Hervey, 'for wishing the King's life, he would wish it every day more than another, as it is a reason that, I fear, will be ever increasing, as long as the King and he shall live. And since Your Majesty has mentioned this, I must say one thing, which I have often thought of with great anxiety, and that is the danger there is of the King's days somehow or other being shortened by those profligate usurers who lend the Prince money upon these terms. I am sure, if I guess right, there are some who deal with the Prince for money payable at the King's death with most extortionate interest, who would want nothing but a fair opportunity to hasten the day of payment; and the King's manner of exposing himself a thousand different ways would make it full as easy for these fellows to accomplish such a design as their conscience would to form it.'— 'What you say,' replied the Queen, 'is certainly true. But what can be done?'—'Why, if no other means,' said Lord Hervey, 'can be found to put a stop to this every day increasing danger to the King's life, I am sure, for my own part, I would make no scruple of moving for an Act of Parliament to make it capital for any man to lend money for a premium at the King's death.'—'To be sure,' replied the Queen, 'it ought to be so; and pray talk a little with Sir Robert Walpole about it.'

The Queen used to speak to Lord Hervey on this subject with

as little reserve when the Princess Caroline was present, as when alone; but never before the Princess Emily, who had managed her affairs so well as to have lost entirely the confidence of her mother, without having obtained the friendship of her brother. By trying to make her court by turns to both, she had by turns betrayed both, and at last lost both.

Lord Hervey was very ill with her. She had first used him ill, to flatter her brother, which of course had made him not use her very well; and the preference on every occasion he gave her sister, the Princess Caroline, completed their mutual dislike.

The Queen kept the King's birthday in London, but came from Kensington only that morning, and returned thither after the ball at night. There was a very thin appearance, and as little finery as if the same sumptuary law forbidding gold and silver that subsists at this time in the Court of Spain was in force here.

Sir Robert Walpole went the day after the birthday as usual into Norfolk for three weeks, the Duke of Devonshire to Newmarket, the Duke of Grafton and Lord Lifford to fox hunt in Suffolk and nobody being left but the Duke of Newcastle at Court, the Queen desired Lord Hervey, who was to have gone into Suffolk for a fortnight to his father, to make his excuse, to say she had absolutely forbid him to leave her, and not stir from Kensington. Accordingly he did so, and was with Her Majesty not only every day, but almost all the day, talking over in different conversations a thousand particulars relating to the subjects I have here treated in short and thrown together in a loose way, that I might not, by a more accurate manner of ranging them, deviate from the manner in which the conversations passed.

The long-deferred, not much expected, and less wished-for orders of His Majesty for the yachts to set out for Holland at last arrived. The Queen gave these orders this year a very different welcome from that with which she received them the last. Last year she felt a sort of triumph in his return, when all the enemies of the Court had flattered themselves he would then defer his return in the same manner he had done now. The Queen, too, had flattered herself that he would come back from this gallantry as he had done before from former excursions of the same sort, and that in returning to her bed he would return to her arms and his former conjugal attachments. But as she had found herself so terribly deceived in these hopes and expectations the last year, and had so much less reason to form them this, she had nothing before her eyes for this winter but the revolution of the coldness she had felt the last; she considered this return only as a transition from the ease and liberty in which she had passed the summer, to an uninterrupted scene of disquiet and constraint; and knew the change for which she was to prepare was from receiving homage to paying it, and that she was to quit the company of those who were perpetually endeavouring, and with success, to please her, for the company of one whom she should be constantly endeavouring to please, and without success.

Between the 7th and 8th of December, in the night, after a great ball and a great supper, the King set out from Hanover, and arrived on the 11th at Helvoetsluys. The Princess Royal, four days before, after a terrible labour and being in great danger of her life, had been brought to bed at the Hague of a daughter, which Dr. Sands, a very eminent man-midwife sent from hence by the Queen, had been obliged to squeeze to death in the birth, to save the mother.

These circumstances did not, after all his former affection professed for his dear daughter Ann, awaken paternal love sufficient in His Majesty to engage him to make any visit at the Hague. He could say to Madame Walmoden, like Sappho to Phaon, 'all other loves are lost in thine.'

The next Tuesday after he came to Helvoetsluys, whilst the people in England were employed in nothing but looking at weathercocks, and talking of tides and winds and moons, the wind changed on this side of the water for about eight or nine hours to the east, and everybody of course concluded His Majesty at sea. On Tuesday night it changed again, and a violent storm arose, which lasted four days, during which time there was not the least tidings of His Majesty. A hundred messages a day passed between the Admiralty Office and St. James's Palace; and a thousand conjectures were made with regard to the danger and safety of His Majesty, just as the different hopes and fears that were busy on this occasion, led people to wish or apprehend the one or the other. Many wagers were laid, and almost all the seafaring men laid that he was embarked.

The alacrity of the Prince and his Court on this occasion was not so ill-founded as it was indecent, nor so improperly felt as it was improperly shown. The wind continuing very strong and contrary, every hour that brought no news added to the apprehension of bad news. On the Friday, during this consternation, the Prince gave a great dinner to the Lord Mayor of London and all the Aldermen at his house in Pall Mall, on their presenting him with the freedom of the City, a compliment which the Queen told me he had asked of my Lord Mayor by his saddler; Her Majesty adding at the same time the comment of its being in a very princely request, and made in a very princely manner. There was another reflection she made on this occasion, which, though she said it made no impression upon her, one plainly saw it left some. The reflection was this, that King Charles I when he was Prince of Wales, and King James II, when he was Duke of York, were the only two sons of kings that ever had had this freedom of the City conferred upon them. But as this remark was a sign of some relics of that Germanic superstition which the whole nation imbibe in their infancy, and few of them have sense enough to rub off when they are grown up, so I must own it was one which was much more natural for her to make, considering her education than considering her understanding.

Lord Hervey dined this disagreeable Friday at Sir Robert Walpole's. As they were going together in the chariot, Sir Robert seemed full of many melancholy reflections, and to wish the King's safety much less for the sake of the King than for the rest of the family. He said, and very truly: 'If any accident should happen to our sweet master, whom I feel more peevish with than I can express, I do not know, my dear Lord, any people in the world so much to be pitied as that gay young company with which you and I stand every day in the drawing-room, at that door from which we this moment came, bred up in state, in affluence, caressed and courted, and to go at once from that into dependence on a brother who loves them not, and whose extravagance and covetousness (*alieni appetens, sui profusus*) will make him grudge every guinea they spend, as it must come from out of a purse not sufficient to defray the expenses of his own vices. On the other hand, what a situation is the Queen's, between the Scylla and Charybdis of falling into the hands of a son who hates her, or receiving a husband whom

she has as much reason to hate; and who, if one was to see her heart,
perhaps she loves the least of the two, as she thinks she has not been
better used by him when she has deserved everything from him!
What will be the Prince's case? A poor, weak, irresolute, false,
lying, dishonest, contemptible wretch, that nobody loves, that nobody believes, that nobody will trust, and that will trust everybody
by turns, and that everybody by turns will impose upon, betray,
mislead, and plunder. And what then will become of this divided
family, and this divided country, is too melancholy a prospect for
one to admit conjecture to paint it.'

Lord Hervey said that, with regard to the avarice and profusion
of the Prince, he agreed it would make him do a thousand wrong
things, and by the by said he wondered that that part of Catiline's
character drawn by Sallust should be thought so extraordinary a one,
when, in his opinion, there were no two qualities often went together. 'But, Sir,' continued Lord Hervey, 'there is one very
material point in which I differ from you, and that is concerning
the influence the Queen would have over the Prince if ever he
came to be King; I am far from believing her interest there would
be so low as you imagine.' 'Zounds, my Lord,' interrupted Sir
Robert, very eagerly, 'he would tear the flesh off her bones with
hot irons; the notion he has of her making his father do everything
she has a mind to, and the father doing nothing the son has a mind
to, joined to that rancour which those about him are continually
whetting against his mother, would make him use her worse than
you or I can foresee; his resentment for the distinctions she shows
to you too, I believe, would not be forgotten. Then the notion he
has of her great riches, and the desire he would feel to be fingering
them, would make him pinch her and pinch her again, in order
to make her buy her ease, till she had not a groat left.'

This conversation broke off by their arrival at Sir Robert's house.

The Queen, at St. James's, passed her common evenings just
as she had done at Kensington; that is, in her private apartment
at quadrille with her lady-in-waiting, Mrs. Schutz, and Lady
Charlotte de Roucy; whilst the Princess Caroline, Miss Dives (one
of her maids of honour), and Lord Hervey played pools at cribbage
and the Duke, Princess Emily, and the rest of the chance-comers
of the family played at basset. Mondays and Fridays, however, there

were public drawing-rooms in the great apartments, in the same manner as when the King used to be in London. This Friday, therefore, that the Queen might betray no apprehension or disquiet, there was a public drawing-room as usual, to which neither the Prince nor Princess came. The Prince made no excuse, the Princess pleaded a cold, but the only marks of it that appeared was a black hood.

The next morning the Queen sent for Lord Hervey earlier than usual, and nobody but the Princess Caroline being by, they talked very freely of the present situation of affairs. The Queen asked Lord Hervey if he had heard any of the particulars of yesterday's feast in Pall Mall, whether he knew if the Prince went thither to toast in the afternoon, and what healths were drank. Lord Hervey said he had heard the Prince's speech in the morning was the most ingratiating piece of popularity that ever was composed, and that, if he did go to his guests after dinner, he concluded the healths were in the same style; and neither the 'Prosperity of the City of London'—'the Trade of this Country'—'the Naval Strength of England'—'Liberty and Property'—nor any popular toasts of that kind were omitted. 'My God,' says the Queen, 'popularity always makes me sick; but Fretz's popularity makes me vomit. I hear that yesterday, on his side of the house, they talked of the King's being cast away with the same sang-froid as you would talk of a coach being overturned, and that my good son strutted about as if he had been already King. Did you mind the air with which he came into my drawing-room in the morning, though he does not think fit to honour me with his presence or ennui me with his wife's of a night? I swear his behaviour shocked me so prodigiously, that I could hardly bring myself to speak to him when he was with me afterwards; I felt something here in my throat that swelled and half-choked me.' 'I presume,' said Lord Hervey, 'Your Majesty and the Princess Caroline are not of that opinion still, on which I disputed with you at Kensington. You do not imagine, I believe, now, that the Prince has all that horror of being King which you then supposed.' 'Oh!' replied the Queen, 'he is such an ass that one cannot tell what he thinks; and yet he is not so great a fool as you take him for neither.' 'There is one thing in which I think of him very differently from Your Majesty, and which proves I think him wiser than you do.' 'What is that?' said the Queen. 'It is,' replied Lord Hervey, 'that Your Majesty in a month, if he came to the Crown, would have more weight with him than anybody in England.' 'Jesus!' interrupted the Princess Caroline, 'my good Lord, you must know very little of him if you believe that; for in the first place he hates Mama; in the next, he has so good an opinion of himself that he thinks he wants no advice, and of all advice no woman's; for the saying, no woman ought to be let to meddle with business or ever did any good where they did meddle, is perhaps the only thing in which I have not heard him ever contradict himself.'

The Queen exclaimed, too, against Lord Hervey's opinion, and asked him upon what it was possible for him to found it. He said: 'Upon knowing, Madam, how susceptible he is of impressions, and how capable Your Majesty is of giving them. He is, Madam, a mere bank of sand, and anybody may write upon one as easy as the other.' 'And what one writes is as easily too,' said the Queen, 'rubbed out of one as the other. Besides, they would never let him come near me.' 'They would try, I acknowledge,' replied Lord Hervey, 'if they were wise, and not your friends, to hinder him coming near you, for fear that, like Archimedes if you got one inch of footing you might disturb the motions of their little globe; but it would not be in their power to hinder him.' 'For my part,' interrupted the Princess Caroline, 'I should desire to run out of the house *au grand galop*, as fast as I could.' 'No,' said the Queen, 'I would not stir before my proper time out of the house; but supposing I stayed in it,' continued Her Majesty, turning to Lord Hervey, 'why do you imagine I should see him?' 'Because I am sure,' answered Lord Hervey, 'I know just how he would think and reason upon that occasion. He would think to conciliate the great king and the dutiful son, and would say he would come and show Your Majesty all the respect due to a mother; but if you offered to meddle with business, he would insist on the respect due to the dignity of his own character as king, and impose an absolute silence upon you with regard to any matters of that sort; and as I know the prevalence of truth, and the art Your Majesty has of letting it lose none of its weight in your hands, you would, under a justification of your past conduct, make him see the things he had most objected to in so different a light from that he had before viewed them, and make him so sensibly feel the propriety and necessity of those parts of your conduct which he had most disliked, that you would soon bring him to hear you on present circumstances after you had reconciled him to past occurrences. You would let him know that the prompt violences of the King's temper, and the factious turbulent spirit of this nation, had made the part you had to act so difficult, that, in order to make the whole go on, you had been often forced to suffer several particular wheels to take a course which, if it had not been with a view to the not obstructing the motions of others, you would certainly have tried to turn differently; and as the good of the whole had always been your primary view, you would then appeal to his recollection whether anything you had ever done had not tended to the welfare and security of your family in general, and whether you had ever submitted to anything that had lessened the dignity and rights of the Crown, or attempted anything that might hurt the liberties or infringe the privileges of the people. You would bid him then reflect on your conduct either as a queen, a wife, or a mother, and desiring him to lay all general charges and insinuations aside, which might always be endless, and consequently unanswerable, you would ask him to name any particular action where you had acted unbecoming the duties of those several stations. It would afterwards be very natural for Your Majesty to add, that as you could have nothing at heart but the quiet continuance of your family upon this throne, whilst every other body about him must have some private views and interests of their own to serve, so it could never be of any prejudice to him to hear what you had to tell him, whether he paid any regard to it or not; and it would then be as natural for him to hear you as it must be for everybody to regard you when they have heard you.'

'My Lord,' said the Queen, 'you have spoken a great deal better for me than I could do for myself; but could I speak as well, I promise you it would be to no purpose. The chief objection he makes to the King's conduct at present is the confidence the King has in me.' 'Supposing that to be the present case,' replied Lord Hervey, 'there is no judgment to be made from thence of his future conduct; for his opinions are so fluctuating, and his sentiments so variable, that if one body had saved his life at the peril of their own, and another had been suspected of bribing one of his pages to infuse arsenic in his chocolate, and the King were to die a week after these incidents, one of these people would stand just as good a chance as the other to be employed by him. Besides, Your Majesty being *au fait* of all transactions both foreign and domestic for these last ten years, he would naturally come to you for intelligence, if not for advice; and as the manner of giving intelligence is often advice without wearing the appearance of it, I am very apt to believe Your Majesty would often be able to mix what he would not be able to separate.' The Queen said Lord Hervey imagined she should give herself much more trouble about these matters than he would find, if ever the case happened, that she should be inclined to do. Lord Hervey answered, that he imagined he should always find Her Majesty acting the part that became her; and as it would be her duty to her son, to herself, and her whole family, her adherents, and, indeed, to the nation to speak her mind freely on these things, to check the indiscretions of her son by showing him the risks he ran, and convince him of his errors by representing truth to him, he was very sure he should never see the Queen indolently looking on whilst the Prince was endangering the whole, but that she would endeavour to prevent the wreck which so unskilful a pilot left to himself would, in all probability, bring upon all that were embarked in the same bottom. The Queen sighed, and said she hoped all this was mere speculation, and that she should never live to see the case happen; but that if she did, she was sure she would never silently be witness to his taking such steps as might shake her family's possession of the throne, but would certainly do all she could to prevent his pursuing any measures that she thought led to such dangerous consequences. 'But what do you think of the King's being embarked,' continued the Queen, 'from all you have heard? For my part I own I am sometimes staggered.' Lord Hervey said he firmly believed he was not at sea.

In the afternoon, however, that is this Saturday, the 18th, the Prince came to the Queen with a letter he had got, written to one Mrs. Cowper, from a correspondent of hers at Harwich, in which it was said that in the middle of the foregoing night, during the storm, guns had been heard at sea, which were taken for guns of distress, and that there was no doubt made at Harwich but that these guns belonged to part of the fleet that was to come with the King, and had been dispersed, if not to the yacht on which the King was himself on board. Lord Baltimore, who was a great sailor himself, and thought to have great skill in sea-affairs, told Lord Hervey this very night, at the Opera, that it was impossible but that the King must have been embarked, and advised Lord Hervey to speak to the Queen for some ships to be immediately sent out to see what was become of him. Lord Hervey said it was impossible, he thought, if the King had set sail, that the whole fleet should be lost, or that some one ship should not have made to shore in some part of the island, by which it would have been known at least that the King had left the Dutch coast. Lord Baltimore said that in this storm, with a full westerly wind, which had now lasted four days and nights, it was absolutely impossible for any ship to have put in to any port on the English coast. From the Opera Lord Hervey went directly to the Queen's apartment, where she was already at play, as usual, to tell her what he had heard; but he had not been in the room three minutes before a messenger, in his dirty boots, arrived, to the great joy of the whole company, with a letter to the Queen from the King, to let her know he had never stirred out of Helvoetsluys, and that the weather was so uncertain he did not know when he should. This messenger had been three days at sea, and, with this storm full in his teeth, had landed by miracle (as all the skilful in maritime affairs called it) at Yarmouth. The joy the Queen was in when she saw this messenger come into the room, and heard everybody crying 'The King is safe! The King is safe!', showed that her apprehension had been greater than she ever owned it; for upon reading the King's letter, she said: 'Ja'i toujours dit que le Roi n'était pas embarqué: on a beau voulu m'effraier cet après-dîner avec leur lettres, et leur sots gens de Harwich; j'ai continué à lire mon Rollin, et me moquois de tout cela.'

Sir Robert Walpole was gone to Richmond Park (which, by the by, the Queen did not take very well), so Lord Hervey despatched a messenger immediately to him to let him know the good news, but did not venture to tell him that he found the Queen looked upon his retirement with Miss Skerret to Richmond Park just at this juncture as a piece of gallantry which, considering the anxiety in which he left Her Majesty, might have been spared, as well as the gallantry of His Majesty's journey to Hanover which had occasioned that anxiety.

As the Prince's fears for the King's safety had been so busy in communicating themselves this afternoon to the Queen, Her Majesty thought the least she could do for so dutiful a son was to take the first opportunity to quiet them. As soon as ever she had read the King's letter, therefore, she sent Lord Grantham (her Lord Chamberlain) to the Prince's apartment to communicate the most material part of the contents of it, which was His Majesty being safe in the harbour of Helvoetsluys.

The joy of this news lasted not long, for early on the Monday morning following (which was the 20th), the wind coming easterly, and continuing so till night, there was now no doubt made by anybody of the King's being embarked; and upon the wind changing at night to north-west, and blowing a most prodigious storm, as little doubt was made of his being in great danger.

Till Friday, the 24th, there was no news of him at all, and then none that was very agreeable; for a sloop, with some clerks belonging to the secretary's office on board, that had sailed with His Majesty from Helvoetsluys on Monday, and continued with the fleet till the storm arose, brought intelligence (being thrown without masts and extremely shattered on this coast) that the master of this sloop had seen the King's yacht tack about, but they knew nothing more either of him or any other ship in the fleet. In order to give the Queen as little alarm as possible, Sir Robert Walpole and Lord Harrington agreed to prevent the Queen seeing these clerks, and to take their account in writing, which was barely this, that on the first shifting of the wind they had seen the yacht on a signal tack about for Helvoetsluys, and that no doubt was to be made of the King's being now there. The next day (which was Christmas Day) four of the men-of-war that made part of His Majesty's convoy were thrown upon this coast, and made shift, after being obliged, too, like the sloop, to cut all their masts, to scramble into four different harbours. All the news any of these ships could give of the King or the rest of the fleet was that about six o'clock on Monday night a gun was fired by Sir Charles Wager's order as a signal, on this stress of weather, for every ship to take care of itself, and that soon after they were all separated, the tempest continuing its violence (the wind still at north-west) for forty-eight hours after. One of the letters that brought this intelligence was written by Lord Augustus Fitzroy, second son to the Duke of Grafton, who, though but twenty years of age, was captain of one of these men-of-war, and had with great difficulty this morning got into Margate. There was another to the Duke of Richmond from Mr. Clayton, one of the King's equerries, who was waiting with His Majesty's relays at Harwich, that gave the same account of this prodigious tempest, from the captain of another ship that had put in at Harwich. And as there were many other accounts, all to the same effect, from several other seaports, the whole town was in agitation, inquiring what was become of the King, some hoping, others fearing, and most people believing, he was at the bottom of the sea.

As there could be nothing done immediately, either to get certain intelligence what was become of the King, or to provide for his safety, it was determined not to tell the Queen this news to-night, as it could have no effect but keeping her awake all night to no purpose. She and her daughters therefore passed this, like other evenings, at play; whilst Sir Robert Walpole, the Dukes of Newcastle, Grafton, Montagu, Devonshire, Richmond and Lord Hervey, with very heavy hearts put on the cheerfulest countenances they could, and talked of many things, whilst all their thoughts were employed only on one.

The next morning (Sunday, the 26th) Sir Robert Walpole came at nine o'clock to the Queen, and acquainted her with all he knew and all he feared.

The Queen no longer endeavoured to constrain herself and wear the appearance of ease on this news, but gave a loose to her tears, which indeed flowed in great abundance. On the Prince's side there was nothing to be seen but whisperers, messengers running backwards and forwards, and countenances that seemed already to belong to those who had the dominion of this country in their hands, and the affairs of Europe revolving in their minds.

The Queen determined she would go to chapel as usual, for no good reason, in my opinion, since it was just as natural for the anxiety and concern she was in to keep her in her apartment, as it was for her to feel that anxiety and concern in the present uncertain state of the King's welfare. The reason she gave to some about her for setting herself up to be stared at in public in these disagreeable circumstances was that she would not suppose her husband drowned before it was sure he was so; and that, as he had given the Government into her hands, she would perform the duty of those who had that honour till the law took it from her and transferred it to another; but this manner of reasoning was, I think rather dictated by her pride than by her understanding.

She had not been half an hour in the chapel before an express arrived from the King to Her Majesty to let her know that, after setting sail from Helvoetsluys on Monday morning at eight o'clock, he had with great difficulty regained that port the next day at three in the afternoon; that the storm had been very violent, and he very sick; that one of the yachts, called the Charlotte, was missing; and that they knew nothing of any of the men-of-war, but were in hopes, as they were better able to resist the tempest than the yachts, that they had by this time made some harbour. The King in his letter said, too, that he had not insisted on embarking when he did, but had done it in pursuance of Sir Charles Wager's directions, who had sent to him twice to make what haste he could on board, the wind and tide being then favourable.

The Queen, after communicating the principal contents of this letter (which was the King's safety) to everybody about her at chapel, and after chapel in the circle in the drawing-room, owned she had gone to chapel with a heavier heart than she had ever before felt in her breast; that she really thought the King had been lost, and would willingly have compounded for his being in Norway or any the remotest part of the world; and that all she wished was to be sure that he was still in being. These are exactly her own words.

To many she said that to be sure her particular loss would have been very great, but that the King's death would have been a loss which not only she, but this whole kingdom, and Europe itself at this injuncture, would have felt most sensibly, and that her chief concern had been not so much for any particular consideration as for the whole.

She then told everybody how glad she was to find by the King's letter that the damage that had been done, the danger of so many lives, and the loss of some, had not been owing to the King's impatience to set sail, for that His Majesty had submitted himself entirely to Sir Charles Wager's government, and embarked in consequence of his directions.

But this account of the King's patience and ductility nobody believed; by which means the Queen on this occasion, as it often happens on many others, weakened the King's justification by endeavouring to strengthen it; for had she stuck to the truth of the fact, and not to the letter of his account, it would have been a much better, as well as a sufficient apology for the King; it would have thoroughly disculpated His Majesty, and not left him chargeable with any of the disagreeable consequences of his embarkation; for the real state of this case was that he had been very impatient to set sail for England, and Sir Charles Wager as obstinate in preventing him till it was proper he should; and when he did embark, the wind had been fair for several hours.

What made the Queen's account of the King's patience more ridiculous was that there was nobody in the room who had not heard, and few who had not seen, accounts from all about His Majesty at Helvoetsluys that his impatience was insupportable; Sir Charles Wager's and Horace Walpole's letters were full of nothing else; examples, too, were given of it. It was known by everybody from these letters that the King had declared if Sir Charles Wager would not sail, His Majesty would go in a packet-boat; that he had told Sir Charles he would go; and that Sir Charles, in his laconic Spartan style, had told him he could not; that the King had said: 'Let it be what weather it will, I am not afraid'; and that Sir Charles Wager had replied, 'If you are not, I am'; that His Majesty had sworn he had rather be twelve hours in a storm than twenty-four more at Helvoetsluys; upon which Sir Charles had told him he need not wish for twelve, for four would do his business; and that, when the King by the force of importunity had obliged Sir Charles Wager to sail, Sir Charles had told him: 'Well, Sir, you can oblige me to go, but I can make you come back again.' These dialogues and bon-mots were in all the private letters but His Majesty's and in everybody's mouth; so what faith any report of

His Majesty's patience met with is easy to be imagined. Even the King in his letter owned to the Queen that he had told Sir Charles Wager he wished to see a storm at sea, and that Sir Charles, immediately on his return to Helvoetsluys, had asked him if his curiosity was satisfied, to which His Majesty said he had answered: 'So thoroughly satisfied that I do not desire ever to see another.' Sir Charles Wager, in his letter that gave this account of what had passed between him and the King subsequent to this storm, added that His Majesty was at present as tame as any about him, an epithet for his behaviour that His Majesty, had he known it, would, I fancy, have liked, next to the storm, the least of anything that happened to him. As to his danger, by all accounts that I heard of it, it is impossible for any I can give to exaggerate it. After the report made by the ships that came in on Saturday, there were very few people who imagined it possible His Majesty should have escaped. They were knocking the fine apartment built for him in his own yacht on the quarter-deck all to pieces, and threw all the wood materials as well as all the rich furniture overboard. The skill and conduct of the captain of His Majesty's yacht, as well as Sir Charles Wager's behaviour, was extremely commended.

The King's danger did not in the least soften the minds of the people towards him; a thousand impertinent and treasonable reflections were thrown out against him every day publicly in the streets, such as wishing him at the bottom of the sea, that he had been drowned instead of some of the poor sailors that had been washed off the decks, and many other affectionate douceurs in the same style. Somebody asking, two or three days after the tempest, how the wind was now for the King, was answered: 'Like the nation— against him.'

There was a fellow too, who, coming into an ale-house where several soldiers were drinking, said: 'I suppose you are all brave English boys, and therefore conclude you will pledge me,—"Here is damnation to your master." ' The soldiers at first suspected it was somebody sent to try and ensnare them; but the fellow persisting, and saying the King hated the nation, and he saw no reason why the nation should not hate him, that he was gone to Hanover only to spend English money there and bring back a Hanover whore here, the soldiers began to believe him thoroughly in earnest;

upon which a serjeant among them went and fetched a constable, and had him apprehended. When the serjeant went and told Sir Robert Walpole what had passed, Sir Robert rewarded him, but bid him, in the affidavit he was to make, leave out the account of the English money and Hanover whore, the rest being enough to make the fellow punishable without descending into these particulars.

The Queen, notwithstanding she was not unacquainted with this almost universal dissatisfaction of the nation towards the King, was in great spirits for two or three days after the news came of his being safe returned to Holland; and perhaps the apprehension she had been in for His Majesty's life was the only thing that could have made her look on his return to England not as the greatest misfortune that could befall her.

She said the agitation she had been in twice within this fortnight, first for fear of her daughter's dying in childbed, and next for fear of her husband being drowned, had left her so stupefied that she could not recover her spirits, though her fears no longer subsisted. She owned, too, that what she felt for the King was so much more than what she had felt for the Princess Royal, that from the Friday when the sloop came in (notwithstanding the account it brought had been so softened to her) till the messenger came on Sunday, she had entirely forgot that the Princess Royal was in her bed, or that there was any such body in the world. It is sure that nothing could exceed the apprehension the Queen had at this time of her son's ascending the throne, as there were no lengths she did not think him capable of going to pursue and ruin her.

Lord Hervey, when she told him of these apprehensions, still persisted in saying, as he had done before, that he was sure there would be nobody in a week who would have had so good an interest in the Prince, if this accident had happened, as herself; and that he was so convinced of it, and thought it so advantageous not only for her own family but for the whole nation that she should have that interest with her son, that he had determined to absent himself from her for some time, in case the King had been lost, that the partiality she showed him might have been no additional irritation of circumstances between her and her son. He was going on, but the Queen stopped him short, and said: 'No, my Lord; I should never have suffered that; you are one of the greatest pleasures of my life. But did I love you less than I do, or like less to have you about me, I should look upon the suffering you to be taken from me, or the suffering you to take yourself from me upon such an occasion, after the manner in which you have lived with me and behaved to me, to be such a reflection upon me, and to betray such a meanness and baseness in me, that I assure you, you should not have stirred an inch from me. You and yours should have gone with me to Somerset House; and, though I have neither so good an apartment for you there as you have here, nor an employment worth your taking, I should have lodged you as well as I could, and given you at least as much as you have now from the King; and should have thought this the least I could do for my own honour, and the best thing I could do for my own pleasure. Sir Robert Walpole, too, I know, said he would retire; but I assure you I would have begged him on my knees not to desert my son.' Many more things passed on these subjects in this conversation; but, as I have already extracted the quintessence in what I have said, I pass over the rest of the particulars, to avoid prolixity and repetition.

The letter the Queen wrote to the King on his danger and her fears, his escape and her joy, was full of all the blandishments which ingenuity, art, insinuation, and flattery could suggest; with a most ample account not only of the conduct but even of the countenances of everybody belonging to the Court, each being particularly specified by name. I did not see this letter; but the King's answer was so minute to every article which the Queen's letter had contained, that, the style and turn of the phrases excepted, anybody was as well acquainted with the one by seeing the other as if they had read both. The passion and tenderness of the King's letter to her, which consisted of thirty pages, must be incredible to anyone who did not see it. Whoever had read it without knowing from whom it came, or to whom it was addressed, would have concluded it written by some young sailor of twenty to his first mistress, after escaping from a storm in his first voyage. 'Malgré tout le danger que j'ai essuié dans cette tempête, ma chère Caroline, et malgré tout ce que j'ai souffert, en étant malade à un point que je ne croiois pas que le corps humain pourroit souffrir, je vous jure que je m'exposerois encore et encore pour avoir le plaisir d'entendre les marques de votre tendresse que cette situation m'a procuré. Cette affection que vous me témoignez, cette amitié, cette fidélité, cette bonté inépuisable que vous avez pour moi, et cette indulgence pour toutes mes foiblesses, sont des obligations que je ne sçaurai jamais récompenser, que je ne sçaurai jamais mériter, mais que je ne sçaurai jamais oublier non plus.' His Majesty then spoke of his extreme impatience for their meeting, and in a style that would have made one believe him the rival of Hercules's vigour, and her of Venus's beauty, her person being mentioned in the most exalted strains of rapture, and his own eagerness to feed, after these three weeks of total abstinence, in the warmest phrases that youthful poets could use in elegies to their mistresses. Added to these things, there was an exact diary in this letter of everything he had heard, done, or said for five days, which concluded with a pathetic petition to the Queen not to believe the length of this letter was owing to idleness and leisure, but to the earnest desire he always had of hiding no thought from her, and that he never was more desirous than at that moment of opening his heart to her, because it had never felt warmer towards her.

Whoever reads this account of the King's conduct and letters can possibly make no other comment upon it than: 'Quel galimatias! quel potpourri!'

When the Queen gave Sir Robert Walpole the King's letter to read she said: 'Do not think, because I show you this, that I am an old fool, and vain of my person and charms at this time of day. I am reasonably pleased with it, but I am not unreasonably proud of it.' When Sir Robert Walpole and Lord Hervey talked over this letter, they both agreed they had a most incomprehensible master, and (though neither of them were very partial to His Majesty) they also agreed that, with a woman who could be gained by writing, they had rather have any man in the world for a rival than the King. Nor, indeed, in the gift of writing love-letters do I believe any man ever surpassed him. He had the easiest, the most natural, and the warmest manner of expressing himself that I ever met with, with the prettiest words and the most agreeable turns I ever saw put together.

By the accounts from both sides of the water it appeared, though there had been many men lost in the late storm, that all the vessels were safe, though excessively shattered. The Charlotte yacht was the last heard of; but after being a fortnight missing, they had an account of her from a port she had made in Zealand. But whilst the King remained at Helvoetsluys, he had the mortification of seeing the 'Princess Louisa,' one of the ships ordered back to Holland from hence to convoy His Majesty to England, together with a merchant ship, lost on the sands, just as they were entering the port, by the fault of a drunken pilot. Seventeen men were drowned.

The water was not the only element at present that made its rigour talked of; for a fire at this time breaking out at the Temple, it burnt for several hours with such fury, that it was feared the whole building would have been consumed. The Prince went at nine o'clock at night, and stayed till five in the morning, to assist with his skill, advice, and authority to extinguish it; and to his timely care in ordering a hundred and fifty men from the Savoy he and many others imputed the Temple being saved, after the loss of five or six houses. The Queen had ordered a guard from St. James's on the first news of the fire breaking out; but all merit of assistance was given to the Prince. He exerted himself so much there, that, as he and his people said, several of the mob cried out: 'Crown him! crown him!' but whether this really happened I am unable to affirm; it is certain it was reported to have happened among all ranks of people through the whole town, and generally believed. But what induces me to think it was not true is, that the Princess Caroline told Lord Hervey she knew her brother or some of his people had said, about a fortnight ago, that the same exclamation of 'Crown him! crown him!' was made at the play; and that she knew from people who had been there that it was a lie, and nothing like it had happened. The Prince, the morning after the fire had happened, when he came to give an account of it to the Queen, said not one word of this crowning incident, though in no other particular did his report at all diminish the honours which had been paid him, the pains he had taken, the use he had been of, or the great service he had done the public. Among other things, he pretended to have received two great blows on his head whilst he was assisting the firemen to convey the water; and, upon the

Queen's asking whereabouts he had received those blows, he directed her fingers through his periwig to the places where he pretended to have been struck; whilst she (who told Lord Hervey afterwards that she felt nothing at all) cried out, 'Really that is no jest: there are two bumps as big as two eggs.'

Lord Hervey told the Queen he did not at all wonder at the Prince's conduct, or that he was drunk with vanity, considering the cordials with which the people about him were perpetually plying that passion; nor was it at all surprising he should believe (when it had been so often by these creatures inculcated) that he was so much beloved by the nation, and the King so much hated, that it was nothing but the popularity of the son that kept the father upon the throne; to which she very pertinently answered that according to reports at present of the son's popularity, that popularity, instead of keeping the father upon the throne, was to depose him.

This naturally brought on again the conversation of what a deplorable situation this country would have been in had the King been drowned; for, as the Prince was known to be so unstable, so false, and consequently so dangerous, few people, it was agreed, who were not very necessitous in their circumstances, if they had sense, till they saw the first turbulency of his reign a little subsided, would have coveted being employed under him, as it would be staking their head against the poor prospect of a temporary power, and very uncertain gain. The Queen said her son's situation would not be more to be envied than the nation's; for, as he would at first think himself capable of managing and conducting everything, and soon find himself capable of managing and conducting nothing, so his timidity—'for you know,' said she, 'he is the greatest coward in the world'—will make him commit his affairs to anybody that happens to be next him, and will take the charge of them, and, when he has done so, it is a hundred to one it is to somebody that would not be capable of serving him if he would allow them the proper means, and very sure that, if they had the capacity, his impatience would not allow that capacity time to operate. She intimated that his betters had found themselves in the same difficulties; though, by a prudent and happy choice of a minister to do what they had vainly fancied they could do alone, they had extricated themselves out of them, as well as by a firmness, which was the quality in the world most necessary to support a Prince in this country, and one which she feared her son could never be reasoned into. Lord Hervey said that everybody knowing beforehand in that case how short the opportunity they were to profit by was likely to be, they would certainly do by the Prince as the mob do at a funeral: everyone would enrich themselves with any bit of him they could catch, and not care a farthing what they tore or spoiled. The Queen told Lord Hervey that it behoved everybody who had any valuable possessions in this country, or any regard to the quiet of it, to prevent that havoc, whether they had any regard for the Prince or not; for as he could not be ruined without endangering their security, so, when once he was King, it would be wise and prudent in everybody to keep him from tottering, as it would be for a ship's crew to take care of the main-mast to which the principal sails and tackle were fastened, and that could not fall without endangering many lives, and making not only the course of the ship less steady, but even its safety very precarious. Lord Hervey said in some storms at sea, though it was a desperate remedy, people found themselves obliged to cut away the main-mast; and, though danger attending the doing it, there was more sometimes in letting it alone. 'In short,' said the Queen, 'a popish King will be surer ruin to this country than any other can bring upon it; and whenever you change a King of this family, it will neither be for no King, nor for any other Protestant King. All sensible people, therefore, must think of the Prince in this way: there he is, he must be King, and we will make the best we can of him, though we cannot make him so good as we would.'

Lord Hervey did not tell the Queen that this was at present the case of the father, and that those who seemed most attached to his interest, were really so only upon this foot; but had he made her this answer, it would only have been improper, not untrue, His Majesty's character with all ranks of people being fallen so low that the disregard with which everybody spoke of him, and the open manner in which they expressed their contempt and dislike, is hardly to be credited. The enlightened state of the nation with respect to any reverence due to the Crown further than the merit of the head that wore it might claim made very little come to His Majesty's share. His conduct of late had convinced the distant part of the nation of what those who had the honour to be more near him had discovered long ago, which was his preferring his German to his English subjects at least as much as his father had done. Those about him knew, too, that he cared for no one of them, that he thought them all overpaid in their several stations for whatever service they did him, and as he looked upon them all with as little mixture of favour as he did on his chairs or tables, or any piece of necessary furniture, so he was perpetually grumbling at Sir Robert Walpole on account of the price he paid for the one, in the same manner as he would have done at a joiner for having charged him too much in any article of his bill for the other. This made even the most sensible people about him feel no affection for him; and those who were less so were fond of declaring the opinion they had of him for fear of being thought his dupes, and ran into the other extreme, as some people declare themselves atheists for fear of being thought bigots.

On Saturday morning at four o'clock an express arrived at St. James's to acquaint the Queen that the King had landed the day before at noon at Lowestoft, after having been detained five weeks at Helvoetsluys, and now obliged at last to come with a contrary wind all the way. The Queen had been ill the day before, had not rested in the night, and when Sir Robert Walpole came at nine in the morning to concert what was to be done on the King's arrival, Her Majesty was trying to sleep, with the Princess Caroline only with her reading at her bedside. At the same time of the Prince coming to wish his mother joy of this good news, and meeting Sir Robert in the antechamber, he made him sit down, and they two, with the Princess Emily only present, had a conference that lasted till the Queen waked and called for them in, which was at least two hours and a half. Many things were discoursed of, but the quintessence of the conversation, which Sir Robert Walpole related to me in detail, was that the Prince told Sir Robert he had always looked upon him as one of the ablest men in England, that he had always had the greatest regard for him imaginable, and that, if ever his looks or actions seemed to speak his sentiments to be different from what he now professed, they were neither what he would have them to be, nor faithful interpreters of his thoughts. Sir Robert thanked him for his good opinion, and the honour he did him; said he had always endeavoured to serve the King to the best of his ability; that all Kings were obliged to take measures which often they could not, and often they would not, explain their motives for, though the more those motives were explained, perhaps the more justifiable the measures would appear; but though that sometimes should happen not to be the case, he would venture to affirm that, considering the disputed title to this Crown, considering the temper of this nation, their readiness to disapprove, and their love of change, it could never be in the interest of the Prince of Wales to quarrel with his father for private reasons, and that whoever flattered the Prince by telling him he could be a gainer by opposing his father's measures must either be the worst or the weakest of mankind.

chapter six

The Prince of Wales's £100,000

15 Jan, 1737

THIS DAY ABOUT two o'clock the King arrived at St. James's. The Queen attended by all her children and servants went down into the colonnade to receive him just as he alighted from his coach, and the whole ceremony of the meeting passed, kiss for kiss (the Prince's cheek not excepted), just as it had done the year before. But His Majesty's temper was very different, for as last year nobody had the good fortune to catch one smile from His Majesty, so now there was nobody who had the mortification to meet with one frown.

Everybody was astonished at all this unexpected sunshine, but the warmest of all his rays were directed towards the Queen. He said no man ever had so affectionate and meritorious a wife, or so faithful and able a friend. He took Sir Robert by the hand next morning in the circle at his levée, and whispered him in the ear that the Queen had given him a full account of his behaviour at every juncture, that he knew that he had behaved like a great and good man, and that he should always remember it and love him for it.

When Sir Robert told me this he said, to be sure one had always rather the Prince one served was kind to one than brutal; but for dependence on his favour he never had any, for he knew he loved nobody. 'Therefore,' said he, 'the only real pleasure I had in this fine speech was the certain proof it gave me of Her Majesty's present way of thinking of me; for how great or how little soever my real merit may be, I know he could see none she had a mind to hide, nor I could want none she had a mind to show.'

The day after the King arrived Sir Robert Walpole coming just from the Queen and meeting Lord Hervey at the foot of the backstairs, the sentinel being close to them, Sir Robert said to him in Latin: 'Optime, Optime, omnia rident.' To which Lord Hervey answered:

> Prisca redit Venus
> Diductosque jugo cogit aëneo
> Flava excutitur Chloe
> Rejectaeque patet janua Lydiae,[1]

and then Sir Robert replied: 'Dixit ad uxorem, "quamquam sidere pulchrior illa est, tecum vivere amem, tecum obeam libens." '[2] Upon which they both laughed, parted, and agreed to meet the next morning to talk this matter over in plain English. But after Sir Robert was in his chair he called out to tell Lord Hervey he did not believe that Mr. Bis had been above, notwithstanding all this rant; to which Lord Hervey replied that if Mr. Semel had been there, it was better company than he believed had been at Kensington last year on the same occasion.

There was nobody triumphed more in this honeyed behaviour of His Majesty towards the Queen than the Princess Caroline, as she bragged to Lord Hervey that she had always told him it would be so. To which Lord Hervey replied there was an English proverb that said, 'All's well that ends well,' which he believed was more applicable to present circumstances than the Italian one of 'Chi ben comincia, a la meta del opera.' He said the King was a mere *enfant gaté*, and that his having been whipped for five weeks together at Helvoetsluys, had made him just supportable now, but that he'd be hanged if his good Majesty would not be as intractable and insufferable in a week as ever he had been in his life.

The Parliament which was to have met the Friday after His Majesty arrived, was further prorogued to the Tuesday se'night following.

There was a little epigram made by Mr. Pulteney on its having been appointed to meet on a Friday, which I think worth reciting and Lord Chesterfield worth owning, for when it was given to him, he received the insinuation with the same sort of avowing denial that he generally put on when verses were ascribed to him which he had not written, or mistresses that he had not lain with. The verses were these:

[1] Horace, Odes III, 9.   [2] *Ibid*.

> The King this summer having spent
>   Amoribus in teneris,
> Appoints his loving Parliament
>   To meet him Die Veneris.

There was another epigram made whilst the King was at Helvoet-sluys by the same author, and claimed by the same plagiary, on the Sheriffs that were to be appointed, which was as follows:

> What shall we do! (quoth Walpole to the Queen)
>   Unless the wind turn quick?
> The sheriffs in all times have been
>   Still chosen by a prick.
> *Answer*. Queen
> The instrument that does the job
>   The King he has about him;
> But can't you help me good Sir Bob,
>   To do the thing without him?

The two epigrams I have already transcribed Pulteney himself told Lady Hervey were written by him, though given to and not denied by the little chattering cur, which was the name by which he generally distinguished Lord Chesterfield.

The two coarse and virulent satires that follow were really written by Lord Chesterfield:

> Great George escap'd from narrow seas and storms
> Now rides at large in Carolina's arms.
> Bold Jonah thus, as holy writ will tell ye,
> A whale received at once into her belly.

ON THE SAME SUBJECT

> What! just escaped from Cleopatra's charms
> To souse at once into your Fulvia's arms?
> With equal violence of haste to run
> From blooming twenty to fat fifty-one.
> Was it for this the youth abroad was sent,
> And so much gold unprofitably spent?
> So travelled Hottentot, refined in vain,
> Returns with rapture to his Gutts[1] again.

Sir Robert Walpole, with all his dexterity on some occasions, and his knowledge of those he had to deal with, sometimes made as

[1] Hottentots were supposed to wear 'bracelets of guts' (see Bolingbroke, *Letters on the Study and Use of History*, Letter IV).

gross mistakes as if his natural sagacity had given him no share of the first of these qualities, nor his long experience any proficiency in the last. An affectation of too much familiarity with people of the highest rank and a very coarse manner of being familiar drew him into these scrapes; and his way of talking to and of the Princesses Emily and Caroline on occurrences to which he should not only have shut his mouth, but his eyes, went so far at this time that a message was sent to him from them in form by the Duke of Grafton to desire he would discourse no more in that strain. The Duke of Newcastle's coquetry to the Princess Emily, and Her Royal Highness's coquetry back again to him, as the only male creature who made up to her, had been often the topic of very little-understood raillery, in very gross terms, uttered by Sir Robert Walpole, and not very privately. He has often, and before many people, in the expressions of a porter, told the Duke of Newcastle he would certainly draw himself into some scrape, for as the Princess Emily thought of nothing but the main point and his Grace of nothing but the outwork Her Royal Highness would certainly catch him alone one day and ask him the question; upon which his Grace would be frighted out of his wits and run away, whilst she would hate him for so doing, and tell her papa and mama to be revenged of him, that he had offered to ravish her.

Sir Robert Walpole had not said this once or twice, or in private only, but it had been almostly his daily topic of conversation to and of the Duke of Newcastle for these last seven or eight months; and often rather more than hinted by him in mixed companies at dinner, even before servants.

The last conversation of this nature, that occasioned the messages which I have mentioned, was part of it in the Queen's morning drawing-room, and the rest in the apartment of the Princesses, where Sir Robert went to fetch the Duke of Newcastle away to dinner. If I were to relate all the particulars they would be incredible, considering by whom these things were said and to whom; but how strong they were may be guessed when Sir Robert, who loved hunting and often took his metaphors from that science, carried on an allegory on this occasion between the apartment of the Princess and a dog kennel, in which he made the Duke of Newcastle one of the principal puppies of his parable and the two

Princesses what, I believe, is as unnecessary as unfit to repeat, when I say he called them in plain terms, during this every way ill-understood raillery, what a hackney coachman would think the last affront he could offer in words to an apple-woman.

All this was told by the Princesses to the Queen, who was very angry with Sir Robert Walpole for what had passed, but never spoke to him about it, expecting, I suppose, what did indeed happen, that the message by the Duke of Grafton would suffice to reform him.

Nor was this the only subject on which Sir Robert Walpole at this time ruffled the temper of the Queen towards him; for whilst Her Majesty, with a little female and conjugal pride united, was every day telling Sir Robert Walpole in private how uninterruptedly kind the King's behaviour had been towards her ever since his arrival, Sir Robert used to shake his head, shrug his shoulders and laugh, and to tell her: 'Madam, do not flatter yourself. For pleasure of the body there must be youth on one side; and believe me, marriage is never so properly called one flesh as after twenty years' marriage, for no husband then knows his wife's from his own.'

It was in vain for Her Majesty to give him instances of the King's expressions of kindness and affection towards her. Sir Robert still persisted, and told her: ' 'Tis compensation, Madam, for the sins of the summer; and he thinks to expiate the crime of real fondness to his mistress by putting it on to his wife.'

The King, having got a violent cold in his journey and taken no care of it at his first arrival, was extremely out of order, too, at this time, having at once the piles, a violent pain in one side of his head, and a little fever. This disorder, for which the King was at last forced to shut himself up and keep his bed, Sir Robert Walpole would insist to the Queen was principally occasioned by the disorder of his mind; that it was pining and fretting; and that he would never be well till she would send for Madame Walmoden to nurse him.

Whilst he grew every day worse and worse, it was every day by the Queen and Princesses given out that he was better and better. Very few people saw him, and all those who did had more than hints given them before they went in to be sure to take care not to ask him how he did. Poor Lord Dunmore, one of his Lords of the Chamber, the first day of his week's waiting, having not received these instructions or neglecting them, as soon as he went into the King told His Majesty how extremely sorry he had been for his indisposition, and said he hoped His Majesty was much better; to which the King made not one word of answer, and the moment Lord Dunmore went out of the room he sent for Lord Pembroke, and bid him as Groom of the Stole to say he would take this week's waiting, His Majesty adding that his reason for giving these orders to Lord Pembroke was that he might not see any more of those troublesome, inquisitive puppies who were always plaguing him with asking impertinent, silly questions about his health like so many old nurses.

Sir Robert Walpole continued every day plaguing the Queen, and whenever she told him the King was better than he had been, or better than people thought him, he used to answer her only with shaking his head and saying: 'Do you flatter me, Madam, in telling me what you do not believe, or do you flatter yourself and believe what you say?' This often made the Queen peevish with him and complain of him to Lord Hervey, telling Lord Hervey at the same time: 'You often pity me for the snubs and rebukes I meet with from the King, but I assure you the affronts I meet with there are nothing compared to what I receive from your friend Sir Robert. I cannot imagine what ails him, or who it is he listens to. In the first place, he wants to persuade me the King is dying; in the next, that he knows him better than I do; and what is more extraordinary still, is telling me every time he sees me that my being from morning to night in the King's room is owing to my forcing myself upon him, and that he had much rather be without my company.'

Lord Hervey did not tell Sir Robert Walpole again what the Queen had said in the last article, but in general let him know that he often found the Queen dissatisfied with the incredulity she said she always found in Sir Robert Walpole when she made any reports from the King's bedchamber; to which intimations from Lord Hervey Sir Robert Walpole always answered with complaining of her unreasonableness, her blindness or hypocrisy in all these points, and said he would continue to tell her the truth, let her take it as she would; but notwithstanding this way of talking to Lord Hervey, and defending what he had done, he changed his manner of acting towards the Queen, which plainly showed he thought he had been in the wrong; which at the same time demonstrated that, as difficult as it is for people to correct their faults, it is more difficult still to own they want correction, since he could bring himself to the one though he could not to the other.

During February, an affair of yet greater moment was brought on the tapis, the Prince and his friends having determined to lay his dispute with his father about the £100,000 a year before the Parliament.

Lord Hervey was the first who told the Queen that it was certainly a measure agreed upon. The way he came to know of it was this. The Prince, who solicited every mortal to be for him on this occasion, sent the Duke of Marlborough to Mr. Henry Fox (the younger of the two brothers, Lord Hervey's most intimate friends, often mentioned in these papers[1]) to desire him to vote for him; and at the same time sent Mr. Hamilton, a brother of Lady Archibald Hamilton, to Mr. Stephen Fox, the elder brother. The Duke of Marlborough meeting with Mr. Henry Fox before Mr. Hamilton found the other brother, Mr. Henry Fox came immediately to Lord Hervey, told him what had passed, and said the answer he had given to the Duke of Marlborough (and he never wanted a quick and a proper one) was that he should certainly do as his brother did, whatever that should be.

Lord Hervey said this affair had been so often talked of, and so often dropped, that he could not believe it would be brought into Parliament; but Mr. Henry Fox assured him it certainly would, and that the Prince's people must have conducted their affairs very secretly and cleverly, or the Ministers have been fast asleep, or had very bad intelligence, if they did not know it would be so, since he believed there was not one man in opposition who had not been already spoken to and solicited. He gave Lord Hervey leave to tell the thing to the Queen, but not to name the Duke of Marlborough. Accordingly, Lord Hervey went directly to Her Majesty, waited till she came on some errand out of the King's bedchamber (where she was shut up all day), and then told her of this measure being certainly taken. She would not at first believe it, gave the same

[1] Possibly in the missing portion, relating to 1730–1732. Hitherto they have been seldom mentioned.

reasons for her incredulity to Lord Hervey, that he had done for his to Mr. Fox, but at last, like him too, began to change her opinion. Lord Hervey begged her not to tell the King of it that night, as it could be of no service, and would certainly set him a fretting, probably keep him awake, and of course increase his fever, which would answer one of the ends he believed was proposed by the timing this measure; which was, knowing the King's warm prompt temper, to put him in such a passion as, in his present weak condition, and which they thought weaker than it was, might go a good way towards killing him.

The Queen assured Lord Hervey she would not name it to the King that night, and Lord Hervey said it was as silly as well as impertinent for him to pretend to direct her what was the best way to behave on any occasion to the King; but that he could not help adding on this, that when she did break it to him, he hoped it would be in the gentlest way she could, or it would certainly do him more hurt than his fever and piles put together, and prevent all the surgeons, doctors, and apothecaries in town doing him any good.

The Queen bid Lord Hervey be sure to go early the next morning to Sir Robert Walpole, to tell him all he knew about this affair, and wished him a better night than she said she hoped to have herself; she was very lavish in her abuse on her son, but not more so than her daughter Caroline to whose apartment Lord Hervey went directly from the Queen, to communicate what had passed.

The next morning Lord Hervey went to Sir Robert, who told him he had from two channels the night before had intelligence that confirmed all Lord Hervey reported, and said he had long told both the King and Queen that this measure would sooner or later infallibly be taken, and that the many douceurs shown to people in the son's conduct, and the few in the father's, would make this a troublesome point to the latter, notwithstanding his superior power.

Lord Hervey went back immediately to St. James's to acquaint the Queen with what Sir Robert had desired him to tell her, and found her at least as impatient as he expected to receive further intelligence of the true state of this affair. She said she had not yet broken it to the King, but would go and prepare him for Sir Robert's arrival, who, Lord Hervey told her, would come to Court that morning at the usual hour.

The King took the first notice of this business with more temper and calmness than anybody expected he would; and the Queen, from the beginning of this affair to the end of it, was in much greater agitation and anxiety than I ever saw her on any other occasion.

Nothing was ever more universally talked of, or more strongly solicited; the Prince himself was as busy as his emissaries, closeted as many members of either House as he could get to come to him, and employed all his servants and friends to speak to every mortal on whom they thought they could possibly prevail, and many even where there was not that possibility.

The general tenor of his applications was, how sorry he was to have it so little in his power at present to show his goodwill to his friends, and offering carte blanche for promissory notes of payment when he came to the Crown, with strong insinuations at the same time how near the King's health seemed to bring that happy day.

Many on the King's side fearing the Prince would carry this point in the House of Commons, if it came to be tried there, all means were used to prevail on the Prince to desist. Lord Hervey advised the Queen to send for the Prince, and speak to him herself, to set forth how dear the victory would cost him, supposing he could gain it, and how little he would get by it; to tell him it would weaken, if not destroy the interest of his family in general in this country, and that it would be impossible for him to get anything by it, as the King would certainly part with his crown rather than give him what he wanted or demanded; to tell him too that the King, if he should be brought to the disagreeable necessity of not complying with an address of Parliament, would still have the resource of dissolving that Parliament and calling another; and that by changing hands the King would always have it in his power to get the better of him, as there were none of those who now seemingly stood by him, though they only in reality made a fool of him, who would not give him up to come into power; and that the King, if driven to extremities, would buy them to give up his son, not his son to give up them, since the danger was in the party, not in him; and as it was, he made use of their strength, not they of his; the yielding, if there was any, would be to them, not him.

The Queen told Lord Hervey that her speaking to the Prince

would only make him more obstinate; and besides that objection, that he was so great a liar it made it extremely unsafe for her to venture any conference with him, as there was nothing he was not capable of asserting had passed between them, not even that she had attempted to murder him. The excise year she said she had sent for him, and on that occasion she was so sensible of his being capable of denying everything he had said or had been said to him, and relating what had never been mentioned, that she had left the door from her bedchamber into her dressing-room (where she saw him) half open, and placed the Princess Caroline behind it, to hear and be a witness to everything that passed, as the Princess Caroline had before told me.

The Queen therefore determined she would not see him, though Sir Robert Walpole did all he could too to persuade her, and told Lord Hervey, when Lord Hervey reported to him what I have here related, that he had spoken to the Queen to the same effect, and that he believed besides the reasons she had given to them for not speaking to her son, that she had two more which she had not given—the one her pride, the other the apprehending the King on this occasion might have some jealousy of any private conference between the Prince and her at this juncture.

It being thought that the report of the King's state of health, which was imagined by everybody out of the palace, and many in it, to be much worse than it really was, aided the Prince's solicitations, everybody about the Queen who had her ear advised her to persuade the King, if it was possible, to keep himself no longer locked up in his bedchamber, but to come out and show himself; as the belief of his being in a declining condition made many people less willing to resist the importunities of the heir apparent to the Crown on this occasion, than better informed of the state of the King's health they possibly would be.

The King therefore was prevailed upon to have levées, and see everybody in a morning as usual; and though he looked pale and was much fallen away, he looked much better than those who had not seen him during his confinement expected. He was much more gracious too, to everybody, than he used to be; and from the first day he came out began to recover his looks, flesh, and strength much faster than could have been expected.

But notwithstanding all this, there were few on his side so sanguine as not to apprehend his son's carrying his point in the House of Commons. All the lists made by the Prince's people gave him a majority of near forty; and by Mr. Winnington's list, who was reckoned one of the best calculators on the King's side, the Prince had a majority of ten. These calculations alarmed Sir Robert Walpole, who thought, not unreasonably, that his fate, at least as a Minister, depended on this question.

The King behaved in public with great seeming unconcern, and even in private with unaccountable temper; the Queen well in public, but to those before whom she appeared with less constraint her invectives against her son were incessant and of the strongest kind, and her concern so great, that more tears flowed on this occasion than I ever saw her shed on all others put together. She said she had suffered a great deal from many disagreeable circumstances this last year—the King's staying abroad, the manner in which his stay had been received and talked of here, her daughter the Princess Royal's danger in lying-in, and the King's danger at sea—but that her grief and apprehensions at present surpassed everything she had ever felt before; that she looked on her family from this moment as distracted with divisions of which she could see or hope no end—divisions which would give the common enemies to her whole family such advantages, as might one time or other enable them to get the better of it; and though she had spirits and resolution to struggle with most misfortunes and difficulties, this last she owned got the better of her; that it was too much for her to bear; that it not only got the better of her spirits and her resolution, but of her appetite and her rest, as she could neither eat nor sleep; and that she really feared it would kill her.

The Princess Caroline, who loved her mother and disliked her brother in equal and extreme degrees, was in much the same state of mind as the Queen, her consideration and regard for her mother making her always adopt the Queen's opinions, as well as share her pleasures and her afflictions. They neither of them made much ceremony of wishing a hundred times a day that the Prince might drop down dead of apoplexy, the Queen cursing the hour of his birth, and the Princess Caroline declaring she grudged him every hour he continued to breathe, and reproached Lord Hervey with his weakness for having ever loved him, and being fool enough to think that he had been ever beloved by him, as well as being so great a dupe as to believe the nauseous beast (those were her words) cared for anybody but his own nauseous self, that he loved anything but money, that he was not the greatest liar that ever spoke, and would not put one arm about anybody's neck to kiss them, and then stab them with the other, if he could get five guineas for it and run no risk of being found out. She protested that from the time he had been here six months—so early had she found him out—she had never loved him better or thought better of him than at that moment.

The day before that which was appointed for the great debate of this important question in the House of Commons, all hopes being now lost of preventing its coming there by any methods which had hitherto been tried, Sir Robert Walpole, who feared extremely, unless something was done to alter the present situation of things, the King's party would be beaten, resolved to persuade the King to send a message to the Prince to make a sort of treaty of composition.

He sent for Lord Hervey early in the morning, communicated this design to him, and told him the particulars of this overture of accommodation were for the King to tell the Prince he would settle a jointure forthwith on the Princess (which really had been under consideration), and at the same time to let the Prince know he would settle the £50,000 a year he now gave him, out of his power.

Lord Hervey said in the first place he believed Sir Robert would find great difficulty in bringing the King into this measure; in the next, that he did not believe it would alter a vote—that everybody would call it a show of yielding in the King, and giving nothing; but that what he feared most of all was, lest the King and Queen, who hated their son so inveterately, might construe it to be a management for their son in Sir Robert Walpole, and never forgive it him.

To this Sir Robert answered that without a measure of this kind he should certainly to-morrow lose the question: that the great cry of the most moderate people was composed of the injustice of having yet given the Princess no jointure, and the Prince being only a pensioner at pleasure on the King, by having nothing secured to him; and though, in reality, what he proposed was, as Lord Hervey said, giving the Prince nothing, and the £100,000 was the chief point, yet these two objections and complaints which he had mentioned being removed by the King's sending this message, it would disarm the Prince's party of two arguments against which there was no answer to be found; that as to the umbrage the King and Queen might take at it, and the jealousies it might infuse in their minds of having underhand any management for the Prince, he must risk it and do as well as he could to combat these consequences; 'and as it is my way, you know, my dear Lord, and when you come to be in my place I advise you to make it your way too, to provide against the present difficulty that presses, I think I shall by this message either get the Prince to postpone to-morrow's affair and enter into treaty, or have it to say for the King to-morrow that he had made the first step to peace, and that his son had refused to parley, and sounded this Parliamentary trumpet to battle.'

Lord Hervey said Sir Robert Walpole was a much better judge what to do in this case than he pretended to be, but it was his opinion the message would neither put off the battle, nor get him one deserter; and that to his own troops it would have an air of diffidence and retreat; besides the danger which he mentioned before, and what he thought most to be avoided, which was giving a distrust of his favouring the Prince to the King and Queen, who were too apt to be suspicious on all occasions, and were particularly so he knew wherever their son was concerned.

Sir Robert said he had talked of this measure last night to the Pelhams, and that they were both extremely for it. 'You will say, I know (says he), they are always of the temporising and palliating side, and I grant you they are so, and generally there are points too on which we differ, but I really think now it is all we have left for it; and as there is no time to be lost, I will dress, go to Court this moment, and go to work upon our stubborn master.'

Accordingly they went together to St. James's, where Sir Robert Walpole, by the same arguments I have already mentioned, first brought the Queen into this measure, and then the King. The Dukes of Grafton and Devonshire (Lord Chamberlain and Lord

Steward) were first sent to the Prince to let him know the Cabinet Council had a message to deliver to him from the King, and to desire to know when they might wait on him; and the Prince saying they might come whenever they pleased, the Lord Chancellor, Lord President, Lord Steward, Lord Chamberlain, Dukes of Richmond, Argyll and Newcastle, Earls of Pembroke and Scarborough, and Lord Harrington, repaired immediately to the Prince's apartment, and Lord Chancellor from a written copy read the following message to His Royal Highness:

> His Majesty has commanded us to acquaint Your Royal Highness in his name that, upon Your Royal Highness's marriage, he immediately took into his royal consideration the settling a proper jointure upon the Princess of Wales; but his sudden going abroad, and his late indisposition since his return, had hitherto retarded the execution of these his gracious intentions; from which short delay His Majesty did not apprehend any inconvenience could arise, especially since no application had in any manner been made to him upon this subject by Your Royal Highness; and that His Majesty hath now given orders for settling a jointure upon the Princess of Wales, as far as he is enabled by law, suitable to her high rank and dignity, which he will, in proper time, lay before his Parliament, in order to be rendered certain and effectual for the benefit of Her Royal Highness.
>
> The King has further commanded us to acquaint Your Royal Highness that, although Your Royal Highness has not thought fit, by any application to His Majesty, to desire that your allowance of fifty thousand pounds per annum, which is now paid you by monthly payments, at the choice of Your Royal Highness, preferably to quarterly payments, might, by His Majesty's further grace and favour, be rendered less precarious, His Majesty, to prevent the bad consequences which he apprehends may follow from the undutiful measures which His Majesty is informed Your Royal Highness has been advised to pursue, will grant to Your Royal Highness, for His Majesty's life, the said fifty thousand pounds per annum, to be issuing out of His Majesty's Civil List revenues, over and above Your Royal Highness's revenues arising from the Duchy of Cornwall; which His Majesty thinks a very competent allowance, considering his numerous issue, and the great expenses which do and must necessarily attend an honourable provision for his whole family.

To this message His Royal Highness returned a verbal answer, which the Lords of the Council who attended him, immediately after they received it, withdrew to put into writing to the best of their recollection, and delivered it to the King in the following words:

> That His Royal Highness desired the Lords to lay him, with all humility, at His Majesty's feet, and to assure His Majesty that he had, and ever should retain, the utmost duty for his royal person; that His Royal Highness was very thankful for any instance of His Majesty's goodness to him or the Princess, and particularly for His Majesty's intention of settling a jointure upon Her Royal Highness; but that as to the message, the affair was now out of his hands, and therefore he could give no answer to it.
>
> After which His Royal Highness used many dutiful expressions towards His Majesty; and then added: 'Indeed, my Lords, it is in other hands; I am sorry for it': or to that effect.
>
> His Royal Highness concluded with earnestly desiring the Lords to represent his answer to His Majesty in the most respectful and dutiful manner.

It was very plain by this answer that the Prince was very willing and ready to receive any favour the King pleased to bestow upon him, and to return as good words as he received, but not to take words instead of money, or to recede from any step he had taken, or to slacken his pace in what he had resolved to pursue.

The King and Queen were both extremely enraged at this reception of the message. The King reproached Sir Robert Walpole a little roughly for having persuaded him to send it; to which Sir Robert Walpole answered that the good he expected from it was to be reaped to-morrow, not to-day; and that he had proposed to bring the House of Commons to reason by it, not the Prince.

The Queen was more particularly piqued at the Prince's behaviour on this occasion from a circumstance that did not appear in the drawing up the Prince's answer, which was his stepping forward, whilst the Lords of the Cabinet Council were with him, and saying in a sort of whisper to my Lord Chancellor that he wondered it should be said in the message that he had made no application to the King on this business, when the Queen knew he had often applied to His Majesty through her, and that he had been forbidden by the King, ever since the audience he asked of His Majesty two years ago at Kensington relating to his marriage, ever to apply to him again any way but by the Queen. To which speech of the Prince's Lord Chancellor very prudently made no other answer than asking the Prince aloud if what he had said to him was part of the answer he designed should be conveyed to the King, and if it was, he desired His Royal Highness would be so good to repeat it to all the Lords of the Council. But the Prince said: 'No, my Lord; I only said it to inform you how that matter stood.'

The Queen said on this occasion she had always known her son to be the most hardened of all liars, but did not imagine even he was capable of exposing himself as such on so solemn an occasion to all the Lords of the Cabinet Council; and did protest that directly nor indirectly he had never desired her at any time to speak to the King about the increase of his income; and that if he persisted in saying he had, she would be glad to have him asked where and when and who was by; or, if he said it had been always at tête-à-tête, the dispute must then remain on the evidence of her word against his; but that it was very odd if he had made this application so often, nobody should ever happen to have been present, especially when she did not remember she had ever seen him so often alone as to make frequent applications with nobody present possible. She said before he was married he had, before his sisters, often talked to her of his debts and his expenses and his poverty, but never even then desired her to speak to the King to increase his allowance; but since the increase of it at his marriage he had not even talked to her in that strain.

The next morning after the message, which was the day this great point was to be opened in the House of Commons, the Queen sent for Lord Hervey the moment she was up, to inquire what people said in the town of the message that had been sent the day before; expressing herself great disapprobation of the measure, and saying: 'All you other great and wise people were for it, and so one was forced to give way; but I knew *canaille* my good son so well that I was sure he would only be more obstinate on any step taken to soften him. You know as well as I that he is the lowest stinking coward in the world and that there is no way of gaining anything of him but by working upon his fear. I know, if I was asleep, or that he could come behind me, he is capable of shooting me through the head, or stabbing me in the back; but if he had ten swords and pistols and came to murder me, though I was quite alone, if I was awake and saw him and held up this pin and said: "You villain!

touch me if you dare!" he would tremble and cry and fall at my feet and ask forgiveness and then wait for another opportunity when I had no pin in my hand to murder me. But what do people say of the impertinent, silly answer he sent yesterday? And of the King's message? Do not people think it was great condescension in the King?' 'Madam,' replied Lord Hervey, 'those that are with us magnify the merit of it extremely; and those that are against us say it has an air of condescension, but, in reality, is giving nothing; for as the King could not have taken away the £50,000 a year and leave his son to starve or beg, nor could the Parliament have suffered it, so the settling it is only making a show of a new concession, without really having made any; and as to the jointure, they say there is no sum named, consequently that part of the message is worth as little as the other; and if there is any advantage accrues to the Prince by this concession (as it is called), I suppose those who have put the Prince upon bullying have sense enough to impute all the merit of it to themselves; and to tell the Prince if anything is got by it, it is those who put him upon bullying who have got it for him. I suppose they tell him (at least I would in their place if I had a mind to keep him warm) that he sees the only way to get anything is to bully; that he would never have been married if he had not frightened the King into it by the audience they made him ask two years ago at Kensington; that by marrying he got his allowance more than doubled; that if he had not frightened the King by this step of appealing to Parliament, he never would have got even his £50,000 a year secured to him, nor a jointure for the Princess; and that if he will listen to them and go on menacing, and bullying, and fighting, and appealing, he will at last get everything he wants.' 'Why, then' (said the Queen) 'you do not approve the message?' 'I cannot say,' replied Lord Hervey, 'I approve or disapprove it; it is above me; and to be able to determine whether it was a proper measure or not, I must have talked to as many members of the House of Commons as Sir Robert Walpole has done, must be able to know what effect it will have on their opinions and conduct, and what alteration it is likely to produce in the calculation made before this measure of the votes which are to be given this day; of all which things there is nobody in England but Sir Robert who can be a competent judge.'

'But was there ever anything so weak' (said the Queen) 'as saying, as he does in his answer, that the affair is no longer in his hands, and that he is sorry for it? Is not that saying that he is to be governed by these people, not they by him? In whose hands is he? and how came he so much in their power!' Lord Hervey said: 'The worse his answer is, Madam, the better for those to whom it was sent. Had I been to have given it, it should have been very different, and embarrassed the Court much more than it will now do. In the first place if the Prince had had any sense or any good advisers, he would have desired time to give his answer in writing to a written message, and upon mature consideration, and consulting all the best heads about him, I doubt not but he would have been advised to express himself with the utmost duty to the King, to bewail his hard fate in having his designs represented to the King as undutiful, which appears by the words in the King's message had been his misfortune, and that nothing but the King's absolute commands should or could have hindered him from applying to His Majesty in the first place either for any favour or justice he thought he might expect from his goodness, and that any round-about way (which was the only one His Majesty's injunctions had left him) he had found so fruitless and ineffectual, that a modest and humble request to the Parliament of England, who had given the Crown to his family, and who had given all that was to support the honour and dignity of it, he hoped could never be construed an indecent step, especially when it was to ask nothing of them but to explain their own acts; and that if there was any dispute between him and his father, that he knew no mediator so proper as the Parliament, nor any arbitrator to whose decisions he should so cheerfully and implicitly submit, especially since he could not hope to find any proper ambassador about the King to plead his cause, after the fatal experience of those who had his ear having advised him to forbid his son making any application to him in person, and representing his conduct in so unjust and false a light as to provoke the King to give it the hard and false undeserved title of undutiful.' The Queen interrupted and said there was enough, and that she was very glad he had not been so advised, or rather that he had thought his own wise head so able to guide him, as to have allowed himself no time to ask any advice. 'But tell me, do you think the fool can have interest enough to carry this point? Do not people know him? What do they think of him and what do they say of him?' 'Madam,' replied Lord Hervey, 'whatever they think of him or whatever they say of him, the people in Opposition will doubtless, for two reasons, be glad to have him join them; in the first place to swell their party, and in the next to wipe off the imputation of Jacobitism.' 'These are your nasty favourites the Whigs,' said the Queen; 'they are always squabbling with one another. The King has shown he would stand by them and would support them; but if they will not stand by him and support him, he has but one party to take—he must employ the Tories. The Tories are ready to come; there they are; he has but to beckon them, and there is not one but will come to St. James's the moment he calls. The Whigs have forgotten the four last years of Queen Anne's reign; they want to feel the oppression again of Tory masters to teach them what they owe to a King that has supported them; and if they are of such a nature as never to know the value of the favour of the Crown, whilst they enjoy it, they may thank themselves for being taught their duty by ill-usage.'

Lord Hervey said: 'There is nobody, to be sure, Madam, who wishes well to the present Establishment, who could advise Your Majesty to continue the Whigs in power, if it appeared they were so broken among themselves as to be unable longer to carry on the King's business; but hitherto, I own, I can see no foundation for that complaint, or that they have not been as ready to support all the rights of the Crown as any set of people who boast their zeal for prerogative the most. It is true, whenever I speak to any Whigs to influence them in this disputed point between the King and the Prince, I always try to alarm them by saying, if the Prince should carry this point, the King must afterward look upon this Parliament as his son's Parliament, not his; that he would consequently be obliged to dissolve it; and that nobody can imagine he would dissolve one Whig Parliament to choose another Whig Parliament, but would certainly employ the Tories. But I am far from thinking the King need be driven to this desperate remedy merely on losing this question, unless the same majority distressed him in others; and I call taking the Tories a desperate remedy, because I believe they will never be long found willing to support a Revolution

Government, nor will Your Majesty find any disputes among the majority, that may arise in a Tory Administration, to be about one branch of your family against another, but against your whole family in favour of another. If this was the case in the four last years of the Queen's reign, you will find it again so whenever the same party is in power; for as the majority of the Tories are certainly Jacobites, so when they act as a party they must act according to the principles and sentiments of the majority of that party, not of the few.'

While Lord Hervey was speaking (the Queen and he both standing at the window of her dressing-room), the Prince happened to walk undressed across the court. The Queen spied him, and said, reddening with rage: 'Look, there he goes—that wretch!—that villain!—I wish the ground would open this moment and sink the monster to the lowest hole in hell.' Lord Hervey was quite astonished to see the looks and hear the tone in which these words were uttered; which the Queen perceived and said: 'You stare at me; but I can assure you if my wishes and prayers had any effect, and that the maledictions of a mother signified anything, his days would not be very happy nor very many.'

The debate lasted till past eleven o'clock; and on the division, the question for an address (to the King to settle £100,000 a year on the Prince of Wales) was lost by a majority of thirty.

The King and Queen were extremely pleased with this victory and by so unexpected a majority. Most people thought it cost a great deal of money, but Sir Robert Walpole and the Queen both told me separately that it cost the King but £900—£500 to one man and £400 to another; and that even these two sums were only advanced to two men who were to have received them at the end of the Session had this question never been moved, and who only took this opportunity to solicit prompt payment.

When the King after this complained of the usage he met with from the Whigs in distressing his measures and maintaining his rascally puppy of a son (as he called the Prince) against him, Sir Robert said it was not altogether just to reproach any party with a distress brought upon him merely by his own family, and desired the King to reflect that £900 was all this great question had cost him; 'And to show you, Sir, how little this was a party or a ministry point, I am very sure if I had lost the question relating to the Prince, the very next moment a question would have been put upon me; and I am as sure I should, though I had lost the other, have carried that by 100. And what must have been the consequence? I must have quitted Your Majesty's service to show I was not betraying you, and giving you up to secure myself; for how can any minister serve a Prince and say he can carry his own points and not his master's?'

Both King and Queen were inclined at first to proceed to the last extremities against the Prince, and for turning him immediately out of St. James's. Sir Robert Walpole dissuaded them from taking this step; said it would put their son more out of their power, increase his party, give him the éclat of a separate Court, furnish many people with arguments to inveigh against their rigour and keep up the spirit of this dispute in the world, if not in their family, much longer than otherwise it would subsist; that the suffering their son to remain in the palace would have an air of lenity in the eyes of some, of contempt in the opinion of others; and that the pushing things to extremity after they had already carried their point, would put them in the situation which hitherto Their Majesties' friends had represented the Prince, and perhaps make the Parliament itself less willing to support them both when they were oppressing their son than it had been to maintain Their Majesties' cause when they were only defending themselves.

Sir Robert Walpole prevailed, and the Prince remained in St. James's. He came to the drawing-rooms as usual, led the Queen, dined with the King and Queen in public, and sometimes too came to the King's levée, but the King never seemed to see or know he was in the room, and the Queen, though she gave him her hand on all these occasions, never gave him one single word in public or private.

The next difficulty Sir Robert Walpole lay under was to bring the King to perform what he had promised in his Message, which was the settling a jointure on the Princess and the giving the £50,000 per annum to his son out of his own power to be resumed or stopped.

The King said in common sense or reason everybody, considering when this Message was sent and how it was worded, must look upon it as an offer made by him of accommodation with his son, and these points as articles of treaty on his part to prevent the Prince's bringing this affair to be discussed in Parliament; that since the Prince, notwithstanding, had proceeded, and, like a silly puppy and undutiful, insolent rascal, had brought the question into Parliament, this non-compliance on the part of the Prince with the offer made by His Majesty must be looked upon, the King said, as a release from obligation of performing the conditions on his part, and that he would leave things just where they were.

Sir Robert said that no such condition was actually expressed in the Message, nor had it been so opened or argued upon by those who had pleaded it in Parliament; nor would the Parliament, he feared, any more than the rest of the world, look upon the Message as anything more than a temporary trick to amuse, if the promises therein contained were not performed. And if this matter should another year be brought into Parliament, how would those who had now carried this point for His Majesty by a majority only of thirty be able to support it, divested of those arguments which (he must in justification of the Message say) he believed were the only arguments which could have given His Majesty the victory? He further added, that all that part of mankind who did not cry out against His Majesty receding from what he had promised must at least be silent, for that it was impossible to justify it; neither would His Majesty gain anything by receding, since the allowance to the Prince, whether secured or left at large, could never be stopped; and that a jointure on the Princess must be given, and the whole world would say ought to be given, let the Prince's behaviour be what it would.

The King said: 'I see my affairs, then, are upon that foot that I must yield in everything.' And Sir Robert was extremely alarmed and hurt at this answer; looking upon this victory over the King as the King did on his over his son, which was a victory that gave him little pleasure, and was more an indication of future mortification than a subject for present triumph.

Sir Robert Walpole's misfortune at this time was that he had not now the resource he used to have on all other occasions, which was making use of the alkali of the Queen's temper to sweeten the acid of the King's; for Her Majesty needed an alkali to take off the sharpness of her own as much as His Majesty; and Sir Robert found her not as usual an auxiliary on his side, but another opponent he had to conquer: and though he could make the conquest, he apprehended himself to be in the same sort of situation with Louis XII after the Battle of Ravenna, who said, when he was felicitated on his victory, that such another would ruin him.

Sir George Oxenden, a Lord of the Treasury, having voted for the Prince on this question, was turned out just before the Parliament rose. Nobody was sorry for him, for he was a very vicious, ungrateful, good-for-nothing fellow. He passed his whole life, in all manner of debauchery and with low company; he had, too, committed incest with his sister; that is he had had two children by his wife's sister, who was married to his most intimate friend Mr. Thompson, from whom, upon Sir George Oxenden's account, she was separated, and died in childbed not without Sir George's being suspected of having a greater share in her catastrophe than merely having got the child. Besides this, Sir George Oxenden had debauched the wife of the eldest son of his friend, benefactor, and patron, Sir Robert Walpole, for Sir Robert had always been partial to Sir George Oxenden, taken him from his first entrance into the world under his protection, and by his favour early and undeservedly raised him into this office in the Treasury. This intrigue with Lady Walpole, and her having but one son, which the world gave to Sir George Oxenden, is alluded to in these two lines in a copy of verses written by Lady Mary Wortley, wherein she supposes Sir Robert Walpole speaking of Sir George Oxenden:

> Triumph enough for that enchanting face,
> That my damnation must enrich his race.[1]

But supposing it were so, I do not imagine, since this boy would, as well as any other, transmit the name of Walpole to posterity, with the title Sir Robert had got for his son, that Sir Robert cared very much who had begot him; and I have the more reason for being of this opinion, as Sir Robert Walpole more than once, in speaking of this child to me, has, with all the sang-froid imaginable, called him that boy, got by nobody knows who, as if he had been

[1] These lines would make more (though still not much) sense if the pronouns were transposed.

speaking of a foundling. But had Sir Robert Walpole been more solicitous about the father of this boy he would not have been without comfort; for though the public, from the little propensity it has to err, had always rather give a child to any father than the man whose name it bears, and did pretty currently impute this to Sir George Oxenden, yet from the extreme aversion my Lady Walpole showed to this poor little animal from the very hour of its birth all judicious, candid, and unprejudiced commentators sagaciously and naturally concluded that she, at least, who must be the ablest judge, entertained no doubt of its being her husband's.[1]

As soon as the Parliament was up, the Court removed to Richmond; and though it was rumoured among people in the town, and suspected by some in the palace, that the King would go to Hanover this year, yet it was by those only who knew nothing of the present *carte du pays*, for Madame Walmoden seemed to those who knew the King best to be quite forgot. Nobody had named her these six months; not the King himself had this great while mentioned her to the Queen; and he seemed so thoroughly easy that those who observed His Majesty most narrowly imagined he thought as little as he spoke of her. The child she had had by him (as he thought at least) was dead, and the most incredulous now began to cease doubting of His Majesty's tasting all the pleasures with Lady Deloraine which she was capable of bestowing, not merely from her taking Lady Suffolk's place in the evening, in the country, next the King at the commerce-table among the maids of honour; but her walking tête-à-tête with him often at Richmond, and her own manner of talking, at this time, at last convinced everybody of what she had long taken infinite pains to prevent their being deceived in. She told Lady Sundon, with whom she was very little acquainted, that the King had been very importunate these two years and had often told her how unkind she was to refuse him; that it was mere crossness, for that he was sure her husband (Mr. Wyndham, who was Sub-Governor to the Duke) would not take it at all ill. Lady Sundon was so extremely surprised at this very

---

[1] This is clearly the origin of the much later story that Sir Robert Walpole's youngest son, Horace, was really the son of Lord Hervey's elder brother (see Lady Louisa Stuart's *Introductory Anecdotes* to the letters of her grandmother, Lady Mary Wortley Montagu).

communicative conversation of Lady Deloraine's, that she knew not what answer to make to her, and told me she muttered something, but could not really remember what. Lady Deloraine, speaking one day at Richmond to Lord Hervey of the King in a room full of company, said to him, in the midst of her conversation, in a very abrupt whisper: 'Do you know the King has been in love with me these two years?' To which Lord Hervey, a little embarrassed for fear of shocking her vanity by seeming to doubt it, or drawing on further marks of her confidence by giving seriously in to this, only answered with a smile: 'Who is not in love with you?' Sir Robert Walpole one day, whilst she was standing in the hall at Richmond with her little son of about a year old in her arms, said to her: 'That's a very pretty boy, Lady Deloraine; who got it?' To which her Ladyship, before half-a-dozen people, without taking the question at all ill, replied: 'Mr. Wyndham, upon honour'; and then added, laughing, 'but I will not promise whose the next shall be.' However, in private, when she spoke seriously to Sir Robert Walpole, she pretended not to have yet yielded and said she was not of an age to act like a vain or loving fool, but if she did consent that she would be well paid; adding, too, that nothing but interest should bribe her, for as to love, she had enough of that, as well as a younger man, at home, and that she thought old men and kings ought always to be made to pay well; which, considering whom she spoke of, as well as whom she spoke to, made this speech doubly well judged. To many people, from whom it used to come round in a whisper to half the inhabitants of the palace, she used to brag of this royal conquest, and say she thought England in general had great obligations to her, and particularly the Administration; for that it was owing to her, and her only, that the King had not gone abroad. Everybody knew, she said, that Sir Robert Walpole and the Queen had done all they could to hinder his journey to Hanover the year before to no purpose; and they would have attempted it again to no purpose this year had it not been for the King's attachment to her. In short, her daily and hourly conversation was all in the same strain; for which reason, I think, it would be great tautology in me to add to this account that her Ladyship was one of the vainest as well as one of the simplest women that ever lived. But to this wretched head there was certainly joined one of the prettiest faces that ever was formed, which, though she was now five-and-thirty, had a bloom upon it, too, that not one woman in ten thousand has at fifteen and what is more extraordinary a bloom which she herself never had till after she was twenty-five and married. She was of a middle stature, rather lean than fat, neither well-made, nor crooked, not genteel, and had something remarkably awkward about her arms which were long and bony, with a pair of ugly white hands at the end of them. Such was the lady who at present engrossed the dalliance of the King's looser hours, His Majesty having chosen not from any violence of passion, but as a decent, convenient, natural, and unexceptionable commerce, to make the governess of his two youngest daughters his whore, his two eldest daughters convenient,[1] and the guardian director of his son's youth and morals his cuckold.

The Queen affected not to be at all uneasy at this engagement, but she only affected it, for though she was glad to find His Majesty's attachment to Madame Walmoden weakened, she could not help repining at his being only gone another way abroad, and not come home, though nobody paid any court to Lady Deloraine, nor had this new mistress the appearance of any power. All people at a distance, and some who were nearer, imagined the Queen had put Lady Deloraine in His Majesty's way, on purpose to engage him at home, and to find him some employment, out of her own apartment, to keep him in England and from Madame Walmoden. Perhaps she might do so and, as it happens to many people, afterwards mourned the success of her own schemes; but I am inclined to think, what was yet more unreasonable for her to propose as it was so improbable to expect, that she hoped her coquet husband should talk, and laugh, and play at quadrille, with this pretty fool, and never go further.

The two eldest Princesses, in whose apartment in town the King played every night with Lady Deloraine, were very innocently accessory to this amour, and, as they were very different in the turn both of their tempers and understandings, behaved very differently on reflecting upon the situation they were in and the part they had acted. The Princess Emily, who cared for nobody nor anything, laughed, and the Princess Caroline, who cared both for her mother's

[1] *Sic.*

ease and her own character, sighed. To the Princess Caroline Lady Deloraine's behaviour was still more extraordinary and absurd than it had been to anybody else. Lady Deloraine had formerly been a great favourite of the Princess Royal's and was one of the legacies the Princess Royal had left to the Princess Caroline when she went to Holland, desiring her sister always to be kind to her for her sake. The Princess Caroline, always faithful and steady in her friendships, had, for the sake of this charge and this recommendation received from her sister, been most particularly kind and essentially serviceable, to Lady Deloraine, having by her interest with the Queen prevailed on Her Majesty to suffer Lady Deloraine to remain at Court after she had married Mr. Wyndham, though the Queen had always told her Ladyship, if she could not live a widow she should not live with her daughters. In short, the Princess Caroline having always shown so much favour to Lady Deloraine, that fool concluded she might as properly make her the *confidente* of her amour with the King as her marriage-affair with Mr. Wyndham, and used often, after setting forth the violence of the King's passion, and the urgency of his attacks, to ask the Princess Caroline's advice what she should do. To which the Princess Caroline, bursting almost with a smothered anger (for her fear of the King made her not dare to give a loose to it), used with the best appearance she could put on of sang-froid to say: 'Ah, my dear fly' (which was a nickname Lady Deloraine went by at Court), 'you must really know your own affairs better than me. You are a great deal older, as well as wiser, and therefore you must know the world much better. Besides, my dear fly, you have had two husbands, and I never had one, so you must know how to act the part of a wife better than I can tell you.' Lady Deloraine once desired the Princess Caroline to tell Mr. Wyndham the embarrassment she was in, pretending she was ashamed to do it herself, and in short put the Princess Caroline into so many difficulties, between the fear of her father, the love of her mother, and regard to herself, that she wanted all the good sense, temper and dexterity she was mistress of to extricate herself out of the perpetual disagreeable situations in which this idiot put her.

The King as usual talked to the Queen of his lying with Lady Deloraine, and the Queen to Lord Hervey and Sir Robert Walpole talked of it with little ceremony. Sir Robert Walpole said to Lord Hervey he was not sorry the King had got a new plaything but wished His Majesty had taken somebody that was less mischievous than that lying bitch. Lord Hervey said: 'I wonder, Sir, you give yourself any uneasiness about that. What matter how mischievous she is, or what lies she tells? If she got the ear of anybody that had power it might be of very bad consequence, but since 'tis only the King, I think it is of no great signification.' Sir Robert Walpole laughed extremely, and seemed almost as well pleased with this little stroke of satire upon His Majesty as he was with the flattery to himself that followed it, when Lord Hervey added that what Miss Skerret said of people was of importance to every man in England, but that for Lady Deloraine she might say her worst or do her best, he thought neither the one nor the other was anybody's business but her own and the King's. His Lordship liked this bon-mot so well, that he employed the former part of it, relating to the King's power, in a conversation on the subject with the Queen; and varied the flattery by saying if Her Majesty had taken Lady Deloraine as Dr. Lamb's successor, to pare her nails, to be sure the good courtiers would have taken alarm at anybody so mischievous being in the way of doing so much harm, but as she only went to bed to the King, lying *with* him or *to* him was much the same as her lying *to* or *with* Mr. Wyndham.

chapter seven

The Princess's Accouchement

1737

I AM NOW come to a very extraordinary occurrence in which I shall be very particular. It had been long talked of that the Prince intended the Princess should lie-in in London; and the King and Queen having resolved she should not, measures were concerting to prevent her doing so. It was at last resolved—that is, the King and Queen and Sir Robert Walpole had agreed—that the King should send a message to the Prince to tell His Royal Highness that he would have the Princess lie-in at Hampton Court. Lord Hervey told the Queen and Princess Caroline that, notwithstanding this message, he would answer for it the Princess would not lie-in where the King and Queen resided. The Queen asked him how he could imagine, as insolent as the Prince was, that he would venture to disobey the King's positive commands on this point. Lord Hervey said the Prince would pretend it was by chance; for as Dr. Hollings and Mrs. Cannons would be made to say that exercise was good for the Princess in her condition, she would be carried once or twice a week to Kew or London, and, whichever of these two places the Prince intended she should lie-in at, he would make her, when she was within a month of her time, affect to be taken ill; and as nobody could disprove her having the pains she would complain of, the King and Queen could not take it in prudence upon them to say she should be removed; and there, of course, Her Royal Highness would bring forth. 'Well, if it is to be so,' replied the Queen, 'I cannot help it; but at her labour I positively will be, let her lie-in where she will; for she cannot be brought to bed as quick as one can blow one's nose and I will be sure it is her child. For my part, I do not see she is big; you all say you see it, and therefore I suppose it is so, and that I am blind.'

The Queen was every day pressing Sir Robert to have this message sent to the Prince, saying: 'Sir Robert, we shall be catched; he will remove her before he receives any orders for her lying-in here, and will afterwards say that he talked so publicly of his intentions, he concluded if the King had not approved of them he should have heard something of it.' Sir Robert said, as the Princess did not reckon till the beginning of October, that it was full time enough; and in this manner, from day to day, this intended message was postponed, till it never went; for on Sunday, the 31st of July, the Princess was taken in the evening, after having dined in public that day with the King and Queen, so very ill, with all the symptoms of actual labour, that the Prince ordered a coach to be got ready that moment to carry her to London. Her pains come on so fast and so strong, that her water broke before they could get her out of the house. However, in this condition, M. Dunoyer, the dancing-master, lugging her downstairs and along the passages by one arm, and Mr. Bloodworth, one of the Prince's equerries, by the other, and the Prince in the rear, they, with much ado, got her into the coach; Lady Archibald Hamilton and Mr. Townshend remonstrating strongly against this imprudent step, and the Princess begging, for God's sake, the Prince would let her stay in quiet where she was, for that her pains were so great she could not set one foot before the other, and was upon the rack when they moved her. But the Prince, with an obstinacy equal to his folly, and a folly equal to his barbarity, insisted on her going, crying 'Courage! courage! ah, quelle sottise!" and telling her, with the encouragement of a toothdrawer, or the consolatory tenderness of an executioner, that it would be over in a minute. With these excitations, and in this manner, after enjoining all his servants not to say one word what was the matter, for fear the news of the Princess's circumstances should get to the other side of the house and their going should be prevented, he got her into the coach. There were in the coach, besides him and her, Lady Archibald Hamilton, and Mrs. Clavering and Mrs. Paine, two of the Princess's dressers; Vreid, his *valet de chambre*, who was a surgeon and man-midwife, was upon the coach-box; Mr. Bloodworth, and two or three more, behind the coach; and thus loaded he ordered the coachman to drive full gallop to London. About ten this cargo arrived in town.

Notwithstanding all the handkerchiefs that had been thrust one after another up Her Royal Highness's petticoats in the coach, her clothes were in such a condition with the filthy inundations which attend these circumstances that when the coach stopped at St. James's the Prince ordered all the lights to be put out that people might not have the nasty ocular evidence which would otherwise have been exhibited to them of his folly and her distress. When they came to St. James's, there was no one thing prepared for her reception. The midwife came in a few minutes; napkins, warming-pan, and all other necessary implements for this operation, were sought by different emissaries in different houses in the neighbour-hood; and no sheets being to be come at, Her Royal Highness was put to bed between two table-cloths. At a quarter before eleven she was delivered of a little rat of a girl, about the bigness of a good large toothpick case, none of the Lords of the Council being present but my Lord President Wilmington, and my Lord Godolphin, Privy Seal. To the first of these the Prince, at leaving Hampton Court, had despatched a messenger to bring him from his villa at Chiswick; and the last, living just by St. James's, was sent for as soon as the Prince arrived in town. He sent also to the Lord Chancellor and the Archbishop; but the one was gone into the country, and the other came a quarter of an hour after the child was born.

In the meantime, this evening, at Hampton Court, the King played at commerce below stairs, the Queen above at quadrille, the Princess Emily at her commerce-table, and the Princess Caroline and Lord Hervey at cribbage, just as usual, and separated all at ten of the clock; and, what is incredible to relate, went to bed all at eleven, without hearing one single syllable of the Princess's being ill, or even of her not being in the house. At half an hour after one, which was above two hours after the Princess had been brought to bed, a courier arrived with the first news of her being in labour. When Mrs. Titchburne, the Woman of the Bedchamber, came to wake the King and Queen, the Queen as soon as she came into the room asked what was the matter that occasioned their being waked up at so unusual an hour; and, as the most natural question, in-quired if the house was on fire. When Mrs. Titchburne said the Prince had sent to let Their Majesties know the Princess was in labour the Queen immediately cried: 'My God, my nightgown! I'll go to her this moment.' 'Your nightgown, Madam,' replied Mrs. Titchburne, 'and your coaches too; the Princess is at St. James's.' 'Are you mad,' interrupted the Queen, 'or are you asleep, my good Titchburne? You dream.' When Mrs. Titchburne insisted on its being certainly true, the King flew into a violent passion, and, in German (as the Queen told me afterward), began to scold her, saying: 'You see, now, with all your wisdom, how they have out-witted you. This is all your fault. There is a false child will be put upon you, and how will you answer it to all your children? This has been fine care and fine management for your son William; he is mightily obliged to you; and for Ann, I hope she will come over and scold you herself; I am sure you deserve anything she can say to you.' The Queen said little, but got up, dressed as fast as she could, ordered her coaches, and sent to the Duke of Grafton and Lord Hervey to go with her; and by half an hour after two Her Majesty set out from Hampton Court with the two eldest Princesses, two of their ladies, the Duke of Grafton, Lord Hervey, and Lord Essex (the King's Lord of the Bedchamber in waiting), who went to be despatched back again by the Queen, as soon as she got there, to acquaint the King how matters went. By four o'clock they all got to St. James's. When they arrived they asked how the Princess did, and, being told very well, concluded either that everything had not been ready for a trick, or that the Princess's pains were gone off, and that they had taken their journey for nothing. Lord Hervey told the Queen, as she was going upstairs, that he would order a fire and chocolate for her in his own apartment, concluding she would not stay long with her son. 'To be sure,' replied the Queen, 'I shall not stay long; I shall be mightily obliged to you'; then winked, and said in a lower voice, 'nor you need not fear my tasting anything in this side of the house.'

When they came upstairs the Prince, in his nightgown and night-cap, met the Queen in the Princess's ante-chamber, kissed her hand and her cheek according to the filial fashions of Germany, and there told her the news of the Princess's being brought to bed of a daughter, as well as who was present when she was delivered, and at what hour. The Queen expressed some little surprise that no messenger should have reached Hampton Court with the news of the Princess's being brought to bed before Her Majesty came from thence, when there had been three hours between the one and the other; upon which the Prince assured Her Majesty the messenger had been despatched as soon as ever he could get his letters to her and the King ready, and, as he had written but three lines, they had been finished in three minutes. The Queen knew this must be a lie, but did not *éclaircir* upon it, having determined (as she said afterward at Lord Hervey's lodgings) not to dispute or contradict anything His Royal Highness should advance, let it be ever so extravagantly absurd, or ever so glaringly false. I must observe, too, that these were the first words Her Majesty and His Royal Highness had exchanged since the day his affair had been moved in Parliament. The Queen went into the Princess's bedchamber, wished her joy, said she was glad she had escaped so well; and added: 'Apparemment, Madame, vous avez horriblement souffert.' 'Point du tout,' replied the Princess, 'ce n'est rien.' Then Lady Archibald Hamilton brought in the child, which had yet no clothes but a red mantle and some napkins, nor any nurse. The Queen kissed the child, and said: 'Le bon Dieu vous bénisse, pauvre petite créature! Vous voilà arrivée dans un désagréable monde.'

The Prince then began to tell the whole story of the labour and the journey; and not only owned that on the Monday and Friday before he had carried the Princess to London, upon thinking, from some slight pains she then complained of, that her labour was coming on, but also wisely acquainted the Queen that the water was broke before the Princess left Hampton Court, that her pains in the coach were so strong he thought he should have been obliged to carry her into some house upon the road to be brought to bed, and that, with holding her and her pillows in the coach, he had got such pains in his own back he could hardly stir. He added many more particulars, on which the Queen made no comments, never asking why he did anything he had done, or left undone anything he had not done; and only said, at the end of His Royal Highness's every way absurd narrative, it was a miracle that the Princess and the child had not been both killed. Her Majesty then added: 'At the indiscretion of young fools, who knew nothing of the dangers to which this poor child and its mother were exposed, I am less surprised; but for you, my Lady Archibald, who have had ten children, that with your experience, and at your age, you should suffer these people to act such a madness, I am astonished; and wonder how you could, for your own sake as well as theirs, venture to be concerned in such an expedition.' To this Lady Archibald made no other answer than turning to the Prince, and saying aloud to him: 'You see, Sir'; which was so prudent and so judicious an answer, as it intimated everything that could be urged in her justification, without directly giving him up, that I cannot help thinking chance put it into her mouth. The Prince, immediately upon this, began to talk to the Queen in German; which she afterwards said was nothing more than to repeat again all the nasty particulars of what had passed in the coach more in detail. The Duke of Grafton, Lord Essex, and Lord Hervey, were called into the Princess's bedchamber to see the child; and the door, both before and after, being open, they could hear everything that passed there. The Queen stayed not long in the Princess's apartment, saying rest was the best thing for the Princess in her present circumstances; and, just before Her Majesty went away, she went up to the bedside, embraced the Princess, and said to her: 'My good Princess, is there anything you want, anything you wish, or anything you would have me do? Here I am; you have but to speak and ask; and whatever is in my power that you would have me do, I promise you I will do it.' The Princess thanked Her Majesty, said she had nothing to trouble Her Majesty with, thanked her for the honour she had done her, and hoped neither she nor the Princesses would be the worse for the trouble they had been so kind to give themselves. All this passed in German, but the Queen and the Princess Caroline told it me just in the words I have related it.

The Prince waited on the Queen downstairs, and said he hoped Her Majesty and the King would do him the honour to christen his daughter; and the Queen promised him to take care of that affair. He then said he intended to come to Hampton Court that day, to ask this honour of the King and her in form. To which the Queen replied: 'I fancy you had better not come to-day; to be sure the King is not well pleased with all this bustle you have made; and should you attempt coming to-day, nobody can answer what your reception may be.' The Prince then named Thursday, and the Queen said Tuesday or Wednesday she thought would be better. The Prince being in his undress, the Queen insisted on his not coming out of his house, advised him to go to bed, and walked, herself, across the courts to Lord Hervey's lodgings. As soon as she got thither she wrote a short letter to the King, and despatched Lord Essex with it back to Hampton Court. She then said to the Duke of Grafton and Lord Hervey (nobody being present but the two Princesses): 'Well, upon my honour, I no more doubt this poor little bit of a thing is the Princess's child, than I doubt of either of these two being mine, though, I owe to you, I had my doubts upon the road that there would be some juggle; and if, instead of this poor, little, ugly she-mouse, there had been a brave, large, fat, jolly boy, I should not have been cured of my suspicions; nay, I believe they would have been so much increased, or, rather, that I should have been so confirmed in that opinion, that I should have gone about his house like a madwoman, played the devil, and insisted on knowing what chairman's brat he had bought.' Lord Hervey said he really did believe, too, from what he had seen, that it was the Princess's child; though not in the least because it was a girl; for, as a girl would do just as well for the Prince's purpose as a boy, and that it would give less suspicion, so anybody who had advised him wisely would have advised him to take a spurious girl rather than a spurious boy. 'But, altogether,' said the Queen, 'was there ever such a monstrous conduct? such a fool, and such an insolent, impertinent fool? and such an impudence, to receive us all with such an ease, as if nothing had happened, and that we were the best friends in the world?' The whole company were very free in their comments on His Royal Highness's behaviour throughout this whole affair; all abused him very freely, and said, very truly, that they believed, take all its absurdities together, nothing like it ever had happened before, or ever would happen again; since His Royal Highness had at once contrived to be guilty of the greatest piece of inhumanity, as a husband and a father, with regard to his wife and his child, the greatest impertinence and insolence, as a son and a subject, to his father and his mother, his King and his Queen, and the most egregious folly, as a Prince of Wales and heir to the Crown, by doing all he could contrive to make the birth of that child suspected, which he proposed should give him such additional weight in the kingdom, and make him of so much more importance than he had hitherto found himself. They all agreed that he had done much more towards making the world believe this was a spurious child than Queen Mary had done at the Pretender's birth; and, consequently, wisely contrived, if ever this Crown came to be fought for, to have the dispute be whether the people would have the Whig bastard or the Tory bastard.

After the Queen had passed about an hour at Lord Hervey's lodgings in drinking chocolate and expatiating on these particulars which I have related, Sir Robert Walpole arrived, who had been sent for from Richmond Park; but a little before he came, I must not forget to relate that, the Duke of Grafton and the Princess Emily being gone into the next room to drink some tea with the Princess's two Ladies of the Bedchamber, the Queen said to Lord Hervey (the Princess Caroline only being present): 'Be sure you do not ever say you foretold this would happen. I foresaw it too, and told it to Sir Robert Walpole, who was certainly in the wrong to delay sending the message to order the Princess to lie-in at Hampton Court, since, if that message had gone, they would have been still more in the wrong, and we had had still more reason to resent what they have done; and no longer ago than when he went away from Hampton Court last Friday, I said: "Pray, Sir Robert, think of this message; indeed we shall be catched; you do not know my filthy beast of a son so well as I do." And he only answered: "Pray stay a little; indeed, Madam, 'tis time enough." And now you see—but, in short, it is over—and Sir Robert Walpole will take it ill if you ever talk of this omission; so be sure you never name it.' As soon as Sir Robert came into the room, the Queen laughed, and only said, 'Here we are, you see; am I in the right? what do you say now?' Sir Robert smiled too, but looked vexed and out of countenance, and said: 'When anything very improbable happens, Madam, I do not think it is a great disgrace for anybody not to have foreseen it would happen.' He then told the Queen that Lord Harrington, having lain this night at Petersham, was sent for at the same time that he had been, and that they came to town together. The Queen asked him what they had said to all this as they came along: to which Sir Robert answered, that Harrington, as usual, had lent his ear. 'But, to speak in the sportsman's style,' said he, 'Madam, he has not given tongue often.' He then told Her Majesty that the Prince (informed as he supposed by some of his servants that Lord Harrington and he were there) had ordered them to be called up; that the Prince was in bed, and had desired them to sit down by his bedside, which they had declined, not caring to enter at present into conversation with him; but that notwithstanding this endeavour to shorten the interview, the Prince had told them all the same particulars (except that of the breaking of the water) which he had before told the Queen—that is, of all that passed in the coach, who had been present at the labour, of the Princess having been ill Monday and Friday, and his having brought her to London both these days, thinking her complaints were the symptoms of approaching labour. 'Take it altogether,' said the Queen, 'do you think there ever was so insolent as well as silly a behaviour? Really they must be made to feel a little, for one is quite weary of being so very prudent and so very tame.' 'It is true,' replied Sir Robert; 'it is really, Madam, too much; it is intolerable. Here was the Princess, in the first place, within a month of her time before her being with child (was) notified to Your Majesty[1]; and then on the 29th, without any notification either of her departure or of her being in labour, she is hurried away from under the roof where Your Majesty and the King reside, and brought to bed in an hour after at St. James's; whilst the first news you have of her being gone, or her being in labour, comes two hours at least after the time you ought to have had the news of her being brought to bed.' 'My God!' interrupted the Queen, 'there is really no human patience can bear such treatment; nor indeed ought one to bear it; for they will pull one by the nose in a little time, if some stop is not put to their impertinence. Besides, one is really ashamed for the figure one makes in foreign Courts, when such a story is told of the affronts one receives in one's own family. What must other Princes imagine of one? I swear I blush when I think of the post going out, and carrying the account of such a transaction into other countries.' 'It is all very true, Madam,' said Sir Robert Walpole; 'but then consider a little whether you would just take this opportunity of quarrelling openly with the Prince, and turning him out of your house, when an heir to the Crown is born. People already talk enough of the partiality the King and Your Majesty have for the Duke; and should all your anger break out at this time, they

[1] This had been notified by the Prince on 5th July.

will be apt to say that your anger is principally occasioned by the Prince's having a child to disinherit your favourite.' 'My God!' interrupted again the Queen, 'if one is always to bear affronts because something false may be said of one for resenting them, there are none one must ever resent.' 'Nay,' replied Sir Robert, 'I give no opinion yet, Madam; I only speak my present thoughts just as they occur, and quite unweighed.' Lord Hervey said there was nothing contradictory in what Sir Robert Walpole had said to what the Queen proposed; since paying all the honours to the child that were possible to be shown to it, at the same time that a resentment was shown to the Prince's conduct, would take off Sir Robert Walpole's objection and would demonstrate that the King and Queen did not confound the innocent with the guilty, nor punish the sins of the father upon the child, but felt as they ought to do towards both. Sir Robert again repeated that he as yet gave no opinion, and that it was a matter that required being very maturely considered. 'However,' said the Queen, 'I am glad we came; for though one does not care a farthing for them, the giving oneself all this trouble is *une bonne grimace pour le publique*; and the more impertinences they do, and the more civilities we show, the more we shall be thought in the right, and they in the wrong, when we bring it to an open quarrel.' 'That is so true,' said Lord Hervey, 'that upon the whole I think their behaviour is the luckiest affront any Court ever received, since everybody must condemn their behaviour in this particular, which will consequently put them, who were on the attack in the quarrel, now upon the defensive; and if they do bring their money question next year into Parliament, his asking for an augmentation of a father he has not only offended but affronted will not be thought quite so reasonable a request as when he could pretend to have never failed in his duty.'

The Queen then sent for Lord Harrington, saying he would take it ill if she did not see him; and when he came, in the midst of all this anger and bustle, she began to joke with him upon his gallantry, and said she believed it was the first time he had ever been sent for at midnight to a young lady in the Princess's circumstances. She stayed not long in Lord Hervey's lodgings after Lord Harrington came, and by eight o'clock got back again to Hampton Court. Sir Robert Walpole, before he followed the Queen, was to go to Lord Godolphin to ask an account from him of what had passed whilst he was present at the Princess's delivery. Just as they were all separating, Lord Hervey sent Mr. Harry Fox to desire Sir Robert Walpole, the first thing he did when he came to Hampton Court might be to send for him, that he might speak to him before he saw the King. Mr. Harry Fox Lord Hervey had sent for the moment he came to town, thinking there would be some juggle (as the Queen apprehended) about a false child, and that he should want some sensible, clever body he could trust to employ in making discoveries.

Lord Godolphin told Sir Robert Walpole that Lord Wilmington and he had been in the Princess's bedchamber a quarter of an hour at least before the child was born; that they were on the same side of the bed with the midwife, and very near her, and the Prince close to the bed on the other side; that the Princess, in her manner of complaining, marking one pain she had much stronger than any of the former, the Prince said: 'Is the child born?' to which the midwife replied: 'Don't you hear it cry?' and then immediately brought it from between the sheets and gave it into my Lord President's hands. The Prince then asked if it was a boy or a girl; and the midwife said the Princess, in her present circumstances, must not be surprised with either the joy or the mortification of knowing which it was.

As soon as Sir Robert Walpole had learnt these particulars from Lord Godolphin, he set out for Hampton Court, and, as soon as he arrived there, sent for Lord Hervey. In this conference Lord Hervey reminded Sir Robert how often he had told him that within these few months, on many occasions, both the King and the Queen had seemed to relax a little in the degree of favour they had formerly shown him; that it had always been on their son's chapter they had done so, and from his appearing either too unwilling to gratify their resentment against him, or too forward in proposing palliatives to an evil to which they were so strongly inclined to apply more violent medicines. 'And though,' continued Lord Hervey, 'you can divert them from pursuing the measures they are inclined to, you cannot cure them of their desire to pursue them, nor make them relish those which you have interest enough to persuade them to follow in their stead.' 'My Lord,' replied Sir

Robert, 'I have seen and felt the truth of what you say; and the King is never out of humour with me on these occasions that he does not recur to the message sent to the Prince last winter, and tell me 'tis I who have made his son independent; 'tis I have put it in the Prince's power to dare to use him as he does, and put it out of his power to punish him for it. I then tell him: "Sir, the giving the £50,000 at that time and in that manner saved your £100,000." But, my Lord, I know the meaning of all this; it is the single thing I ever did against the Queen's will and without her consent, and that is the reason this sin against the Holy Ghost is not forgiven. She begged, that morning the message was sent, I would defer the measure at least till next day. I said: "Madam, to-morrow it will be too late: there is no time to deliberate; we must act." She then said: "It is such a mean condescension in the King to follow this advice that I can never consent to it." I then told her: "Madam, 'tis all you have for it"; and went out of her room directly to the King's closet; where, after reasoning, and hearing him bluster and swagger, I was forced to say, when he had done nothing but oppose me: "Sir, I ask your pardon; I must not give you time to retract your consent; the Lords of the Council are in the next room, and I will give them your orders this minute, for time presses—you have none to lose." And in this manner, my Lord, supposing him to have given consent when he had given me nothing but contradiction, I got the thing done.'

I must here remark that Sir Robert Walpole, as often as he had talked of this transaction of the message to Lord Hervey, had never related it in this manner before. He had always spoke of the Queen's consent as extorted, but not denied; and I believe he only put it in this light now that he might make people think it was her pride, not her judgment, that made her still condemn a measure he could not retract and would not give up.

Lord Hervey said: 'Sir, you will certainly ruin your interest here if you go on in combating the King and Queen's inclinations in this quarrel. Those who have a mind to hurt you will take such advantage of their passions and what they will call your phlegm, that they will either say your conduct proceeds from management of the Prince, or that old Ministers dare venture on no vigorous measures, that new ones can do anything they please at setting out,

and that, if the King and Queen will give them power, they will
lay their son in tears and penitence at Their Majesties' feet.' 'What
then,' interrupted Sir Robert Walpole, 'would you have me say?
Would you have me advise a separation, and the turning the Prince
out of St. James's?' 'No,' replied Lord Hervey; 'if you give it as
your judgment and your advice, you charge yourself with the consequences, and lose the merit of the compliance. I would therefore in
your place tell them that though in public matters and parliamentary affairs it is your business to advise, yet in their family
affairs it is your duty to obey; and that, as you are always ready to
give counsel in the one, you are equally ready to receive orders in
the other. In any point where abilities, penetration, or judgment
are requisite, I am sure, Sir, I am unable to offer anything that can
be of use to you; but as the present point, with regard to you, turns
chiefly on the temper of the King and Queen, I see so much of
them, and hear so much of their sentiments in this question (for
you know they talk or think of nothing else), that it is impossible,
unless I was deaf and blind, but that I must be able to guess a little
how they stand affected, more perhaps even than they suffer to
appear to you, and more even perhaps than they would have appear
to me.'

'You are so much in the right,' said Sir Robert Walpole, 'that
I know, even after the question last year was carried against the
Prince, upon my desiring them to be satisfied with victory, and not
to push victory to oppression, upon my advising the execution of
the articles of the message, and saying that execution was unavoidable, I know the King and Queen deliberated whether they should
not at once change the Ministry, disavow me in that step, and make
the supporting them in a non-performance of those articles the first
condition with my successors. But here, my Lord, lies the disagreeable difficulty of my situation: when I tell them if they will arm
me with power I will conquer and humble their son, I receive such
a flow of grace and good words, such a flood of promises and
favour, that I could dictate nothing stronger; yet, whenever I propose anything particular, I am answered by the King: "I will not
do that." How many people there are I could bind to me by getting
things done in the army you may imagine, and that I can never get
any one thing done in it you perhaps will not believe; but it is as

true as that there is an army, that I never ask for the smallest commission by which a Member of Parliament may be immediately or collaterally obliged, that the King's answer is not "I won't do that; you want always to have me disoblige all my old soldiers; you understand nothing of troops; I will order my army as I think fit; for your scoundrels of the House of Commons you may do as you please; you know I never interfere, nor pretend to know anything of them, but this province I will keep to myself." Now, if I, my Lord, should advise, or, without advising only obey orders in separating the Courts, there is all the Prince's family, be they more or less, thrown in every question into the Opposition, and how is the loss of those votes to be replaced?' Lord Hervey replied: 'Sir, I do not pretend to counsel or to judge; I only state the facts I know, and represent some circumstances which may escape you, and leave you afterward, as the fittest and ablest judge I know, to weigh those particulars with others, and make your own determination. I can see your difficulties, but I am sure I am incapable of helping you in the least to extricate yourself out of them.' 'In short, my Lord,' interrupted Sir Robert, 'the King, on one hand, is so peremptory in what he will have done, and so costive in furnishing the means to do it, expects so much and furnishes so little, and the Queen, on the other, is so suspicious of one's sincerity, and gives one so much reason to doubt of hers, fancies often she sees so much more than there is to see, and gives me often occasion to see so much more than I dare own I see, that I am quite weary of my situation, and have been much nearer than you think of throwing it all up and going to end my days at Houghton in quiet.' Lord Hervey said: 'To be sure, Sir, there are things in your situation you would be glad to alter, but what Minister has not such things? And sure, since it is impossible not to meet with some difficulties, you ought to reflect with pleasure and satisfaction that your good fortune has exposed you to as few as any Minister ever had, and your good sense enabled you to get better through them. Besides, Sir, you have so many people dependent upon you that your good-nature to them will hinder you from leaving them to shift for themselves.' 'I know,' replied Sir Robert, 'that chance and concurring circumstances have put me in such a situation that (as much vanity as there may seem in saying it) I am certainly at present in a situation that makes me of consequence to more people than any man before me ever was, or perhaps than any man may ever be again; but yet, my Lord, to anybody at my age, who has been plagued with the thorns and glutted with the fruits of power as long as I have been, ease and safety are considerations that will, one time or other, outweigh all others.'

The ninth day after the Princess was brought to bed the Queen with her two eldest daughters went again from Hampton Court to see the Princess. The Prince, when they came to St. James's, went no further than the door of his wife's bedchamber to meet Her Majesty, and the whole time she stayed (which was about an hour), spoke not one single word either to her or his sisters, but was industriously civil and affectedly gay with all those of their suite who were present. Lady Archibald Hamilton brought in the child, and showing the Queen its hands, asked Her Majesty if she did not think the Princess had the prettiest little hand she had ever seen, and exactly like the Prince's. The Queen asked once or twice for her coaches, which were gone to have the horses changed, and said she feared she was troublesome, fears which nobody in the room endeavoured to remove, by saying one word in answer; and when she went away, the Prince, who could not avoid leading her to her coach, though he had not spoken one word to her, yet at the coach door, to make the mob believe he was never wanting in any respect, he kneeled down in the dirty street, and kissed her hand. As soon as this operation was over, he put Her Majesty into the coach, and then returned to the steps of his own door, leaving his sisters to get through the dirt and the mob, by themselves, as they could; nor did there come to the Queen any message either from the Prince or Princess, to thank her afterwards for the trouble she had taken, or for the honour she had done them in this visit.

It is easy to imagine, after such a reception, that the Queen made no more of these trips to St. James's, and the King told her she was well enough served for thrusting her nose where it had been shit upon already. This extraordinary expression of His Majesty's (though none of the cleanest) I could not help relating just in the words the Queen reported it to me.

chapter eight

The Separation of the Courts

1737

ON THE 29th of August the christening was performed. The Duke of Grafton stood for the King, Lady Burlington for the Queen, and Lady Torrington, one of the Princess's ladies, for the Duchess-Dowager of Saxe-Gotha. The young Princess was christened Augusta; and the Prince, as soon as the christening was over, sent his treasurer, Mr. Herbert, to tell everybody belonging to his family then at Court that the Prince would not have his daughter called Princess Augusta, but according to the old English fashion, the Lady Augusta, and that she should be called Her Royal Highness, though his sisters had not been so when his father was Prince of Wales. This Mr. Herbert was a commoner of a great estate, who had voted for the Prince last year in the question of the £100,000; and to reward that service, Mr. Hedges dying just at the rising of the Parliament, the Prince nominated, the day Hedges died, Mr. Herbert to succeed him; though Mr. Herbert had not voted against the Court in any one vote but that of the £100,000, and declared he never would.

The day after the christening, the Prince sent Lord North with two letters to Hampton Court to the King and Queen, to thank them for the honour they had done his daughter.

The Queen sent these letters by Lord Hervey to Sir Robert Walpole, and bid Lord Hervey tell Sir Robert not to fail to let her see him before he saw the King. What Her Majesty wanted with Sir Robert was, to agree with him on the substance of a message to be sent to the Prince to turn him out of St. James's, before Sir Robert spoke to the King upon it. When Sir Robert Walpole came back from this interview with the Queen, having been also afterward with the King, he told Lord Hervey that the resolution was to leave the child with the Princess, and not to take it (as the late King had taken this King's children, upon the quarrel in the last reign) lest any accident might happen to this royal little animal, and the world in that case accuse the King and Queen of having murdered it for the sake of the Duke. Besides that the Queen, to give her her due, though she always spoke of the Princess as a driveller, always spoke of her, too, as one whom she would not displease, one who had never offended her, or done anything wrong; and, consequently, one who did not deserve such harsh usage as the being separated from her only child.

Sir Robert Walpole told Lord Hervey he liked, on every occasion, to hear other people's opinions whilst he was forming his own, and, therefore, desired him to put down in writing what, if he were to advise the King on this occasion, he would have him say. And though the other messages[1] had been all drawn in the third person, in the nature of memorandums only for the messenger, yet, as this was to go in the King's own name, and to be signed by him, Sir Robert Walpole bid Lord Hervey draw it up in the form of a letter, which Lord Hervey did in the following words; not a little pleased with a commission that put it in his power to make use of the King's character and authority to express and gratify his resentment against the Prince:

> It is in vain for you to hope I can be so far deceived by your empty professions, wholly inconsistent with all your actions, as to think they in any manner palliate or excuse a series of the most insolent and premeditated indignities offered to me and the Queen, your mother.
>
> You never gave the least notice to me or the Queen of the Princess's being breeding or with child till about three weeks before the time when you yourself have owned you expected her to be brought to bed, and removed her from the place of my residence for that purpose. You twice in one week carried her away from Hampton Court with an avowed design of having her lie-in in town without consulting me or the Queen, or so much as communicating your intentions to either of us. At your return you industriously concealed everything relating to this important affair from our knowledge; and, last of all, you clandestinely hurried the Princess to St. James's in circumstances not fit to be named, and less fit for such an expedition.
>
> This extravagant and undutiful behaviour in a matter of such great consequence as the birth of an heir to my Crown, to the manifest

[1] Not printed in this edition.

peril of the Princess and her child (whilst you pretend your regard for her was your motive), inconsistent with the natural right of all parents, and in violation of your double duty to me as your father and as your King, is what cannot be excused by any false plea, so repugnant to the whole tenor of your conduct, of the innocence of your intentions, or atoned for by specious pretences or plausible expressions.

Your behaviour for a long time has been so void of duty and regard to me, even before this last open proof you have given to all the world of your contempt for me and my authority, that I have long been justly offended at it; nor will I suffer any part of any of my palaces to be longer the resort and refuge of all those whom discontent, disappointment, or disaffection have made the avowed opposers of all my measures; who espouse you only to distress me, and who call you the head, whilst they make you the instrument of a faction that acts with no other view than to weaken my authority in every particular, and can have no other end in their success but weakening the common interest of my whole family.

My pleasure, therefore, is that you and all your family remove from St. James's as soon as ever the safety and convenience of the Princess will permit.

I will leave the care of my grand-daughter to the Princess till the time comes when I shall think it proper to give directions for her education.

To this I will receive no reply. When you shall, by a consistency in your words and actions, show you repent of your past conduct and are resolved to return to your duty, paternal affection may then, and not till then, induce me to forgive what paternal justice now obliges me to resent.

Sir Robert Walpole, after two days' consideration, made several alterations in this paper, and then showed it again to Lord Hervey, desiring him, at the same time, not to own to anybody, not even the Queen, that he had seen it. 'I need not tell you,' said he, 'that she is main good' (that was his expression) 'at pumping; but be sure you do not let her get it out of you. I shall not show it to her herself till the Duke of Newcastle and my Lord Chancellor have seen it. I shall only talk with her again upon the matter which it is to contain; for should I show her the paper itself, the Chancellor and his Grace would complain they were tied up from giving any opinion on alterations, because it would be combating hers; and, therefore, I will be able to say to them it is open to their free correction.'

On the other hand, the Queen, telling Lord Hervey of this paper, gave him the same injunctions Sir Robert had done, not to own to anybody, not even to Sir Robert, that she had spoke to him about it; and by her, too, Lord Hervey found, notwithstanding what Sir Robert had said of concerting only the substance with her, that she had seen it in writing. These sort of transactions often put Lord Hervey in a very disagreeable, as well as delicate, situation, from his hearing so many things from Sir Robert and the Queen, some of which he might confer upon in common with them, others which he might not; some that had particular circumstances only which he was to seem ignorant of, others which he was often at a loss to remember who had told him; but the most general rule he had to go by was never to begin any of these subjects before the King, and always, when they were begun, to seem as if it was the first time he had heard of them.

As the Queen's confidence in Lord Hervey every day increased, Sir Robert Walpole's jealousy of him increased too, not from his being in the rank of a rival in his power, but from a weakness in this great man's composition, which made him grudge this show of favour even where, I believe, he had not the least suspicion, or where, I am very sure, at least, he had no reason given him to justify suspicion, that this favour would ever be employed to his disservice. For Lord Hervey always looked upon Sir Robert as his benefactor, who had placed him in that situation; as an able master, from whom he had learned all he knew in the beginning of the secrets of the Court, and most of what he knew of the policy requisite for his conduct there; and was sensible it was to his favour, protection, and commendations, that he owed originally his having any credit there. But that credit was now higher than Sir Robert wished it; and though Lord Hervey did not know that he endeavoured to destroy or weaken it, yet he plainly perceived, after the Queen had accidentally told Sir Robert Walpole of her having talked of things to Lord Hervey which Sir Robert had not communicated to him, or sent messages by him to Sir Robert, that Sir Robert did not like it, which made Lord Hervey always cautious of bragging of such favours. But he could not venture to desire the Queen to be more cautious in concealing them; and as Sir Robert knew he did not want any assistance from Lord Hervey, he was uneasy at his having any power to hurt him, though he was not apprehensive of its being so employed.

When the Lord Chancellor and the Duke of Newcastle had perused and cooked this message, it was shown to the King; and the Cabinet Council, the day before it was to be sent, was summoned to make it their act. At this meeting of the Cabinet Council Sir Robert Walpole, who did this sort of work with more strength and perspicuity than any man I ever knew, ran through every step of the Prince's conduct this summer, by way of preface to reading the paper which he said he had drawn up in pursuance of the King's positive commands, who was determined to suffer the Prince no longer to reside in any of his palaces. There were many of the Cabinet, as the Duke of Newcastle, the Duke of Richmond, and Lord Pembroke, who spoke as if they wished this measure had not been insisted on by the King, and that some means could be found out to make up the quarrel; and all were for softening as much as possible, if it was absolutely necessary these orders should go, the terms in which they were sent.

Sir Robert Walpole said the Cabinet Council being summoned by the King, not to give advice whether these orders should be sent or not, but to agree upon the form, it was unnecessary to deliberate on objections to their being sent; and though in this situation he might be very naturally excused giving his opinion on the expediency and propriety of sending such orders, yet he was very free to declare, if his advice was asked even on that point, he should be for sending them. 'I wish,' continued he, 'as zealously as any of your Lordships can do for a reconciliation; but I think (as paradoxical as it may sound) this thorough breach the likeliest way to attain that end. Should the King seem to receive these letters from the Prince as an atonement for the fault he has committed and send to-morrow to St. James's to say he will see him, what advantage would the King reap from it? Or would anybody call this a reconciliation? Would the Prince recede for this reason from pushing his money dispute in Parliament? Or would he be less afraid after this of offending his father or opposing his measures, when he saw his father so afraid of coming to an open rupture that nobody dare advise His Majesty not to take words as a compensation for actions, or not to show himself as ready on every offence to compound as his son to irritate, and as desirous to retreat as the Prince to attack? The King, my Lords, if he is in the right, must stand the battle and must conquer, and those who advise him to decline it must advise him to show he thinks himself in the wrong, or the weakest. When he has conquered he may forgive, but forgiving before he has conquered, is being conquered and patching up a peace neither honourable in present nor possible to be lasting.'

Though Sir Robert Walpole told Lord Hervey as soon as he came from council, what he had said there, he refused to tell him who had made it necessary to say so much; and told Lord Hervey, as the King and Queen would never forgive those people if they knew them, he intended not to report to them what he had reported to him, for fear they should ask the same question Lord Hervey had done, 'who had made it necessary?'—and would therefore sink the opposition to this measure and the defence, losing the merit of the last himself, to save others from the demerit of the first. But he bragged of a lenity he did not practise, for he told it all to the Queen and the Queen to Lord Hervey.

The morning before the message went, the Queen at breakfast talking the whole over, said several times, lifting up her eyes to Heaven, that watered not with the remains of any maternal affection: 'I hope in God I shall never see the monster's face again. Thank God it is over, and if I should have the misfortune ever to be in his house, I promise you I will not stay to be turned out.' 'You once thought,' said she to Lord Hervey, 'you fool, to be so imposed upon, that he loved me.' 'I did indeed,' replied Lord Hervey, 'but I never thought people may not alter.' 'You thought, too,' said the Queen, 'that he loved you, poor my Lord Hervey. He laughed at you all that while for believing him and for fancying you had any interest in him. I told you he never loved anybody; he cannot love anybody. But you will all fancy you know him better than me, and when I say he is worse than any of you think him, and yet is not so great a fool as you think him, you will imagine I say it from some silly little pride of a mother, or from some partiality of a mother. God knows my heart, I feel no more of a mother towards him than if he was no relation, and if I was to see him in hell I should feel no more for him than I should for any other rogue that ever went there. And yet once, I say it before one of my children' (the Princess Caroline was by), 'I would have given up all my children for him. I was fond of that monster, I looked upon him as one that was to make the happiness of my life, and now I wish he had never been born.' 'Pray Mama,' interrupted the Princess Caroline; 'do not throw away your wishes for what cannot happen, but wish he may *crever*, and that we may all go about with smiling faces, glad hearts, and crape and hoods for him.'

Whilst the Queen, Princess Caroline, and Lord Hervey were discoursing on this subject, the King came into the room, and the Queen telling him what they had been talking of, he said: 'I am weary of the puppy's name, I wish I was never to hear it again, but at least I shall not be plagued any more with seeing his nasty face. Not but I could forgive him all he has done to me, but I can never forgive him his behaviour to you' (speaking to the Queen). 'I must say you have been an excellent mother to all your children, and if any of them behave ill to you they deserve to be hanged. I never loved the puppy well enough to have him ungrateful to me, but to you he is a monster, and the greatest villain that ever was born.' Then turning to Lord Hervey he continued: 'I have scolded the Queen oftener for taking that rascal's part, and have had more quarrels with her when she has been making silly excuses for his silly conduct, than ever I had with her on all other subjects put together. And now you see,' said he, turning to the Queen, 'how you are repayed for your nonsense. I always told you how it would be, and you deserve it; for it was really a silly weakness in you that was unpardonable. When one's children behave well to one, one certainly must be a brute not to behave well to them; but when they behave ill, they deserve to be worse used than any other people because the ties they break through are stronger. There are degrees in all these things. Bad subjects are very provoking; bad servants are still more provoking; and bad children are the most provoking of all.'

The King then ran through all the faults of the Prince's conduct towards him, and when he spoke of the impertinent manner in which he had asked to be married, said the Prince had excepted against the Princess of Denmark, which was the properest match in Europe, and he believed only for that reason. Lord Hervey said he had heard she was old, ugly, crooked, and a dwarf. The King said she was not handsome, and was low, but very well shaped, and but twenty-seven years old. 'If he insisted on not having a crooked woman,' said the Queen, 'he has chosen but ill.' 'It is certain,' said the King, 'when I saw her at Herrenhausen she did not appear so. It is true she was in a sacque and that might hide it, and she was in nightclothes which become her much better than the frightful dress her women now put on her. She seemed to me an ill likeness of Ann, but I did not desire him to trust to me. I indulged him in sending a servant he said he could confide in to see her, and upon the report of that man he took his resolutions. Besides, for Protestant Princesses there is not great choice of matches. The Princess of Denmark he would not have. The Princesses of Prussia have a madman for their father, and I did not think ingrafting my half-witted coxcomb upon a madwoman would mend the breed.'

The King then named another family I have forgot (I think it was the Duke or Prince of Würtemberg) in which he said the grandmother had had the madness of not letting her husband lie with her after the first child for fear of spoiling her shape, and the great-grandmother the madness of letting anybody lie with her that pleased.

A great deal more passed in this conversation (that was a very entertaining one) which I have forgot.

After the Cabinet Council had on Friday morning agreed on the message and the King that evening signed it, the next day in the evening the following paper was sent.

From the King at Hampton Court to the Prince at St. James's, Sept. 10, 1737, by the Duke of Grafton, Lord Chamberlain, the Duke of Richmond, Master of the Horse, and Lord Pembroke, Groom of the Stole.

The professions you have lately made in your letters of your particular regard to me are so contradictory to all your actions, that I cannot suffer myself to be imposed upon by them.

You know very well you did not give the least intimation to me or to the Queen that the Princess was with child or breeding until within less than a month of the birth of the young Princess; you removed the Princess twice in the week immediately preceding the day of her delivery from the place of my residence, in expectation, as you have voluntarily declared, of her labour; and both times upon your return you industriously concealed from the knowledge of me and the Queen every circumstance relating to this important affair; and you at last, without giving any notice to me or to the Queen, precipitately hurried the Princess from Hampton Court in a condition not to be named. After having thus, in execution of your own determined measures, exposed both the Princess and her child to the greatest perils, you now plead surprise and your tenderness for the Princess as the only motives that occasioned these repeated indignities, offered to me and to the Queen your mother.

This extravagant and undutiful behaviour in so essential a point as the birth of an heir to my crown is such an evidence of your premeditated defiance of me, and such a contempt of my authority and of the natural right belonging to your parents, as cannot be excused by the pretended innocence of your intentions, nor palliated or disguised by specious words only.

But the whole tenor of your conduct for a considerable time has been so entirely void of all real duty to me that I have long had reason to be highly offended with you.

And until you withdraw your regard and confidence from those by whose instigation and advice you are directed and encouraged in your unwarrantable behaviour to me and to the Queen, and until you return to your duty, you shall not reside in my palace, which I will not suffer to be made the resort of them who, under the appearance of an attachment to you, foment the division which you have made in my family, and thereby weaken the common interest of the whole.

In this situation I will receive no reply; but when your actions manifest a just sense of your duty and submission, that may induce me to pardon what at present I most justly resent.

In the meantime it is my pleasure that you leave St. James's with all your family, when it can be done without prejudice or inconvenience to the Princess.

I shall for the present leave to the Princess the care of my granddaughter, until a proper time calls upon me to consider of her education.

The Duke of Grafton, taking place by his office of both the other messengers, was ordered to read the message to the Prince, and then leave it with him. It was said His Royal Highness changed colour several times in this interview, and told the messengers, though he knew it would have been his duty to have sent an answer in writing if the King had not in his letter forbid him, yet, since His Majesty had done so, he had nothing to trouble them with.

His Royal Highness then asked if there was any time fixed by the King for his departure from St. James's, to which Lord Pembroke answered that the King had only in the message said it should be when it could be done without prejudice or inconvenience to the Princess. The Prince then desiring the Lords Messengers to present his duty to the King, and say he was very sorry for what had happened, dismissed them; and they all three returned that night immediately to the King, to let him know what I have related. The first question the King asked was whether the Prince had made them wait, which the Prince had not done; but Lord Pembroke told me if he had, that they had all agreed to lie and say he had not. He told me, too, that the Prince's behaviour had been very civil, and very decent.

The next morning the Queen, at breakfast, every now and then repeated: 'I hope, in God, I shall never see him again'; and the King, among many other paternal douceurs in his valediction to his son, said: 'Thank God, to-morrow night the puppy will be out of my house.' The Queen asked Lord Hervey if he thought the Prince would be mortified. 'For my part,' said she, 'I believe he will be very glad; for I am sure last winter he wished to be turned out.' Lord Hervey said: 'There is a great deal of difference, Madam, between his being turned out on a parliamentary quarrel and for a personal family misbehaviour; and though he might wish it therefore in one case, he may be very sorry for it in the other. Those about him must see and feel this distinction, and cannot fail, though he should not find it out, to represent it to him.' 'Who about him,' says the King, 'will tell it him, or who about him indeed has sense enough to find out anything? Who is there but boobies and fools, and madmen that he ever listens to?' Lord Hervey laughed, and the King went on: 'Why, is it not so? Am I not in the right? There is my Lord Carnarvon, a hot-headed, passionate, half-witted coxcomb, with no more sense than his master; there is Townshend, a silent, proud, surly, wrong-headed booby; there is my Lord North, a very good poor creature, but a very weak man; there is my Lord Baltimore, who thinks he understands everything, and understands nothing, who wants to be well with both courts, and is well at neither and, *entre nous*, is a little mad; and who else of his servants can you name whom he listens to, unless it is that stuttering puppy, Johnny Lumley?'

The day after the message was sent to the Prince, it was signified by the Secretaries of State to all the foreign Ministers that it would be agreeable to the King if they would forebear going to the Prince; and a message was sent in writing to all Peers, Peeresses, and Privy Counsellors, that whoever went to the Prince's court should not be admitted into the King's presence. The guard too was taken away from the Prince[1]; and though Sir Robert Walpole, at the instigation of the Duke of Newcastle and Duke of Grafton, endeavoured to persuade the King and Queen to let the Prince take the furniture of his apartments away with him, it was not allowed. The King said he had given the Prince £5,000, when he married, out of his pocket to set out with, besides £5,000 which was his wife's fortune; and that it had cost him above £50,000 more for one thing or other on that occasion, and positively he would not let his son carry the things away; and the Duke of Grafton was ordered to take care that nothing did go. When Lord Hervey, who was by when these orders were given, said that chests and those sort of things which were not ornamental, but to hold the Prince and Princess's things, must not be understood to be included, as their clothes could not be carried away like dirty linen in a basket, he was answered: 'Why not? A basket is good enough for them.' Sir Robert Walpole, in order to induce the King and Queen to consent to this carrying away of the furniture, had told them it would disarm the Prince's party in Parliament of the argument of the necessary additional expense the Prince had this year incurred by being turned out of his father's house, and being obliged to buy everything new for another; but all would not do. The Queen pretended to consent (as Sir Robert told me), but I am sure she was as much against it as the King; and the King's perseverance in being against it, is a demonstration she was so.

Lord Carteret was at this time at his own house in Bedfordshire; Lord Chesterfield ill of a fever; and Mr. Pulteney gone to take the diversion of shooting in Norfolk; so that there was nobody about

---

[1] Similar measures had been taken by George I against George II as Prince of Wales in 1717; and by William and Mary against Anne, as Princess of Denmark and heir presumptive, in 1692.

the Prince but the minor Council, who were all in the same strain of flattery, talking of the magnanimity and fortitude with which His Royal Highness received this shock. Lord Baltimore (the Queen told me) had compared His Royal Highness's bravery and resolution to that of Charles the Twelfth of Sweden.

All the letters that passed this year and the last between the King or Queen and the Prince or Princess are copied in these memoirs from the originals,[1] which Lord Hervey had many days in his possession, given him by the Queen to range them in order; and whoever hereafter sees the originals will find them all docketed in his handwriting, assisted by the King in some parts, where he had forgotten by whom some particular papers were sent; and those names which are not in his handwriting, though mixed with it, are written by the King himself. The originals Lord Hervey had orders to give to Sir Robert Walpole; and when he obeyed those orders, Sir Robert Walpole told him: 'When the Duke of Newcastle sees these letters indorsed by the King and you in conjunction, it will put him out of humour for a week at least; he'll say you are Closet Secretary to the King, whilst he is only Office Secretary.'

On Monday, September 12, the Prince and Princess and their whole family removed from St. James's to Kew; and Lord Carteret, Sir William Wyndham, and Mr. Pulteney having been sent for by expresses from the Prince as soon as he had received the King's message, they all immediately repaired to Kew. When Lord Hervey, who had met some of these people upon the road going to Kew, told His Majesty of it, the King's remark was that he believed they would all soon be tired of the puppy; 'for, besides his being a scoundrel, he is such a fool,' said the King, 'that he will talk more fiddle-faddle nonsense to them in a day than any old woman talks in a week.'

The Prince took the Duke of Norfolk's house in St. James's Square for his town dwelling, and Cliveden for his country habitation, having given unregarded hints to the Duke of Bedford of his desiring to have Southampton House; but before the Duke of Norfolk would consent to the Prince having his house, the Duchess of Norfolk came to Hampton Court to ask the Queen, whom she saw in private, if it would be disagreeable to her and the King; and

[1] Most of them have been omitted from this edition.

the Queen assuring the Duchess of Norfolk it would not, and thanking her for the civility she had shown to the King and her, the Duke of Norfolk let the Prince know his house was at His Royal Highness's service.

The Prince reduced the number of his inferior servants, which made him many enemies among the lower sort of people, and did not save him much money. He put off all his horses too that were not absolutely necessary; and farmed all his tables, even that of the Princess and himself.

The Queen told Lord Hervey that the three things of which the Prince accused the King, besides the robbing him of the £100,000 a year, were His Majesty's having thrice cheated him, by his sinking the late King's will,[1] and the Duke of York's will, and by seizing the revenues of the Duchy of Cornwall; and as to the two first articles, she said the Prince was not named in either of the wills, and that the Duke of York (who died the year after the present King came to the throne) in his will had left everything he had, which came to about £50,000, to his present Majesty, except his jewels, and his jewels he left to the Queen of Prussia, to whom the King had delivered them, after satisfying the King of Prussia (who before the King showed him the will had a mind to litigate it in favour of his wife) that the will would admit of no dispute; and as to the King's seizing the revenues of Cornwall, all he had done was to take care, on the receiver of the revenues for the Duchy of Cornwall's having embezzled some of the money, that, as His Majesty's arrears was the debt first incurred, that debt should be first paid.

Whilst the Queen was telling this one morning to Lord Hervey, the King opened the door at the further end of her gallery, upon which the Queen chid Lord Hervey for coming so late, saying she had several things to say to him, and that he was always so long in coming after he was sent for, that she never had any time to talk with him; to which Lord Hervey replied, it was not his fault, for that he always came the moment he was called; that he wished

---

[1] This was really a *testament politique*, not an ordinary will. It attempted to provide for the dissolution of the personal union of England and Hanover. It was pronounced by George II's Hanoverian ministers to be illegal and invalid and on this account was suppressed.

with all his heart the King had more love, or Lady Deloraine more wit, that he might have more time with Her Majesty, but that he thought it very hard that he should be snubbed and reproved because the King was old and Lady Deloraine a fool. This made the Queen laugh, and the King asking when he came up to her what it was at she said it was at a conversation Lord Hervey was reporting between the Prince and Mr. Lyttelton on his being made Secretary, and left Lord Hervey, on the King's desiring him to repeat it, to invent one; telling Lord Hervey the next time she saw him: 'I think I was even with you for your impertinence.' To which Lord Hervey replied: 'The next time you serve me so, Madam, perhaps I may be even with you, and desire Your Majesty to repeat as well as report.'

Lord Hervey took occasion among many other things, to say he did not believe there ever was a father and a son so thoroughly unlike in every particular as the King and the Prince, and enumerated several points in which they differed, as little to the advantage of the Prince as to the dispraise or displeasure of the King. The King said he had really thought so himself a thousand times, and had often asked the Queen if the beast was his son. Lord Hervey said that question must be to very little purpose, for to be sure the Queen would never own it if he was not. The King said the first child generally was the husband's, 'and therefore,' says he, 'I fancy he is what in German we call a Wechselbalg. I do not know,' continued he, 'if you have a word for it in English: it is not what you call a foundling, but a child put in a cradle instead of another.' 'That is a changeling,' replied Lord Hervey. The King was extremely pleased with this translation, and said: 'I wish you could prove him a changeling in the German sense of the word as easily as anybody can prove him so in the other; though the Queen was a great while before her maternal affection would give him up for a fool, and yet I told her before he had been here a week he had not common sense.'

Lord Hervey said the Queen had often last year done the honours of His Royal Highness's understanding to him, and was very loth to give it quite up, but that of late he had not perceived she had any hope left of disguising it. 'My dear Lord, I will give it you under my hand,' replied the Queen, 'if you are in any fear of my relapsing, that my dear first-born is the greatest ass, and the greatest liar, and the greatest *canaille*, and the greatest beast, in the whole world, and that I most heartily wish he was out of it.'

The Queen told me at this time she heard the Prince's people intended to print the letters the present King, when he was Prince of Wales, wrote to the late King upon the quarrel in the late reign, and said she concluded, if they did, Lord Chesterfield must have got the copies of them from the Duchess of Kendal[1]; for, as to the originals, all the letters the present King had written to the late King had been found among the late King's papers when he died, and the present King had made her burn all of them except three.

However, soon after printed they were, together with the late King's message to the Prince to turn him out of St. James's, and a sort of circular letter by Mr. Addison, then Secretary of State, by the late King's orders, to all the English Ministers in foreign Courts to give an account of the whole transaction.

There were some more circumstances relating to the letters found in the late King's closet which I never knew till now, and are too curious for me not to relate. One was, that in a letter from Earl Stanhope to the late King, when things were pushing to an extremity against the then Prince of Wales, there were these words: 'Il est vrai c'est votre fils, mais le Fils de Dieu même a été sacrifié pour la salut du genre humain.'

'It is true he is your son, but the Son of God himself was sacrificed for the good of mankind.'

In another letter it was said: 'Il faut l'enlever; et my Lord Berkeley le prendra sur un vaisseau, et le conduira en aucunie partie du monde que votre Majesté l'ordonnera.'

'He must be carried off and my Lord Berkeley will take him on board and carry him to any part of the world Your Majesty will order him.'

It was no wonder, if the King and Queen believed this to be true, that Sir Robert Walpole, weak as his interest was at the beginning of this reign, had power sufficient to remove Lord Berkeley from the head of the Admiralty.[2]

It is certain that Earl Stanhope and Lord Sunderland were both so afraid of the Prince of Wales at that time, and so inveterately

[1] See p. 15. She was his wife's aunt.   [2] See p. 9.

his enemies, that nobody doubted of their being willing and capable to undertake anything to secure themselves, gratify their resentments, and deprive the Prince of the succession to the Crown.

Madame Walmoden's name had not been mentioned for a long time, when Sir Robert Walpole told Lord Hervey that he had had the King's orders to buy one hundred lottery-tickets for His Majesty, to send to her as he supposed, for he had pressed Sir Robert to get them by the Friday following, and given for his reason that Friday was the German post-day. Sir Robert told Lord Hervey, too, that he had acquainted the Queen with this commission, to avoid her suspecting he had any secret managements for this lady, or was employed in any transactions relating to her which he did not communicate to Her Majesty. He also told Lord Hervey that the King, to save making this £1,000 disbursement out of his privy purse, had ordered him to charge the purchase money of these tickets in the secret service; adding that His Majesty, like all other covetous people, fancied always that he gave less when he gave out of a stock which, though equally his own, was money he had never fingered. When first Sir Robert began his account to Lord Hervey, he called Madame Walmoden only the 'King's favourite,' which Lord Hervey mistaking for Lady Deloraine, said he did not think His Majesty went so deep there; to which Sir Robert, setting him right, replied: 'No, I mean the Hanover woman. You are indeed in the right to imagine he does not go so deep to his lying fool here. He'll give her a couple, and think her generously used.'

The Court came to town as usual two days before the King's birthday, and Sir Robert Walpole being in too deep mourning for his wife[1] to appear on that occasion, he set out for Norfolk the day before the King left Hampton Court.

Those who were in the King's service, or espoused his cause in the quarrel with his son, piqued themselves on contributing to make up the crowd on this first show-day after the separation of the Courts, and by these means the drawing-room, to the great satisfaction both of the King and the Queen, was much fuller than ever it had been on any other 30th of October since the first after His Majesty's accession to the Crown.

---

[1] Who had died on the 20th August.

chapter nine

The Death of the Queen

1737

I MUST NOW as well as I can connect the particulars of a diary of the most melancholy fortnight I ever passed in my life, not only from the inquietude of my own mind, but from the scene of distress all around me, not seeing a single creature in the Queen's apartment (out of which I passed very few hours of this fortnight) that either for public or private reasons, and many for both, was not filled with the most careful thoughts, agitated with the greatest anxiety, and giving way without disguise to every symptom of the two most turbulent sensations in a human mind, grief and fear.

On Wednesday, the 9th of November, the Queen was taken ill in the morning at her new library in St. James's Park. She called her complaint the colic, her stomach and bowels giving her great pain. She came home, took Daffy's Elixir by Dr. Tesier, the German and house-physician's advice; but was in such great pain, and so uneasy with frequent reachings to vomit, that she went into bed. However, when the clock struck two, and the King proposed sending Lord Grantham to dismiss the company, and declare there would be no drawing-room, she, according to the custom of the family, not caring to own, or at least to have it generally known, how ill she was, told the King she was much better, that she would get up and see the company as usual. As soon as she came into the drawing-room she came up to Lord Hervey and said: 'Is it not intolerable at my age to be plagued with a new distemper? Here is this nasty colic that I had at Hampton Court come again.' The Queen had twice this summer at Hampton Court been seized with a vomiting and purging, which had lasted in the most violent manner for three or four hours, and then left her so easy and well that she had played the same night in the drawing-room as usual,

231

and talked with almost the same cheerfulness. This made Lord Hervey less alarmed than he otherwise would have been at her present disorder, for she looked extremely ill, and complained much more than was her custom to do when she suffered most. Lord Hervey asked her what she had taken, and when she told him, he replied: 'For God's sake, Madam, go to your own room; what have you to do here?' She then went and talked a little to the rest of the company, and coming back again to Lord Hervey, said: 'I am not able to entertain people.' 'Would to God,' replied Lord Hervey, 'the King would have done talking of the Dragon of Wantley, and release you.' (This was a new silly farce which everybody at this time went to see.) At last the King went away, telling the Queen as he went by that she had overlooked the Duchess of Norfolk. The Queen made her excuse for having done so to the Duchess of Norfolk, the last person she ever spoke to in public, and then retired, going immediately into bed, where she grew worse every moment.

At seven o'clock, when Lord Hervey returned to St. James's from M. de Cambis's, the French ambassador's where he dined that day, he went up to the Queen's apartment and found her in bed, with the Princess Caroline only in the room, the King being gone, as usual at that hour, to play in the Princess Emily's apartment. The Queen asked Lord Hervey what he used to take in his violent fits of the colic; and Lord Hervey, imagining the Queen's pain to proceed from a goutish humour in her stomach that should be driven from that dangerous seat into her limbs, told her nothing ever gave him immediate ease but strong things. To which the Queen replied: 'Pshaw! you think now like all the other fools, that this is the pain of an old nasty stinking gout.' But her vomitings, or rather her reachings, together with such acute pain, continuing in a degree that she could not lie one moment quiet, she said about an hour after to Lord Hervey, 'Give me what you will, I will take it'; and the Princess Caroline bidding him not lose this opportunity, he only said to the Queen he would fetch the strongest thing he could get, telling her at the same time that his former experience of violent fits of the colic was such that he was sure all the angels in heaven together could not procure her immediate ease without it.

He fetched some snake-root and brandy, and asking Dr. Tesier, who was in the outward room, whether he might venture to give it her, Dr. Tesier, who was naturally timid, and made more so by the manner in which he had been talked to in the King's illness last year, said the Queen's pulse was very high and feverish, and as she was unused to drinking anything strong, he could not affirm that this very strong cordial would do her no hurt. Lord Hervey then asked him if he should propose to the King to call in another physician, and if he had any objection to Broxholme; and Dr. Tesier saying he wished it extremely, but did not dare to propose it himself to the King, Lord Hervey told Princess Caroline what had passed; that he did not dare to take upon him to give the snake-root without Tesier's consent; and would, if she approved, propose to the King that Dr. Broxholme might be called in.

The Princess Caroline consented, and Lord Hervey speaking to the King, who was now returned from Princess Emily's apartment, and began to be alarmed, Dr. Broxholme was immediately sent for by Lord Hervey. When he came, Tesier and he agreed to give the Queen immediately some snake-root with Sir Walter Raleigh's cordial; but this cordial being long in preparing, and Ranby, house-surgeon to the King, a sensible fellow and a favourite of Lord Hervey's, telling Lord Hervey that insisting on these occasions upon a cordial with this name or t'other was mere quackery, and that no cordial was better than another in these cases but in propor-tion to its strength, Lord Hervey got some usquebaugh immediately, and telling Princess Caroline what Ranby had said, the usquebaugh was immediately given to the Queen, who kept it about half an hour, which was about twenty-nine minutes longer than she had kept anything else, but then brought it up. Soon after the snake-root, and Sir Walter Raleigh's cordial arrived from the apothecary's; it was taken and thrown up about an hour after. All these strong things, twice Daffy's Elixir, mint-water, usequebaugh, snake-root, and Sir Walter Raleigh's cordial, had without easing the Queen's pain so increased her fever, that the doctors ordered Ranby to bleed her twelve ounces immediately. She took a glister but it came from her just as it went into her.

The Princess Caroline had been extremely ill all this summer at Hampton Court of rheumatic pains, and growing every day worse, notwithstanding all the medicines that had been given her in what the physicians call a regular way, Lord Hervey upon her coming to town had persuaded her to take Ward's Pill, a nostrum belonging to one Ward, an excellent medicine, not only in rheumatisms but in several cases, which all the physicians and surgeons endeavoured to decry for being so.

Princess Caroline, persuaded by Lord Hervey, had taken this medicine since her arrival in London, with the privity rather than consent of the King and Queen, and keeping it a secret to everybody else; but in four times taking only she had found such benefit that, notwithstanding she had been unable to walk or get up from her chair without help when she began it, she was now quite free from pain, and could walk almost as well as she ever could have done in her life. This medicine vomits, purges, and sweats in a great degree. However, her recovery being not yet perfect, the King and Queen were both extremely solicitous to have her go to bed, which she did not do till two o'clock in the morning. The King, inconveniently both to himself and the Queen, lay on the Queen's bed all night in his nightgown, where he could not sleep, nor she turn about easily.

Early in the morning of Thursday the 10th the Queen was blooded twelve ounces more, upon which her fever, that had been very high all night, abated, and everybody but herself thought she was better. When the King went to his own side to change his linen, she told the Princess Caroline it signified nothing what they did to her, for she should certainly die, and added: 'Poor Caroline! you are very ill too; we shall soon meet again in another place.'

Her vomiting was suspended for a few hours this morning; but nothing passed downwards and two glisters she took returned immediately and pure. However, on this amendment, as everybody called it, but few really thought it, the King resolved to have a levée and that the Princess should see the company at the usual hour of the Queen's going out, in her drawing-room; and to show what odd and inconsistent particulars we are all composed of, this being the day the Foreign Ministers came to Court, the King, in the midst of all his real and great concern for the Queen, sent to his pages to bid them be sure to have his last new ruffles sewed on upon the shirt he was to put on that day at his public dressing. Such sort of particulars will seem very trifling to those who do not think, like me, that trifling circumstances often let one more into people's tempers and characters than those parts of their conduct that are of greater importance, from which one frequently knows no more of their natural turn of mind than one does of their natural gait whilst they are dancing.

Mrs. Herbert, sister-in-law to Lord Pembroke, happened to be the Bedchamber-Woman in waiting this week on the Queen, and though she was a personal and warm enemy, and had long been so, to Sir Robert Walpole, yet she was so sensible, so well-bred, so handy, so cheerful, and so agreeable to the Queen, that the Queen desired if she should continue ill longer than that week that Mrs. Herbert would continue in waiting. Mrs. Herbert, Mrs. Selwyn, and Mrs. Brudenel were the only Bedchamber-Women who attended the Queen during her whole illness, Lady Sundon being very ill in Bath, and the rest absent elsewhere. None of the Ladies of her Bedchamber were admitted to her at all.

Lord Hervey asked the Duke of Newcastle this morning if he would not send for Sir Robert Walpole, and the Duke of Newcastle said he had mentioned it, but that the Princess Emily had told him the King and Queen would both dislike he should; but his Grace added he would write that night to Houghton to say how the Queen was, and disguise nothing. He did so, and Princess Emily added a postcript in the letter, softening the state of things, and begging Sir Robert Walpole by all means not to think of coming to town.

Lord Hervey wrote that night, softening nothing, and advising him by all means to come, and did not then tell Sir Robert what he thought he plainly perceived, that the Princess Emily and the Duke of Newcastle had no mind he should come; the Princess Emily hoping, I believe, that the Queen would not take his staying at Houghton well; and the Duke of Newcastle, joined to that reason, proposing perhaps by Sir Robert's absence to have the King more to himself. If that was his scheme, he was disappointed; for after this day the King saw no Minister, nor any one man-servant that belonged to him but Lord Hervey who was never out of the Queen's apartment for above four or five hours at most at a time during her whole illness, and sometimes not two in the twenty-four, and never went from the King without his desiring him to come back as soon as he could.

This evening whilst the Princess Caroline and he were alone with the Queen, she complaining and they comforting, she often said: 'I have an ill which nobody knows of'; which they both understood to mean nothing more than she felt what she could not describe, and more than anybody imagined. Princess Caroline's extreme concern and almost continual weeping gave her a return of her rheumatism, which settled in her back; and added to this, she had from this violent and perpetual weeping a frequent bleeding at her nose, and in great quantities. The King and Queen, therefore, both persuaded her to go to bed, and insisted on her doing so about midnight, Lord Hervey promising her to sit up, and giving his word he would frequently come and inform her how the Queen was exactly, and without the least disguise.

This night two more physicians were called in, Sir Hans Sloane and Dr. Hulse, who ordered blisters and a purge; the purge came up, like every other thing, soon after she had swallowed it, and the blisters, though a remedy to which the King and Queen had often declared themselves very averse, were put upon her legs.

Lord Hervey went once or twice in the night, as he had promised, to Princess Caroline; the King sat up in the Queen's room, and Princess Emily lay on a couch in Mrs. Herbert's.

At six o'clock on Friday morning the Queen was again blooded, upon which her fever went almost entirely off; but the total stoppage and frequent vomitings still continued.

On Friday Lord Hervey again desired the Duke of Newcastle to send an express for Sir Robert Walpole, which his Grace at last thought fit to do; but sending the messenger round by Euston, where the Duke of Grafton then was, and the messenger by accident or order loitering on the road, Sir Robert Walpole had not these letters till Saturday evening, and set not out for London till Sunday morning.

On Friday Lord Hervey, hearing the Prince was come from Kew to Carlton House in Pall Mall, suspected he had done so in order to come to St. James's to inquire after the Queen, and perhaps to ask to see her; and that no resolution on such step might be taken by the King in a hurry, Lord Hervey told the King his conjecture, and asked His Majesty, in case it should prove a true one, what he would have done. The King said: 'If the puppy should, in one of his impertinent affected airs of duty and affection, dare to come to St. James's, I order you to go to the scoundrel and tell him I wonder at his impudence for daring to come here; that he has my orders already, and knows my pleasure, and bid him go about his business; for his poor mother is not in a condition to see him act his false, whining, cringing tricks now, nor am I in a humour to bear his impertinence; and bid him trouble me with no more messages, but get out of my house.'

About an hour or two afterward, whilst Lord Hervey was sitting with the Duke of Cumberland, drinking tea in the Queen's apartment, a message came by one of the Queen's pages to the Duke to tell him Lady Pembroke, the Queen's lady then in waiting, desired to speak with His Royal Highness in the passage. Lord Hervey, telling the Duke he suspected this might prove something relative to the Prince, said he would go with him. Accordingly he went, and Lady Pembroke told the Duke Lord North had just been with her from the Prince to desire her, in the Prince's name, to let the King and Queen know His Royal Highness was in the utmost affliction upon hearing of the Queen's illness, was come to London in order to hear more frequently how she did, and that the only thing that could alleviate his great concern at this time was to be admitted to the honour of seeing her.

The Duke said: 'I am not a proper person, Madam, to take the charge of this message, but there is Lord Hervey, who is the only one of papa's servants that sees him at present, and is just going to him; if you will deliver it to him, he will certainly let the King know.'

Accordingly, Lady Pembroke repeated the message over again to Lord Hervey, and Lord Hervey assured her he would take the first opportunity to acquaint the King with it.

When Lord Hervey told the King what had passed, His Majesty flew into as great a rage as he could have done had he not been prepared. 'This,' said he, 'is like one of the scoundrel's tricks; it is just of a piece with his kneeling down in the dirt before the mob to kiss her hand at the coach-door when she came from Hampton Court to see the Princess, though he had not spoken one word to her during her whole visit. I always hated the rascal, but now I hate him yet worse than ever. He wants to come and insult his poor dying mother; but she shall not see him; you have heard her, and all my daughters have heard her very often this year at Hampton Court, desire me, if she should be ill and out of her senses, that I would never let that villain come near her; and whilst she had her senses, she was sure she would never desire it. No, no! he shall not come and act any of his silly plays here, false, lying, cowardly, nauseous, puppy. Besides, supposing the Queen loved him as much as she hates him, it would be as improper for her to see him in that case as it is now. She is not in a condition to bear the emotion. Therefore, my Lord, you know my thoughts. I have told you already the answer I would have given; you have but to tell it my Lord North, and be sure not to forget to say I will be plagued with no more messages.'

Lord Hervey told the King, if he delivered a verbal message only, that the Prince and his people would certainly engraft a thousand lies upon it, and without a possibility of being disproved.

'It is no matter for that,' replied the King, 'I will not honour him with another written message, nor have the appearance of giving myself at this time so much trouble about him.'

'Nor would I have your Majesty,' answered Lord Hervey; 'but if you will give me leave, as for the help of my own memory, to put Your Majesty's commands down in writing, and only let me read that paper, without delivering it, Your Majesty will at once show that you will neither honour them with a written message nor trust them with a verbal one.'

'You are in the right,' said the King: 'do so. Put down in writing what you are to say, and pray see who are in the rooms, and take two people of quality and credit along with you, to be by when you read the paper to Lord North, that they may be witnesses to what passes; for else that pack of knaves and liars (Cartouche's[1] gang, as the poor Queen always calls them) are capable of reporting you to have said things you never thought of.'

Lord Hervey went immediately to put down what he was to say in writing, and desired the Duke of Newcastle and Lord Pembroke to go along with him to Lord North, telling them that he had already named them to the King for that purpose, and acquainting them at the same time with all the material part of what I have already related concerning this transaction.

[1] A French robber, executed in 1721.

Lord Pembroke, Lord Hervey chose as a man of credit; and the Duke of Newcastle, because he thought it would mortify him to play subaltern in an occurrence where Lord Hervey acted the principal part—a *petitesse* in Lord Hervey's way of thinking, but one he liked to indulge. The message Lord Hervey drew was as follows:

Message delivered by Lord Hervey by word of mouth to Lord North at St. James's, on Friday, November 11, 1737, in the presence of the Duke of Newcastle and Lord Pembroke.

I have acquainted the King with the message sent to Lady Pembroke, and His Majesty has ordered me to say that in the present situation and circumstances His Majesty does not think fit that the Prince should see the Queen, and therefore expects he should not come to St. James's.

The King thought this draft much too mild, but after a little persuasion consented to it; as also (at Lord Hervey's request) to see the Duke of Newcastle and Lord Pembroke only for a minute, to read this paper to them, to tell them he had ordered Lord Hervey to deliver this message, and to order them to be present when he did so; and the King again, in their presence, repeated his commands to Lord Hervey to be sure not to give a copy of that paper, with his reasons, already mentioned, why he would not have it done, as well as those for his ordering the Duke of Newcastle and Lord Pembroke to be witnesses to what passed at this interview, cutting Lord Pembroke very short, who would have offered some palliatives to the wording of the message, and telling him: 'My Lord, you are always for a softening, and I think it is much too soft already for such a villain and a scoundrel; it is much softer than I ordered Lord Hervey to prepare it; so pray go, and let it be given this moment, and be sure I am plagued with no more impertinence of this sort, for I will neither have the poor Queen disturbed with his silly noise, nor will I be troubled with it again myself.'

When Lord Hervey delivered the message, Lord North desired he might have a copy of it in writing, to which Lord Pembroke answered that Lord Hervey had the King's positive commands not to give it in writing; and Lord Hervey added that he would read it as often as Lord North pleased, and after hearing it three or four times, Lord North took his leave.

In the afternoon the Queen said to the King, she wondered the Griff (the nickname of the Prince) had not sent to ask to see her yet, it would be so like one of his filthy *paroîtres*; 'but sooner or later I am sure one shall be plagued with some message of that sort, because he will think it will have a good air in the world to ask to see me; and perhaps hopes I shall be fool enough to let him come, and give him the pleasure of seeing my last breath go out of my body, by which means he would have the joy of knowing I was dead five minutes sooner than he could know it in Pall Mall.'

The King bid her not be under any apprehensions of a trouble of this kind, for that he had already taken care to prevent it; and then related to her every circumstance of the message he had received, and the answer he had returned by Lord Hervey. The King told the Queen, too, that if she had the least mind to see her son, he had no objection to it, and begged her to do just what she liked. 'I am so far,' said the Queen, 'from desiring to see him, that nothing but your absolute commands should ever make me consent to it. For what should I see him? For him to tell me a hundred lies, and to give myself at this time a great deal of trouble to no purpose. If anything I could say to him would alter his behaviour, I would see him with all my heart; but I know this is impossible. Whatever advice I gave him he would thank me for, *pleureroit comme un veau* all the while I was speaking, and swear to follow my directions; and would laugh at me the moment he was out of the room, and do just the contrary of all I bid him, the moment I was dead.

'There is no hope of mending him; it is a sad wretch. And therefore if I should grow worse, and be weak enough to talk of seeing him, I beg, Sir, you will conclude that I doat and rave, and insist upon your promising me now that I shall not see him,' which the King accordingly did. Lord Hervey was not by when all this passed, but the Duke and both the eldest Princesses were, and every one of these told it to Lord Hervey again just as I have related it. The King told it too to Lord Hervey with several other particulars and comments on the Prince's temper and vices which have already on other occasions been often mentioned in these papers.

The Queen often in her illness spoke of him, and always with detestation, and when she has heard hasty steps in the next room has said she was afraid he would watch his opportunity, come privately up the back stairs, and run into her room before anyone could stop him; and as the King and Princess Caroline both told me, the Queen would sometimes when she talked of dying cry: 'At least I shall have one comfort in having my eyes eternally closed—I shall never see that monster again.'

She certainly hated him more and expressed that hate in stronger terms if possible in her illness than ever she had done in health. And indeed his conduct at this time deserved she should do so, for all this while that he was outwardly putting on this grief, making these professions, sending these messages, and pretending this great desire to see her, he was sitting in his house in Pall Mall, with some of his trusty favourites (as I afterward learnt from the Duke of Marlborough) railing at his mother, sending private messages every minute to St. James's to know how she did, and saying perpetually: 'Well, sure, we must have some good news soon. 'Tis impossible she can hold out long. I think I am a very good son, I wish her out of her pain.' And added to speeches of this kind indecent rejoicings, which would have shocked anybody of common humanity to hear, and could only belong to one of the most uncommon barbarity to utter.

This whole Friday the Queen grew worse almost every hour. The Princess Caroline went to bed at night in her own apartment; the Princess Emily sat up in the Queen's bedchamber; Lord Hervey lay on a couch in the next room, and the King had his own bedding brought and laid upon the floor in the little room behind the Queen's dressing-room and there lay till about four o'clock on Saturday morning, when the Queen complaining more than ever of the racking pains she felt in her belly and of a throbbing, he was called, and all the physicians immediately sent for, one only having been appointed to sit up, which they did by turns during her whole illness.

When the King came into the room to the Queen he whispered her, and, as he said afterward, told her he was afraid her illness proceeded from a thing he had promised never to speak of to her again; but that her life being in danger, he could not answer it to her, himself, or his family, not to tell all he knew and all he apprehended. She begged and entreated him, with great earnestness, that he would not, and spoke with more warmth and peevishness than she showed at any other time during her whole illness. However, he sent for Ranby the surgeon, and told him he apprehended the Queen had a rupture at her navel, and bid him examine her. The Queen carried her desire to conceal this complaint so far that when Ranby came to feel her she laid his hand on the pit of her stomach and said all her pain was there; but Ranby, slipping his hand lower, kept it there in spite of her, some little time; and then, without saying one word to the Queen, went and spoke softly to the King at the chimney, upon which the Queen started up, and sitting in her bed, said to Ranby with great eagerness: 'I am sure now, you lying fool, you are telling the King I have a rupture.' 'I am so,' said Ranby, 'and there is no more time to be lost; Your Majesty has concealed it too long already; and I beg another surgeon may be called in immediately.' The Queen made no answer, but lay down again, turned her head to the other side, and as the King told me, he thinks it was the only tear he saw her shed whilst she was ill. The King bid Ranby send immediately for old Busier the surgeon, whom, though four-score years old, the King and Queen had a great opinion of, and preferred to every other man of his profession.

Busier not being immediately to be found, and the King very impatient, he bid Ranby go and bring the first surgeon of any note and credit he could find; and whilst Ranby was absent on his errand, the King told Lord Hervey the whole history of this rupture.

'The first symptoms I ever perceived of it,' said he, 'were fourteen years ago, just after the Queen lay in of Louisa; and she then told me, when I spoke to her of it, that it was nothing more than what was common for almost every woman to have after a hard labour, or having many children. This made me easy, and it grew better, and continued better afterwards for several years. When it grew worse again, I persuaded her to consult some surgeon, which she declined, and was so uneasy whenever I spoke to her on this subject that I knew not how to press her; but when I came from Hanover the last time but one, I found it so much worse than ever that I again spoke to her, told her it was certainly a rupture, and that she ran great risks in taking no care of it. She was so very uneasy upon my saying this, telling me it was no such thing, and that I fancied she had a nasty distemper which she was sure she had not, and spoke so much more peevishly to me on this occasion than she had ever done in her life upon any other, that upon my renewing my solicitations to let somebody see it, and her growing every time I mentioned it more and more hurt and angry, I at last told her I wished she might not repent her obstinacy, but promised her I never would mention this subject to her again as long as I lived.'

The King, in as plain insinuations as he could without saying it in direct terms, did intimate to Lord Hervey that the Queen had received what he had said to her on this subject, upon his return from Hanover, as if she had reproached him with being grown weary of her person, and endeavouring to find blemishes in it that did not belong to her.

I do firmly believe she carried her abhorrence to being known to have a rupture so far that she would have died without declaring it, or letting it be known, had not the King told it in spite of her; and though people may think this weakness little of a piece with the greatness of the rest of her character, yet they will judge partially who interpret this delicacy to be merely an ill-timed coquetry at fifty-four that would hardly have been excusable at twenty-five. She knew better than anybody else that her power over the King was not preserved independent, as most people thought, of the charms of her person; and as her power over him was the principal object of her pursuit, she feared, very reasonably, the loss or the weakening of any tie by which she held him. Several things she afterwards said to the King in her illness, which both the King and the Princess Caroline told me again, plainly demonstrated how strongly these apprehensions of making her person distasteful to the King worked upon her.

When Ranby returned he brought one Shipton with him, a City surgeon, and one of the most eminent and most able of the whole profession. By this time, too, Busier arrived, and these three attended her constantly. After they had examined the Queen, they all told the King she was in the utmost danger. Busier proposed making the operation of cutting a hole in her navel wide enough to thrust the gut back into its place; which Ranby opposed, saying that all the guts, upon such an operation, would come out of the body in a moment into the bed, and that he thought he felt at the bottom of the swelling (which was of an immense size) a softness which he took to be a disposition to making matter and which they might encourage by warm fomentations, till the swelling might break of itself or at least allow them by a slight touch of a lancet to open it without danger. Shipton inclining to Ranby's opinion, this method was pursued.

In the meantime, Lord Hervey telling the King that he had heard it said among some lawyers that if the Queen died Richmond Gardens would come to the Prince, the King ordered Lord Hervey to go immediately to my Lord Chancellor, and ask his opinion upon it. Lord Hervey accordingly went to Westminster Hall, where my Lord Chancellor then was trying a cause in the Court of Chancery. Lord Hervey sent for him off the bench and my Lord Chancellor, stopping the proceedings, retired into a private room with Lord Hervey, and told Lord Hervey he would look into the deeds and Act of Parliament by which Richmond was settled on the Queen, and should then be able to give his opinion more particularly; but in the meantime bid Lord Hervey tell the King, whatever the settlement was, it could not be altered by any will the Queen should make; and that whatever she died possessed of that was unsettled would go to the King if she died without a will, or even with one, if that will was not made in consequence of powers given her by His Majesty.

This answer made the King easy as to everything belonging to the Queen except Richmond; and when my Lord Chancellor had examined all the settlements relating to that, it came out that Richmond would belong to the King for his life, but that after his death nothing could prevent it going to the Prince.

The King told the Queen of this transaction, to set her mind at ease from doubts she had conceived, and fears she had formed, of the Prince being any way pecuniarily the better for her death.

After six o'clock this Saturday evening the surgeons lanced the swelling just at her navel and let out some matter, but not enough to abate the swelling in any material degree or give them any great hope of her recovery.

The Princess Caroline's nose bled so violently and almost constantly this whole day that she was but little in the Queen's bedchamber, but stayed in the outward room of Her Majesty's apartment, and was again blooded with much difficulty, for Ranby was forced to prick her in both arms, and even at both the blood was so thick he could get but little.

However, her mother being so ill, no persuasions could prevail with her to go to her own side to bed; she lay all night on a couch in the outward room. Princess Emily sat up with the Queen, the King went to bed, and Lord Hervey lay on a mattress on the floor, at the foot of Princess Caroline's couch.

About four o'clock on Sunday morning the 13th, the Queen complaining that her wound was extremely painful, and desiring to have it dressed, Ranby and Shipton were called in to her, and upon opening the wound declared it had already begun to mortify. Hulse, whose turn it was that night to sit up, was sent for into the Queen's bed-chamber, and acquainted by the surgeons with the situation she was in. Hulse came to the Princess Caroline, and told her this terrible and dreaded news, upon which she bid him and Ranby go immediately and inform the King.

All this passed in the room without Lord Hervey's waking, who was fallen asleep quite exhausted by concern and watching. Princess Caroline, as soon as the surgeons and Hulse were gone to the King, waked Lord Hervey, and told him if ever he saw the Queen again it must be immediately, for that the physicians and surgeons had declared the mortification already begun, and were gone to tell the King that it was impossible for her to live many hours.

When Hulse and Ranby came back to Princess Caroline (the King being already up, and gone to the Queen), Princess Caroline and Lord Hervey asked Hulse if there was no possibility left of her recovery, and he answered: 'None.' Lord Hervey then asked Ranby if they were never deceived in the signs of a mortification, to which Ranby, shaking his head, replied: 'We know them but too well.'

The Queen finding the wound still so uneasy, sent again to have them open and dress it; but Hulse said it was to no purpose to do anything more, and Ranby assured the Princess Caroline he could do nothing that would not give the Queen more pain without a possibility of doing Her Majesty any good. However, the Queen insisted on having the wound cleaned at least, the King, who had told the Queen all that the surgeons had told him, came out, called in Ranby and Hulse, and made them comply with her request. Lord Hervey went in with them, just to see the Queen once more, looked at her through his tears for a moment, and then returned to his mattress.

As soon as the surgeons had applied some of their lenient ointments and anodyne preparations, they left the room, came to Lord Hervey, and confirmed their former report of the impossibility of her holding out many hours.

Nobody now remained in the room with the Queen but the King, the Duke, and her four daughters, of whom she took leave in form, desiring they would not leave her till she expired. She told the King she had nothing to say to him. 'For as I have always,' said she, 'told you my thoughts of things and people as fast as they arose, I have nothing left to communicate to you. The people I love, and those I do not, the people I like and dislike, and those I would wish you to be kind to, you know as well as myself; and I am persuaded it would therefore be a useless trouble both to you and me at this time to add any particular recommendations.'

To the Princess Emily she said nothing very particular; to the Princess Caroline she recommended the care of her two younger sisters, and said: 'Poor Caroline, it is a fine legacy I leave you— the trouble of educating these two young things. As for you, William,' continued she to the Duke, 'you know I have always loved you tenderly, and placed my chief hope in you; show your gratitude to me in your behaviour to the King; be a support to your father, and double your attention to make up for the disappointment and vexation he must receive from your profligate and worthless brother. It is in you only I hope for keeping up the credit of our family when your father shall be no more. Attempt nothing ever against your brother, and endeavour to mortify him no way but by showing superior merit.'

She then spoke of the different tempers and dispositions of her two youngest daughters, and the different manner in which they ought to be treated, cautioning the Princess Caroline not to let the vivacity of the Princess Louisa (the youngest) draw her into any inconveniences, and desiring her to give all the aid she could to support the meek and mild disposition of the Princess Mary.

She then took a ruby ring off her finger, which the King had given her at her coronation, and, putting it upon his, said: 'This is the last thing I have to give you—naked I came to you, and naked I go from you. I had everything I ever possessed from you, and to you whatever I have I return. My will you will find a very short one; I give all I have to you.' She then asked for her keys, and gave them to him.

All this and many more things of the like nature, whilst she expatiated on the several rules and instructions she gave to her children, according to their different ages, situations, and dispositions, passed in this interview, which the King and the Princess Caroline repeated to me, who told me there were no dry eyes during this conference in the room but the Queen's, who, as they could perceive, shed in all this touching scene not one tear.

It is not necessary to examine whether the Queen's reasoning was good or bad in wishing the King, in case she died, should marry again. It is certain she did wish it, had often said so when he was present, and when he was not present, and when she was in health, and gave it now as her advice to him when she was dying; upon which his sobs began to rise and his tears to fall with double vehemence. Whilst in the midst of this passion, wiping his eyes, and sobbing between every word, with much ado he got out this answer: 'Non—j'aurai—des—maîtresses.' To which the Queen made no other reply than: 'Ah! mon Dieu! cela n'empêche pas.' I know this episode will hardly be credited, but it is literally true.

When she had finished all she had to say on these subjects, she said she fancied she could sleep. The King said many kind things to her and kissed her face and her hands a hundred times; but even at this time, on her asking for her watch, which hung by the chimney, in order to give it him to take care of her seal, the natural brusquerie of his temper, even in these moments, broke out, which showed how addicted he was to snapping without being angry, and that he was often capable of using those worst whom he loved best. For on this proposal of giving him the watch to take care of the seal with the Queen's arms, in the midst of sobs and tears he raised and quickened his voice, and said: 'Ah! my God! let it alone; the Queen has always such strange fancies. Who should meddle with your seal? Is it not as safe there as in my pocket?'

The Queen after this fell into a sort of dozing, during which time the King often said: 'She is dying; she will go away in this sleep; it is over; she will suffer no more.' However, when she waked, she said she found herself refreshed and much better, adding: 'I know it is only a reprieve to make me suffer longer, and therefore I wish it was at an end; for I cannot recover; but my nasty heart will not break yet.' She then added that she believed she should not die till Wednesday, for that all the remarkable occurrences of her life had happened on that day; that she had been born on a Wednesday, married on a Wednesday, and brought to bed of her first child on a Wednesday; that she had heard the first news of the late King's death on a Wednesday, and been crowned on a Wednesday, and for this reason believed she should die of a Wednesday. This I own showed a weakness in her, but one which at this time might be excused, as most people's minds are a little weakened on these occasions, and few people, even of the strongest minds, are altogether exempt from some little taint of that weakness called superstition. Many people have more of it than they care to let others know they have, and some more of it than they know themselves.

On Sunday morning, about nine o'clock, the surgeons, upon opening the Queen's wound, found the mortification was not spread; and upon cutting off what was already mortified, declared she might recover. This appeared so inconsistent with their declarations some few hours before, and in my opinion showed so much ignorance, that if a life of this consequence, committed to the care of four of the best physicians and three of the best surgeons in England, received no better assistance from their skill, how natural it is to deplore the situation of those whose safety depends on the sagacity of these professions and how reasonable to despise those who put their trust in such aids. Not that I am so unjust to surgery as to put that science upon the same foot with physic; and for my own part I firmly believe there was not the least mortification begun, when they ignorantly pronounced there was; and that what they cut off was not mortified, and only declared so to conceal the mistake they had made the night before in saying it was.

On Monday morning Sir Robert Walpole arrived from Houghton. The Queen had mentioned him but twice during her illness: once to say she hoped they would not send for him, and the day before he came, upon hearing he had been sent for, to ask if he was come. The King, when she asked that question, desired to know if she had anything she wanted to say to him, to which she answered: 'No, nothing; my asking if he was come was mere curiosity.'

Lord Hervey told the King Sir Robert was in the outward room, upon which His Majesty ordered Lord Hervey to bring him in. Sir Robert, with some difficulty from his great bulk and natural awkwardness, knelt down and kissed His Majesty's hand; but with much less difficulty (for he was at present thoroughly frighted) dropped some very proper tears and asked: 'How is the Queen?' To which the King replied: 'Come and see yourself, my good Sir Robert'; and then carried him to the Queen's bedside. The interview was short, but what the Queen said was material, for these were her words: 'My good Sir Robert, you see me in a very indifferent situation, I have nothing to say to you, but to recommend the King, my children, and the kingdom to your care.' As soon as Sir Robert came out of the room he told Lord Hervey what had passed, who asking him what he thought of the Queen, he said: 'My Lord, she is as much dead as if she was in her coffin; if ever I heard a corpse speak, it was just now in that room.' He then repeated again what the Queen had said to him in the presence of the King and the Princesses, which Lord Hervey found made a great impression on his pride, whatever it did on his tenderness; for he repeated it to everybody he saw for a fortnight after.

Vain of this reception and presuming upon the strength of it, he came in the evening, without being sent for, into the room where Lord Hervey used to be with the King whenever His Majesty was not with the Queen. Lord Hervey knew the King would not like this, but was afraid to tell Sir Robert so, lest Sir Robert should think him proud of an honour he was not to partake, and fool enough to be pleased with a distinction which had no other consequence than making those who thought it of more importance than he knew it was, envy, fear, and hate him; and indeed the nature of Lord Hervey's interest with the King was such as might make him many enemies but few friends; for as it was much easier to make the King hate than love, so Lord Hervey (had he been disposed to it) could with very little industry have prejudiced His Majesty against whom he though fit, but with no pains whatever could bring him to bestow any material marks of favour on those he loved best.

When the King found Sir Robert Walpole in the evening in his room he gave him a very cold reception, and every time Sir Robert spoke and offered his advice, or told his opinion with regard to the Queen's illness, or the manner in which she was treated, His Majesty gave him very short answers, and not in the smoothest terms. The next morning, however, the King found him there again, and with him the Duke of Grafton, whom the King had not yet seen since his return from the country; he spoke very coldly to both, and going soon back to the Queen's bedchamber, he complained there that the outward room was so full of people one could not stir for them. Upon which the Princess Caroline, by the Queen's order, immediately sent to bid the room be cleared of everybody who did not use to be there; and from this time nobody attempted to come there any more.

Monday and Tuesday the Queen was what the doctors, surgeons, and courtiers called better, there being no threatening symptoms in her wound, and her vomitings being much slackened; but nothing passing through her, those who judged by essential circumstances and not on the hourly variation of trifles, whatever they might say from fashion or to please, could not in reality believe the Queen's condition more hopeful, or less dangerous, whilst that main point of the internal stoppage continued in the same situation; and whenever the King used to tell her how much better the doctors and surgeons said she was and the hopes they gave him, the moment his back was turned she used to look at the Princess, shake her head, and bid them not to flatter themselves, and often in the day used to tell them: 'Believe me, my dear children, it won't do; at twenty-five I might have struggled through it, but at fifty-five I cannot resist.'

During this time the Prince's family had by little and little, under the pretence first of inquiring of the Queen's health from the Prince or Princess, and afterwards for themselves, got into possession of coming every day and all day to St. James's, till there was no part of the day in which there were not three or four of them dangling in that part of the Queen's state apartment where the Lady of the Bedchamber sat to receive all those who came to inquire about the Queen, and give the no-intelligence of the doctor's verdict on Her Majesty's situation.

This evasion of the King's order (which though it only literally forbid those who went to the Prince's Court coming into the King's presence, was certainly meant to forbid them coming to St. James's) made the King extremely angry, and more especially because the King knew they only came to inquire if the Queen was better in hopes of hearing she was worse; and as the Queen herself said (when she heard of their being daily and hourly there), to watch her last breath, in order to have the merit to their master of bringing the first news of her death.

The King sent Lord Hervey to Sir Robert Walpole to know what way he should take to prevent these scoundrels (as he called them) coming every day to St. James's, in defiance of his order, to insult him and the Queen in their present distress. Sir Robert Walpole asked Lord Hervey what he would advise on this occasion; and Lord Hervey, who was always ready to give the Prince a slap, and knew how uneasy their coming to St. James's made the Queen, said that he thought they ought to be forbidden; but Sir Robert Walpole, who had no mind unnecessarily to shock the Prince, especially at this time, when he thought the spur that used to urge him on to those attacks was going to be blunted, told Lord Hervey that the Prince's servants would certainly pretend they came out of respect and concern for the Queen; that therefore there would be an air of hardness in forbidding them at this time, since nobody could disprove that pretended motive. He added, too, that they had not transgressed the literal sense of the order which only forbid them the King's presence; and as the King might very well be supposed to know nothing of their coming, he thought it would be better for the King just at this time not to mix any marks of resentment against his son with those of affection for his wife, nor give people a handle to say: 'No situation of distress can soften him enough to make him forget to hate one moment.'

This advice Lord Hervey conveyed to the King, who took it with as much reluctance as his Lordship brought it; though not with so good an excuse to himself for sacrificing his inclination to his fear, especially when he found it made the Queen so uneasy that she often asked if nobody would turn those ravens out of the house, who were only there to watch her death, and would gladly tear her to pieces whilst she was alive. 'I hope, at least, it will not be thought proper to let them come into my room, if they should have a mind to it.' The Queen guessed very truly the reason of their coming, for the Prince all this while used to sit up at his house in Pall Mall almost the whole night and every night, sending messengers continually to St. James's, showing the utmost impatience for their return, and saying with equal prudence and humanity to the people who were with him: 'Well, sure we shall soon have good news; she cannot hold out much longer'; and talked all day long in the same strain to everybody about him. This the Duke of Marlborough told Harry Fox, and Harry Fox to Lord Hervey; and some time after the Duke of Marlborough told it to Lord Hervey himself. Poor Mr. Hamilton only, when he was told such reports were spread, doubted of the truth of them, and said the Prince was in the utmost concern for his mother; but when Lady Archibald was asked if the Prince was really concerned for the Queen, she laughed, and said: 'He is very decent.'

Many letters were written, and great care was taken by the Princesses, to prevent the Princess Royal making her mother's illness an excuse for coming to England at this time; everybody knowing the very indifferent reception she would meet with on her arrival from her father, who, not being apt to retain much affection for people who gave him any trouble or put him to any expense, and as little addicted to speak of them in a softer manner than he thought of them, had often lately expressed himself upon the Princess Royal's chapter in terms not altogether so paternal with regard to the affection they contained as with regard to the authority they expressed; and positive orders were sent to Horace Walpole, if persuasion failed, to stop her by force, which orders he communicated to the Prince of Orange, who immediately told them (though desired not) to his wife; the consequence of which was her venting all the passion and anger raised against those who had sent the orders on him who received them.

On Wednesday morning the Queen sent for Sir Robert Walpole, who saw her alone but not for above a quarter of an hour. What really passed I know not but by conjecture, but have reason to think it was only to desire Sir Robert Walpole to examine what was to become of Richmond after her death. Sir Robert told the King this was all, and at first he told Lord Hervey so too. The King also told Lord Hervey that the Queen had told him this was all she had sent for him for. But when Sir Robert went from the Queen to the King, the King (as Sir Robert told Lord Hervey) used him worse than ever he had done in his life; and when Sir Robert told him he had been sent for by the Queen, the King forbade him going any more without first acquainting him, and said he would not have the Queen plagued now with business, adding that she was too weak to bear it, which was very true. But he himself, whenever he was in the room, was always asking her so many questions, talking so fast and in so loud a voice, and teasing her to eat and drink so many different things, that the Princesses, by Lord Hervey's advice, got the doctors to make it one of the articles in their written prescription for the Queen that she should not be talked to more than was absolutely necessary, and always in the lowest voice; and this prescription, with the rest, after it had been shown to the King, was pinned up on the curtain of the Queen's bed. But this prescription had as little effect on the King as the rest of their prescriptions had on her.

Sir Robert waited at night at St. James's till Lord Hervey came from the King, and then asked him if he could comprehend what had put the King into such a devilish humour in the morning, when the Queen was so much better. Lord Hervey said he could as little comprehend any turns in the King's temper as he could Sir Robert's giving in to the ill-founded opinion of thinking the Queen better; 'for till a passage is opened,' continued he, 'I cannot think her vomiting a little more or a little less of any consequence, or that it signifies much that the external circumstances of her wound are something less threatening, when all the internal symptoms remain in the same unknown and dangerous condition they were.'

'Oh! my Lord,' said Sir Robert, 'if this woman should die, what a scene of confusion will here be! Who can tell into what hands the King will fall? Or who will have the management of him? I defy the ablest person in this kingdom to foresee what will be the consequence of this great event.' 'For my own part,' replied Lord Hervey, 'I have not the least doubt how it will be. He will cry for her for a fortnight, forget in a month, have two or three women that he will pass his time with to lie with now and then, and to make people believe he lies with them day and night; but whilst they have most of his time, a little of his money, less of his confidence, and no power, you will have all the credit, more power than ever you had, and govern him more absolutely than ever you did. Your credit before was through the medium of the Queen, and all power through a medium must be weaker than when it operates directly. Besides, Sir, all princes must now and then be deceived by their ministers, and as the King is much easier deceived than the Queen, so your task, whenever that task is deceiving, will be much less difficult than it was before. In the first place, because the King is naturally much less suspicious than the Queen; in the next, because he is less penetrating; and lastly, because he cares much less to converse with different people, and will hear nobody talk to him of business but yourself.' 'Oh! my Lord,' interrupted Sir Robert, 'though he will hear nobody but me, do you not know how often he refuses to hear me when it is on a subject he does not like; but by the Queen I can fetch him round with time to those subjects again; she can make him do the same in another shape, and when I give her her lesson, can make him propose the very thing as his own opinion which a week before he had rejected as mine. The many opportunities and the credit she has with him, the knowledge of his temper, the being constantly at him, and the opinion he has both of her judgment and her pursuit of his interest and his pleasure as her first objects, makes this part easy for her; but I have not the same materials to act it, and cannot do without somebody that has leisure to operate slowly upon him, which is the only way he can be effectually operated upon. For he is neither to be persuaded nor convinced; he will do nothing to oblige anybody, nor ever own or think he has been in the wrong; and I have told the Queen a thousand times that it is not to be wondered at that he should be of that mind, when she, whom he believes sooner than any other body in the world, never heard him broach the most absurd opinion, or declare the most extravagant design, that she did not tell him he was in the right.' 'Notwithstanding all this,' replied Lord

Hervey, 'I am convinced if the Queen should die (which I firmly believe she will), that you will have him faster than ever, and yet I am sincere enough to own to you I heartily wish she may recover.' This conversation lasted two or three hours, and kept Lord Hervey out of bed much longer than he desired, this being the first night the Queen was ill that he had been dismissed so early or had a prospect of passing so many hours undisturbed.

The King had been particularly anxious this whole day from what the Queen had said with regard to her dying of a Wednesday, which could not be much wondered at, since a mind much less addicted to superstition than His Majesty's might have been a little affected by a smaller hint that had fallen from one they loved in such circumstances, and on an occasion of so much importance to them. Could it then be surprising that a man who believed in ghosts and witches, should not be proof against a weakness that might have appeared in one exempt from many more than His Majesty's best friends can deny him to labour under?

On Thursday the Queen's vomitings returned with as much violence as ever, and in the afternoon one of the guts burst in such a manner that all her excrement came out at the wound in her belly, though the surgeons could not by any probing certainly tell whereabouts in the gut the fracture was. The running at the wound was in such immense quantities that it went all through the quilts of the bed and flowed all over the floor.

Some ignorant people about her who knew not from what cause this evacuation proceeded, told the Queen they hoped this relief would do her good, to which the Queen replied very calmly, she hoped so too, for that it was all the evacuations she should ever have.

Every day once at least, and sometimes oftener, from the first of her being under the surgeons' hands, they were forced, or thought themselves so, to make some new incision; and before every operation of this kind which she underwent, she always used to ask the King if he approved what the surgeons proposed to do; and when he said they had told him it was necessary, and that he hoped she would consent to anything they thought so, she always submitted immediately and with the utmost patience, resignation, and resolution suffered them to cut and probe as deep and as long as they thought fit. She asked Ranby once, whilst he was dressing her wound, if he would not be glad to be officiating in the same manner to his old cross wife that he hated so much; and if any involuntary groans or complainings broke from her during the operations, she used immediately after to bid the surgeons not mind her, and make them excuses for interrupting them with her silly complaints, when she knew they were doing all they could to help her.

On Wednesday some wise, some pious, and a great many busy, meddling, impertinent people about the Court asking in whispers everybody they met whether the Queen had had any body to pray by her, and wondering at the irreligion of the Queen for thinking she could pray as well for herself as anybody could pray for her, and at those about her for not putting her in mind of so essential a duty, Sir Robert Walpole desired Princess Emily to propose to the King or Queen that the Archbishop should be sent for, in order to stop people's impertinence upon this subject; and when the Princess Emily made some difficulty about taking upon her to make this proposal to the King or Queen, Sir Robert in the presence of a dozen people (who really wished this divine physician for the Queen's soul might be sent for, upon the foot of her salvation) very prudently added, by way of stimulating the Princess Emily: 'Pray, madam, let this farce be played. The Archbishop will act it very well. You may bid him be as short as you will. It will do the Queen no hurt, no more than any good; and it will satisfy all the wise and good fools, who will call us all atheists if we don't pretend to be as great fools as they are.'

After this eloquent and discreet persuasion—the whole company staring with the utmost astonishment at Sir Robert Walpole, some in admiration of his piety and others of his prudence—the Princess Emily spoke to the King, the King to the Queen, and the Archbishop was sent for, who continued afterwards to pray by her morning and evening, at which ceremony her children always assisted; but the King constantly went out of the room before his episcopal Grace was admitted. But all this was thrown away, for the people that had whispered and wondered and clamoured at no prayers were now just as busy and as whispering and as wondering about no sacrament. Some fools said the Queen had not religion enough to ask to receive the sacrament; some other fools said she had asked for it and that the Archbishop had refused to give it to her unless she would first be reconciled to her son; and this many idiots believed, and many who were not idiots told, in hopes of finding credit from those that were. There were some who were impertinent enough to ask the Archbishop himself why he would not advise the Queen to be reconciled to the Prince, and more than hinted to him that he would be wanting in his duty if he did not; to which his Grace very decently and properly answered that whenever the Queen had done him the honour to talk to him upon that unhappy division in the family she had always done it with so much sense and goodness that he never thought she wanted any advice. The Queen desired the Archbishop, if she died, to take care of Dr. Butler, her Clerk of the Closet; and he was the only body I ever heard of her recommending particularly and by name all the while she was ill. Her servants in general she recommended to the King, and in general terms said he knew whom she liked and disliked, but did not, that I know of, name anybody to him in particular.

From the time of the bursting of the gut the physicians and surgeons, who had hitherto, without any disguise or reserve, talked over all the particulars of the Queen's case to anybody that asked them any questions, were absolutely forbidden by the King to reveal this circumstance, or to give any other answer for the future, to anybody whatever who inquired concerning the Queen's health, than the general one of being much as she was. Had these restrictive orders been issued by His Majesty on the first discovery of the Queen's rupture, considering her delicacy on this point and his passion for a mystery on every point, it would have been easy to account for this edict being given out; but after her case had been talked over for five days, as publicly and as minutely as if she had been dissected before St. James's gate, I own I was at a loss to comprehend why these orders were issued, especially when this circumstance was not by the physicians or surgeons pronounced so inevitably mortal as I should have thought it natural for them to judge it. The King told it to Lord Hervey, and Ranby to Sir Robert Walpole. Lord Hervey ventured to reveal it to the Princess Caroline; but the King not telling it himself to any of his children, none of the rest of them knew it, but were extremely surprised, as well as the rest of the Court, at the sudden reserve of the physicians and surgeons in their present accounts of the Queen's situation.

During this time the King talked perpetually to Lord Hervey, the physicians and surgeons, and his children, who were the only people he ever saw out of the Queen's room, of the Queen's good qualities, his fondness for her, his anxiety for her welfare, and the irreparable loss her death would be to him; and repeated every day, and many times in the day, all her merits in every capacity with regard to him and every other body she had to do with. He said she was the best wife, the best mother, the best companion, the best friend, and the best woman that ever was born; that she was the wisest, the most agreeable, and the most useful body, man or woman, that he had ever been acquainted with; that he firmly believed she never, since he first knew her, ever thought of anything she was to do or to say, but in what manner it would be most agreeable to his pleasure, or most serviceable for his interest; that he had never seen her out of humour in his life; that he had passed more hours with her than he believed any other two people in the world had ever passed together, and that he never had been tired in her company one minute; and that he was sure he could have been happy with no other woman upon earth for a wife, and that if she had not been his wife, he had rather have had her for his mistress than any woman he had ever been acquainted with; that he believed she never had had a thought of people or things which she had not communicated to him; that she had the best head, the best heart, and the best temper that God Almighty had ever given to any human creature, man or woman; and that she had not only softened all his leisure hours, but been of more use to him as a minister than any other body had ever been to him or to any other prince; that with a patience which he knew he was not master of, she had listened to the nonsense of all the impertinent fools that wanted to talk to him, and had taken all that trouble off his hands, reporting nothing to him that was unnecessary or would have been tedious for him to hear, and never forgetting anything that was material, useful, or entertaining to him to know. He said that, joined to all the softness and delicacy of her own sex, she had all the personal as well as political courage of the firmest and bravest

man; that not only he and her family, but the whole nation, would
feel the loss of her if she died; and that, as to all the *brilliant* and
enjouement of the Court, there would be an end of it when she
was gone; and that there would be no bearing a drawing-room
when the only body that ever enlivened it, and one that always
enlivened it, was no longer there. 'Poor woman, how she always
found something obliging, agreeable, and pleasing to say to everybody, and always sent people away from her better satisfied than
they came! *Comme elle soutenoit sa dignité avec grace, avec
politesse, avec douceur!'*

These were the terms in which he was for ever now talking of
the Queen, and in which he likewise talked to her; and yet so
unaccountable were the sudden sallies of his temper, and so little
was he able or willing to command them, that in the midst of all
this flow of tenderness he hardly ever went into her room that he
did not, even in this moving situation, snub her for something or
other she said or did. When her constant uneasiness, from the sick-
ness in her stomach and the soreness of her wound, made her shift
her posture every minute, he would say to her: 'How the devil
should you sleep, when you will never lie still a moment? You
want to rest, and the doctors tell you nothing can do you so much
good, and yet you are always moving about. Nobody can sleep in
that manner, and that is always your way; you never take the
proper method to get what you want, and then you wonder you
have it not.' And as the doctors said she might eat or drink anything she had a mind to or could swallow, the King was ever
proposing something or other, which she never refused, though
she knew it would only lie burning in her stomach for half an
hour or an hour and then come up again. When she could get
things down, notwithstanding these effects (which to other people
she said she knew they would have), her complaisance to him made
her always swallow them; and when he thanked her for so doing,
she used the answer: 'It is the last service I can do you.' But when
her stomach recoiled so that it was impossible for her to force anything down her throat which he had given her, and that she only
tasted it and gave it away, he used peevishly to say: 'My God! how
is it possible you should not know whether you like a thing or not?
If you do not like it, why do you call for it; and if you do, why will

you give it away?' To which she would only answer: 'I am very silly and very whimsical, for a *dégoût* takes me in a moment, for what I think, a minute before, I have a mind to.'

Notwithstanding the constant pain she was in, and her great want of rest, the physicians never gave her opium but one night. She herself was not much inclined to take it; and the physicians, thinking it might possibly, from its binding quality, prevent the relief she so much wanted, were not very forward to prescribe it. She had not rested with it all night, and when the King came into her room in the morning, as she lay with her eyes fixed at a point in the air, as people often do in these situations, when they are neither enough at ease to shut their eyes and sleep, nor enough themselves to prevent their thoughts wandering, or to see the things they seem to look at, the King with a loud and quick voice said to her: 'Mon Dieu! qu'est ce que vous regardez? Comment peut-on fixer ses yeux comme ça? Vos yeux ressemblent à ceux d'un veau à qui on vient de couper la gorge!'

There was, besides this mixture of brutality and tenderness towards the Queen, at this time in the King's conduct and conversation another mixture full as natural to him and much less extraordinary, which was the mixing constantly some praises of himself with those he bestowed on her. He never talked of her being a good wife without giving strong hints of his deserving a good one, and being at least as good a husband; and gave people to understand, when he commended her understanding, that he did not think it the worse for her having kept him company so many years. He plainly showed, too, that he not only wished other people should believe, but did himself believe that her whole behaviour to him was the natural effect of an amorous attachment to his person and an adoration of his great genius. When he mentioned his present fears for the Queen, he always interwove an account of the intrepidity with which he waited his own fate the year before, both in the storm and during his illness afterward, giving tiresome accounts with what resolution and presence of mind he talked to his pages on shipboard during the tempest; and for a proof of his own courage, and the want of the same magnanimity in them, told us that when he saw La Chaux, one of his pages, pale and trembling in the corner of the cabin, he said to him: 'Comment as tu peur?'

To which La Chaux (said he) replied: 'Oui, Sire, vraiment, et je crois qu'il n'y a que votre Majesté dans la vaisseau qui ne l'a pas.' From which history the conclusion the King proposed one should draw was much less natural than that which most people would draw, which was that His Majesty had a mind to seem on that occasion to have more courage than he had, and that the *valet de chambre* very adroitly made his court by pretending to have less.

As to his behaviour during his illness, what fears he had I know not, but the Queen and everybody about him said he always seemed to think himself much worse than he was; and for the accounts of his peevishness and impatience, they could with great difficulty, according to his own confession, exceed reality, for he himself told me that he found such an abominable frowardness in himself that in the intermissions of it (which was not easy to catch) he had told his pages not to mind him when he was unreasonably chiding and swearing at them, for that it was part of his distemper and that he could not help it. There was a mixture of good-nature and good sense in this apology, that I own I, who knew him, should rather have taken for an accidental distemper than the other, for it was much less of a piece with his conduct in health than what he endeavoured to excuse.

One night whilst the Queen was ill, as he was sitting in his nightgown and nightcap in a great chair, with his legs upon a stool, and nobody in the room with him but the Princess Emily, who lay upon a couch, and Lord Hervey, who sat by the fire, he talked in this strain of his own courage in the storm and his illness, till the Princess Emily, as Lord Hervey thought, fell fast asleep, whilst Lord Hervey, as tired as he was of the present conversation and his last week's watching, was left alone to act civil auditor and adroit courtier, to applaud what he heard, and every now and then to ask such proper questions as led the King into giving some particular detail of his own magnanimity. The King, turning towards Princess Emily, and seeing her eyes shut, cried: 'Poor good child! her duty, affection, and attendance on her mother have quite exhausted her spirits.' And soon after he went into the Queen's room. As soon as his back was turned, Princess Emily started up and said: 'Is he gone? Jesus! How tiresome he is!' Lord Hervey, who had no mind to trust Her Royal Highness with singing her father's praises in duetto with her, replied only: 'I thought Your Royal Highness had been asleep.' 'No,' said the Princess Emily; 'I only shut my eyes that I might not join in the ennuyant conversation, and wish I could have shut my ears too. In the first place, I am sick to death of hearing of his great courage every day of my life; in the next place, one thinks now of Mama, and not of him. Who cares for his old storm? I believe, too, it is a great lie, and that he was as much afraid as I should have been, for all what he says now; and as to his not being afraid when he was ill, I know that is a lie, for I saw him, and I heard all his sighs and his groans, when he was in no more danger than I am at this moment. He was talking, too, for ever of dying, and that he was sure he should not recover.' All this, considering the kind things she had heard the King say the minute before when he imagined her asleep, Lord Hervey thought a pretty extraordinary return for her to make for that paternal goodness, or would have thought it so in anybody but her; and looked upon this openness to him, whom she did not love, yet less to be accounted for, unless he could have imagined it was to draw him in to echo her, and then to relate what he said as if he had said it unaccompanied.

Whilst she was going on with the panegyric on the King which I have related, the King returned, upon which she began to rub her eyes as if she had that instant raised her head from her pillows, and said: 'I have really slept very heartily. How long had Papa been out of the room?' The King, who had very little or rather no suspicion in his composition, took these appearances for realities, and said: 'It is time for us all to take a little rest. We will all go to bed, for by staying here we do the poor Queen no good, and hurt ourselves.' And so dismissing Lord Hervey, they all retired.

I will relate no further particulars how the two following days passed, as such a narration would be only recapitulating a diary of the two former, without any material variation. The Queen grew so perceptibly weaker every hour, that every one she lived was more than was expected.

She asked Dr. Tesier on Sunday the 20th Nov., in the evening, with no seeming impatience under any article of her present circumstances but their duration, how long he thought it was possible for all this to last. To which he answered: 'Je crois que votre Majesté, sera bientôt soulagée.' And she calmly replied: 'Tant mieux.'

About ten o'clock on Sunday night, the King being in bed and asleep on the floor at the feet of the Queen's bed and the Princess Emily in a couch-bed in a corner of the room, the Queen began to rattle in the throat, and Mrs. Purcel giving the alarm that she was expiring, all in the room started up. Princess Caroline was sent for and Lord Hervey, but before the last arrived the Queen was just dead. All she said before she died was: 'I have now got an asthma. Open the window.' Then she said: 'Pray.' Upon which the Princess Emily began to read some prayers, of which she scarce repeated ten words before the Queen expired. The Princess Caroline held a looking-glass to her lips, and finding there was not the least damp upon it, cried: ''Tis over'; and said not one word more nor shed as yet one tear on the arrival of a misfortune the dread of which had cost her so many.

The King kissed the face and hands of the lifeless body several times, but in a few minutes left the Queen's apartment and went to that of his daughters, accompanied only by them. Then advising them to go to bed and take care of themselves, he went to his own side; and as soon as he was in bed sent for Lord Hervey to come and sit by him, where, after talking some time, and more calmly than one could have expected, of the manner of the Queen's death, he dismissed Lord Hervey, and sent for one of his pages to sit up in his room all night, which order he repeated for several days afterwards. And, by the bye, as he ordered one of them, for some time after the death of the Queen, to lie in his room, and that I am very sure he believed many stories of ghosts and witches and apparitions, I take this order (with great deference to his magnanimity on other occasions) to have been the result of the same way of thinking that makes many weak minds fancy themselves more secure from any supernatural danger in the light than in the dark, and in company than alone.

Lord Hervey went back to the Princess Caroline's bedchamber, where he stayed till five o'clock in the morning, endeavouring to lighten her grief by indulging it, and not by that silly way of trying to divert what cannot be removed, or to bring comfort to such affliction as time only can alleviate.

The King passed every day and all the day (excepting the time he was at dinner, and the hour or two he slept after dinner), till the Court went into mourning, in the apartment of the Princesses, and was only called from thence for a few minutes when any of the Ministers wanted to speak with him about business, whilst every new body who was admitted to him on these occasions threw him into a new flood of tears.

The grief he felt for the Queen, as it was universally known, and showed a tenderness of which the world thought him before utterly incapable of, made him for some time more popular and better spoken of than he had ever been before this incident, or than I believe he ever will be again. He was thoroughly unaffected in his conduct on this occasion, and by being so (as odd as it may seem to say this) perplexed those who were about him more to form an opinion of him than perhaps they would have been had he appeared to them in a less natural shape; for his sudden transitions from tears to smiles, from a sighing pensive silence to a loud talkative conversation on things foreign to what one imagined at other times engrossed all his thoughts; the tender manner in which he related a thousand old stories relating to his first seeing the Queen, his marriage with her, the way in which they lived at Hanover, his behaviour to her when she had the smallpox, and his risking his life by getting it of her (which he did) rather than leave her; and the next moment talking, with the most seeming indifference and calmness, of her being opened and embalmed, of the method of her ladies and maids of honour keeping watch by the body, and all the minutiæ relating to the regulation of the funeral; I say his talking with so much emotion and concern of old stories, and with so little on present circumstances which affected everybody in the room but himself, and perhaps the more for their seeming to affect him so little, puzzled one's judgment of the situation of his mind extremely, and made it vary as often as these circumstances on which it was to be formed.

One day he came into the room at once weeping and laughing, and said: 'Vous me croirez fou, je crois, mais je viens de voir le pauvre Horace Walpole pour la première fois, et il pleure de si mauvaise grace, qu'au milieu de mes larmes il m'a fait rire.'

The King often said, and to many people at this time, that not only he and his family should have a great loss in the Queen's death, but the whole nation; and would instance occasions where he owned her good sense and good temper had kept his passions within bounds which they would otherwise have broken. And during this retirement (in which he was infinitely more talkative than I ever knew him at any other time of his whole life) he discoursed so constantly and so openly of himself that if anybody had had a mind to write the memoirs of his life from his cradle to the present moment the Princesses and Lord Hervey could have furnished them with materials of all the occurrences, transactions, and anecdotes, military, civil, amorous, foreign, and domestic, that could be comprehended in such a work, from his own lips, excepting what related to his mother, whom on no occasion I ever heard him mention, not even inadvertently or indirectly, any more than if such a person had never had a being.

He always spoke well and with respect of her father, the Duke of Zell; said that the Duke of Zell was fond of him, but had often told him, as well as he loved him, if he ever found him guilty of a base action, and that he should prove a liar or a coward, he would shoot him through the head with his own hand.

Of his aunt, the Queen of Prussia, too he spoke well, who, by what I heard from others, and particularly the Queen, was a very vain, good-for-nothing woman.

For his sister, the present Queen of Prussia, he had the contempt she deserved, and a hatred she did not deserve.

What he thought and said of the King of Prussia was much the same as what the King of Prussia thought and said of him; that he was a proud, brutal, tyrannical, wrong-headed, impracticable fellow, who loved nobody and would use everybody ill that was in his power. How far these two Kings were in the right in this point, or how little they were so in every other, is not my business here to determine.

He always spoke of his father as a weak man rather than a bad or a dishonest one; and said though his father had always hated him and used him ill, that on one point he had always done him justice, for that he knew when that scoundrel, and puppy, and knave, and rascal, my Lord Sunderland, had endeavoured to fix some lie upon him (the particulars of which story he had now forgot), that the late King had answered: 'Non, non, je connois mon fils; il n'est pas menteur, il est fou, mais il est honnête homme.'

Whilst the days and evenings passed in these conversations in the apartments of the Princesses, the Ministers and courtiers and politicians without doors were speculating, conjecturing, and reasoning by whom the power and credit the Queen had had was likely to be inherited.

The Dukes of Grafton and Newcastle laboured, by assuring Sir Robert Walpole it would fall upon the Princess Emily, to persuade him to play it into her hands, and by early applications there to secure her, and make her believe she owed that to his assistance, which she would certainly acquire whether he assisted her or not, and which would be employed against him, if she did not imagine in some measure she had obtained it by him. Sir Robert Walpole, in his short, coarse way, asked these Dukes, with more sense and penetration than decency or politeness: 'Does your Princess Emily design to commit incest? will she go to bed with her father? or does he desire she should? If not, do not tell me the King intends to make a vow of chastity, or that those that lie with him won't have the best interest with him. I am for Madame Walmoden. I'll bring her over and I'll have nothing to do with your girls. I was for the wife against the mistress, but I will be for the mistress against the daughter unless you think the daughter intends to behave so as to supply the place of both wife and mistress, which, as I have told you before, I know not how she can do but by going to bed with him.' Accordingly he advised the King and pressed him to send for Madame Walmoden immediately from Hanover; said he must look forward for his own sake, for the sake of his family, and for the sake of all his friends, and not ruin his health, by indulging vain regret and grief for what was past recall. The King listened to this way of reasoning more kindly every time it was repeated; but Sir Robert Walpole tried this manner of talking to the Princesses, not quite so judiciously, respectfully, or successfully; for when he talked to them of looking forward, drying up their tears, and endeavouring to direct their father's melancholy by bringing women about him, and in scarce covert terms persuaded them to bawd for him; when he squabbly and shockingly told them that though he had been for the Queen against Lady Suffolk and every other woman, yet that now he would be for Madame Walmoden, and added that he would advise them in the meantime to bring my Lady Deloraine to their father for the sake of his health, saying, in his polite style, that 'people must wear old gloves till they could get new ones'; when he spoke to them in this absurd style, the pride of the Princess Emily and the tenderness of the Princess Caroline were so shocked that he laid the foundation of an aversion to him in both, which I believe nobody will live to see him ever get over.

When Sir Robert Walpole advised the King to take Lady Deloraine till Madame Walmoden could be brought over His Majesty said she stank of Spanish wine so abominably of late that he could not bear her. But Lady Deloraine, who had formed to herself fine schemes of power and grandeur on being left sole possessor of the King's bed and imagined it was by the management and jealousy of the Princess Emily that she was not permitted to see the King, did in the folly of her sober hours and the extravagance of her elevated conversations break out into such invectives against Her Royal Highness, and on purpose to have them conveyed to her again, that a consultation among the Princess Emily's friends was held what was to be done with her. It was agreed and resolved that the best method the Princess could take was to act ignorance; which Lady Deloraine (who knew she could not be ignorant) construing fear, redoubled her fury, said she would go to the King whether the Princess would or no, that Brinkman (an old *valet de chambre* of the King's) should tell her when he was alone, and that half an hour would suffice to ruin the Princess Emily (whose conduct she would lay open to her father) and to put herself in full possession of that credit which they were all afraid of and all working to prevent.

The true state of this case was that the Princesses were thoroughly indifferent whether the King saw Lady Deloraine or not and had neither tried to forward nor retard their meeting, as they did not love Lady Deloraine enough to desire to introduce her, or fear her enough to take pains to exclude her. The King, therefore, being left to himself and certainly designing to send for Madame Walmoden,[1] as he neither cared to be at the trouble nor expense of a

---

[1] She was brought over in the following year and created Countess of Yarmouth. Lady Hervey undertook the task of preparing her lodgings in the palace and settling her petit cour (Egmont Diary, 22nd May, 1738).

new mistress in the interim, soon after all this bustle saw Lady Deloraine from time to time as he had done before the Queen's death without the least alteration in his manner of talking to her or his manner of paying her, and in short sent for this old acquaintance to his apartment from just the same motives that people send casually for a new one to a tavern.

Lord Hervey, whilst all the world was speaking of him at this time as the King's first favourite, knew his own situation too well to think the interest he had in His Majesty worth anything to one whose vanity could not be pleased with the éclat of appearances, when he knew there was nothing essential to be depended upon at the bottom. The letter he wrote at this time to Sir Robert Walpole will explain his own sentiments of his present situation so well, that I need add nothing by way of comment to the following copy of it.

Lord Hervey to Sir Robert Walpole.
DECEMBER 1, 1737.

SIR,

As I never did nor ever will deceive you by misrepresenting or concealing my thoughts upon any occasion, so I cannot resist troubling you with them upon this, and choose to do it in writing, not only as the surest way of not being prevented in the attempt, but because you should not imagine, what often happens in speaking, that they are sudden starts and not my coolest sentiments and reflections.

That you have had a very sensible and affecting loss is certain; the loss of a great, a good, a wise, a kind, and a powerful friend must ever be esteemed such; but as to the loss it will be in points where people who look from a great distance, and consequently see imperfectly, imagine it will hurt you, you know I told you before this unfortunate event, and I am every hour more confirmed in that opinion, that it will be far from affecting you as some of your sanguine enemies hope, or some of your misjudging friends may apprehend. It may occasion many difficulties in the exercise of your power, but no danger to the possession of it. I need not expatiate on all the particular reasons on which this opinion is founded; you would not like I should, and I have already in conversation told you two which alone would be sufficient to demonstrate the truth of it, and these are, the Queen's recommendations of you, and the King's desire to refute the insinuations frequently made when she was living, that you were her minister, not his, and forced upon him by her influence, not distinguished by his choice.

This being the case, you are as secure as ever, perhaps more so, and you know I have my reasons, and good ones, for saying so; but, indeed, I have often said of you, though never before to you, what I really think true, that your great talents and abilities are so much superior to anybody I ever knew, or I believe ever shall know, that the loss of them is the only essential loss in the ministerial character you can ever feel, and that whilst you keep them you may meet with rubs, but you will never find a stop.

As to my own situation (it is the last time I will trouble you upon it, so bear with me), it is as well known to me as yours. I have long made it my sole business to please the Queen and you. How well or how ill I succeeded in the first is now immaterial; but that I have on every occasion endeavoured to gain your friendship and on some lately to move your good-nature, and have succeeded alike in both, is, I fear, too true. Some honorary trifles you have refused me, and other more essential favours which you have denied, leave me too little room to doubt that either those who have always been giving you ill impressions of me have made you afraid or unwilling to distinguish me, or that your own judgment and knowledge of me have convinced you that I am fit for nothing but to carry candles and set chairs all my life, and that I am sufficiently raised, at forty years old, by being promoted to the employment of Tom Coke and designed, like him, and on the same terms, to die in it. My situation often puts me in mind of three lines in Dryden, where a Prince, speaking of a very contemptible appurtenance to his Court, says—

The Court received him first for charity,
And since with no degree of honour graced,
But only suffer'd where he first was placed.

I promised you I never would ask anything for myself of the Queen but through you, and kept my word; but I own to you I feel my pride so shocked by many things that have happened to me of late, that nothing but my not being able to afford to quit has prevented me. Not that in quitting I should have acted in anything differently from what I have done and shall now do, but would that way only have endeavoured to make you regret the slighting me for the sake of others, whom I wish you may always find deserve as well of you. I once had it in my power to serve you (or my vanity gave me the pleasure of thinking so). That time is over. I know I am now as insignificant as any other of the dignified ciphers about you—as insignificant as their envy can wish me or as anything can make me. For as for the little distinctions the King has shown me during the poor Queen's illness or since her death, they are such as may serve for food to the envy of some fools of our acquaintance, but are not what I am fool enough, I promise you, to think of more value in point of an interest than the sheet of paper I am writing upon. But my interest at Court might have been, though like this paper, of some consequence to me, since you might have written what you pleased upon it, though you have thought fit to leave it a blank.

You will be tired of reading, and I am tired of writing. Do not torture any expression in this letter, for I am not in a situation of mind to weigh or choose my words, and all I mean to say is that I will be refused or disappointed no more, for I will ask and expect no more; that my enemies shall not conquer, for I will not struggle; that I could have made my peace with my greatest enemy if I would have done it at your expense; that I scorned it, and do not repent the part I have acted; that I submit to be a nothing, and wish whoever you honour with your confidence, or benefit with your favour, may always serve you with as honest a mind, as warm a heart, and as unshakable an attachment, as you have been served by your neglected, etc.

To this letter Sir Robert Walpole sent no answer in writing, but by a verbal message desired to speak with Lord Hervey early the next morning, and then told him, with a very well acted concern, that of all the things he had ever met with in business, this letter had surprised and afflicted him the most; that after his own children there was nobody in England he loved so well, nor anybody to whom he thought he had done more obligations than to Lord Hervey. 'As to the opinion I have of your worth and integrity, my Lord, the things with which I have trusted you are a sufficient proof. I mean to serve you, I wish to please you, for God's sake go on with me as you used to do; and leave it to me, pray trust me to show the sincerity with which I speak to you. Let us have no *éclaircissemens* on what is past; commit your future interest to my care, and give me leave to think, what I wish to believe, that all the dissatisfaction expressed in your letter is rather the effect of the melancholy present turn of your mind on this unhappy event, than a distrust of my friendship and sincerity.'

It would be very tedious to relate all the particulars of this long conversation, which ended in an extorted promise from Lord Hervey that he would not alter his conduct, make any complaints to anybody, or relate what had passed between them, unless he thought he had any fresh reason to be displeased with Sir Robert Walpole's behaviour; and though Lord Hervey now began to know Sir Robert Walpole too well to depend much on the most lavish professions of kindness and esteem, yet he had some satisfaction in Sir Robert Walpole's behaviour in a manner that saved him the troubles of coming to a rupture with him at a time when it was certainly his interest as well as his inclination to lie by and be quiet. It will be natural, then, to ask, if these were Lord Hervey's sentiments, why he wrote this letter. The answer to which is that he thought the letting Sir Robert Walpole see he was sensible he had not been well used was the likeliest way to prevent his being worse used, knowing that fear was the only check upon a man who was so apt to conceive jealousies and suspicions, and whose temper, though it could from that motive of fear long suspend resenting, seldom or never failed from any other to annoy and depress those against whom these jealousies and suspicions were conceived.

Several of Sir Robert Walpole's enemies, as well as some of Lord Hervey's injudicious friends, tried to stimulate and persuade Lord Hervey at this time to endeavour to ruin Sir Robert Walpole in the palace, to make use of his perpetual access to the King to this purpose, and told him, as the Princesses were so irritated against Sir Robert, from his ungrateful behaviour to their mother's memory and his indecent conduct towards themselves, that they would certainly join with Lord Hervey in promoting any scheme that tended to the subversion of his power and the punishment of his insolence; at the same time blowing up Lord Hervey's vanity and ambition, by telling him how capable he was of stepping into Sir Robert's place, and how glad the at present broken Whig party would be to unite under his banner, if he would but set up his standard. But these people know little of the true situation of things; the Princess Emily not daring to speak of business to the King, and the Princess Caroline not caring how things went, engrossed by her melancholy, and in so bad a state of health, that nobody imagined, any more than herself, that her life would of any long continuance.

Index

Index